D1525214

HOPE

Also by Arnold A. Hutschnecker

THE WILL TO LIVE
LOVE AND HATE IN HUMAN NATURE
THE WILL TO HAPPINESS
THE DRIVE FOR POWER

HOPE

THE DYNAMICS OF SELF-FULFILLMENT

ARNOLD A. HUTSCHNECKER, M.D.

G. P. Putnam's Sons
New York

The author gratefully acknowledges permission to reprint material from the
following sources:
   American Medical News for material from "Physician Fears Cults May
Spread in '80s," May 9, 1980.
   The Conde Nast Publications, Inc., for material from the article "If You Are
Depressed," which appeared in the January 15, 1972 issue of *Vogue*.
   Hoffman-La Roche, Inc., Nutley, N.J., for material from *This Question of
Coping*. 11. 1976.
   Medical Aspects of Human Sexuality for material from the article "Sexual
Revenge" by Dr. Nathan Roth, February 1979, and from the article "Devel-
opment of Sexual Intimacy in Marriage" by Dr. Raymond Babineau, April
1979.
   Sirgay Sanger, M.D., for material from his article "Treating the Compulsive
Gambler," which appeared in *Behavioral Medicine*, August 1979.
   Alan A. Stone, M.D., for permission to quote from his speech.

LIBRARY OF CONGRESS CATALOGING IN PUBLICATION DATA

Hutschnecker, Arnold A
   Hope, the dynamics of self-fulfillment.

   1. Hope.   2.   Self-actualization (Psychology)
I.   Title.
BF575.H56H87   1981   158'.1   80-25127
ISBN 0-399-12589-2

Acknowledgments

Writing this book was pain and joy. However, I had the good fortune of having an extraordinary editor in Rob Fitz, who helped me develop a heretofore unknown momentum by never looking over my shoulder, never asking where I was going or how I would carry through the main theme of the book. I am grateful for the calm and confident manner in which he handled my manuscript.

My secretary, Evelyn Gruen, picked up the intensity by working long hours deciphering my handwriting and typing the manuscript. Her undeterred devotion deserves my special thanks.

I wish to thank my literary agent, Bill Adler, whose perceptive talent grasped my ideas to a point of being enthusiastic enough to sell the book without demanding written material. Also, I would like to thank Alexandria Hatcher for the devoted preliminary work she did with me, and Marcia Cohen and Jeanne Bernkopf for reassuring me of an average reader's interest in my project.

And then there are my friends who have always proved to be supportive, all renowned psychiatrists: George and John Train, Ferrucio di Cori, James Smith, Harry Perlowitz, Bill Sorrel, Maria Fleischl, Alvin Yapalater, and Irving Salan.

I owe special thanks to Dr. Austin Kutscher, the distinguished founder and president of the Foundation of Thanatology and associate professor at Columbia Presbyterian Medical Center, New York, who so generously contributed to this book by writing a profound summary of his thoughts on modern man's struggle with life and death and the role of hope that I placed before the last paragraph of Chapter I. He was one of the earliest supporters of my concept about death and dying and of my later thoughts on the importance of hope as a psychological concept, a man who, after the death of his first wife, named the dog he acquired "Hope."

But my deepest thanks go to my patients, especially Ariel Sutin, whose story makes up Chapter V of this book. They are the frontline soldiers in the hard battle of reconstructing their lives. Their struggle and suffering, their trust and humaneness have never ceased to move me, as have the moments of sharing the exciting breakthroughs that produced little inner victories in the lives of the patients and a better understanding of their relationship to themselves and their world. At times, they made me feel as if I were a sculptor who was bringing out the best of what was in them the way they were bringing out the best in me as their doctor.

New York
Sherman, Connecticut
1980

This book is dedicated to all people
who live on hope.

Contents

Hope sustains life
Hopelessness causes death

Introduction

WHEN DID I experience the full meaning of hope for the first time? My mind went back to an hour of mortal dread when, as a very young soldier, I was facing a firing squad. Not for cowardice; not for treason but, incredibly, for loyalty.

It was the night of November 1, 1918, at the barracks of an Austrian military training center near L'vov, in the western Ukraine. I had been sent there with some of the men of my unit who had survived an epidemic of typhus. The original Russian front had long since collapsed, due to a separate peace treaty and the Bolshevik revolution raging within Russia. That night I was awakened by machine-gun fire. Automatically I grabbed a rifle, wondering who would be shooting at us? There was no need to get dressed since the barracks were unheated and I was sleeping in my frayed uniform. As we assembled at a hall our unit had shrunk to a dozen men. The rest had deserted. We were unaware that revolutions had broken out November first in Austria, and on November ninth in Germany. Both emperors had fled. Their armies were trudging home.

At the crack of dawn the attack came. Bullets were piercing the wall—spattering mortar over me—near the door I was defending against an unknown enemy. Suddenly, a huge figure leaped out of the dark and held a pistol against my head. Others poured in, in unknown uniforms with armbands. One took my rifle and marched

13

me out to a wide court. Soon, armed escorts brought out the remainder
of our unit into a bitterly cold morning. Finally, an officer appeared,
reading an order in Ukrainian or Russian. Someone translated it into
German. We were told that we had offered armed resistance to the
new (short-lived) Ukrainian Republic, which had decreed that anyone found with a weapon would be executed on the spot.

More trucks and soldiers arrived. We were lined up, several feet
apart, while our executioners formed two lines opposite us. The only
thought in my mind was *I can't die—I won't die—I am too young to
die—*. Reason was pitted against hope. The faint sun's reflection on
the barrels of the rifles held by stony-faced soldiers demonstrated the
hopelessness of our situation. "No chance for escape," said the voice
of reason. But against that grim reality other thoughts were racing
through my brain: *It won't be. At the last minute they will change their
minds. They will realize we are innocent. Or the bullets are dummies.* There
was a cluster of wishful thoughts produced by one theme: Hope.

The human mind at a moment of deadly peril invokes a mental
defense called denial. This is equivalent to saying the whole thing is
not true. Denial is an unconscious defense mechanism that disavows
all that is intolerable or life-threatening. It is a mechanism for
escaping into a childlike fantasy or hope that all will be well.

A miracle did happen. The officer of the firing squad gave an
order. The men were ready to aim when suddenly there was commo-
tion among higher-ranking officers. A legionnaire on a motorcycle
had arrived and had given a message to the commanding officer. He
in turn gave a signal to the officer of the firing squad. It evidently
was a command to stop the execution. We were ordered to break open
a warehouse containing military equipment and load it onto trucks.
While I was on the top floor of the warehouse throwing out leather
boots, I began to make plans for my escape. While this looting was
going on, a second motorcycleman appeared with a message that
prompted the Ukrainians to take to a hasty flight. There was a dead
calm as I came down from my hiding place. As we soldiers debated
what to do next, we saw our captain driving off. "Get away," he
yelled. "Run. You are in the middle of two armies. You should have
left with the others last night. Polish forces are on the march to
capture the city from the Ukrainians."

As we marched off, unarmed, we drew fire each time we tried to
cross the railroad tracks. Sensing that the city might become a trap, I
decided to break away, hoping to reach a train station somewhere
west, while the rest of the group thought of getting into the city to
find a train out. As I marched off by myself, the group, becoming

concerned about my survival, walked back trying to persuade me to join them. "If I have to go a thousand miles by foot to get home, I will walk," I said. They thought I was unreasonably stubborn but finally decided to go with me, and so, although the youngest, I became the leader of a small band getting out of an area of raging civil war. My instinct was right, the city was besieged for over a year, while our experience in getting home was like an odyssey of a "lost battalion." We did ultimately reach the Polish-German frontier in a cattle car, sleeping on filthy straw that had been used for Russian prisoners of war en route from Siberia. We said good-bye, and I, after obtaining a travel order from German military headquarters, went on, in an ironic fashion, sleeping peacefully on the red velvet of a warm first-class compartment of a train to Berlin and my parents' home.

That was a long time ago but the question of hope, which Nietzsche called "the worst of all evils because it prolongs the torments of man," ended happily because of a stroke of good luck. But the memory of hope as an uplifting power remained, as did the awareness that it is this power that sparks the human will into taking intrepid action.

During the decades that have followed, I have seen a multitude of people in pain and confusion, first as a physician and later as a psychotherapist. They could not act and thus could not extricate themselves from their tormented and often hopeless existences. Out of my experiences, and a compelling need to find new ways of helping the sick and the discouraged, I felt motivated to write, in 1951, my first book, *The Will to Live*. In it I dared to give both my colleagues and the public my interpretation of modern man's struggle for survival and, more specifically, how to stay healthy by first recognizing and then changing attitudes of self-destruction.

The experiences of the three decades since *The Will to Live* was published taught me that not all situations can be resolved by will. Even the strongest human will is bound by limitations—those set by the laws of nature and the laws of man, but most significantly and destructively by each individual alone. My experience before the firing squad was one incident in which will, no matter how forcefully exerted, could have been to no avail.

The limitations of will can run from self-defeating inhibitions to abulia, a paralysis of willpower. The inhibitions themselves, in their various degrees, are determined by inner fears and taboos that have the power to cripple our natural spontaneity and self-confidence as well as our feelings of joy and the urge to create. People who fail to attain a mature relationship with the world in which they live remain as inhibited as if they were living in a prison they unconsciously have built by themselves. In these cases there is a diminishment of human will, even a loss of will to act as a motivating force. Indeed, as Schopenhauer said, "Man can do as he will but not will as he will." To ignite the will in a world of reality or fantasy, it is hope that sustains us or creates the momentum that can make us move mountains.

The theme of this book is to present a structure of hope, as well as empirical evidence that demonstrates that *Hope sustains life while hopelessness causes death.*

Before presenting scientific evidence of this statement, we must first clarify the meaning of hope as a concept. There exists confusion about the meaning of hope, because the same term is used for two dynamically opposite human reactions in response to the demands of life. Psychodynamically there is a hope that is positive and optimistic and another that is negative and pessimistic, hence the two opposing sentiments of poets on hope. To clairfy the different uses of the term *hope* as it becomes evident in the way people use their life energy, make their decisions, or set their goals, I decided to name one *active hope* and the other, which is nurtured by fantasy living and an escape existence, *passive hope.* It must be mentioned that there is a third group of people who see no purpose in life and consequently are nihilistic, cynical, and more or less parasitic—they exist with no hope.

Active hope is an inner mental force that triggers the human will into action. It mobilizes an individual's vast energies in order to overcome obstacles that block his or her way toward a chosen goal.

Active hope is also a source of inspiration. It encourages us to believe that we possess the ability to accomplish near or distant goals. But it is also an inner force that sustains us in our struggle toward our objectives. Active hope balances our inner needs with the controlling demands of an often harsh reality. It also supplies us with the energies and reassurance necessary to safeguard the integrity of a healthy ego striving for a state of wholesomeness.

Active hope is essential for happy living. It plays a fundamental role in all human relationships. In thought and feeling it produces the optimist, the man and woman with a positive *Weltanschauung*, a view of life, which is part of our personality and which eventually determines how we use our creative energies. Active hope is beautifully expressed by the memorable words of the late Hubert Humphrey, "Never give in, never give up." Thus, in every successful human interaction, be it adult to adult or child to adult, active hope

16

plays a dominant role because it reassures us that things will work out, that we will win, or that whatever the action we may wish to take will contribute to our survival or betterment of life.

Passive hope is antilife. In its extreme it leads, as stated before, to abulia, the loss of will as it exists in states of deep mental depression. Passive hope is nonaction or incomplete inhibited action. It is the attitude of people who dream their life away. It is the existence of people who waste their life by conducting an unconscious guerrilla war against themselves, against those to whom they feel close, or against a world they consider a strange or hostile place. Dynamically, it is any of these conflicts that cause the wear and tear of our organism, premature aging and the many other destructive effects of mind and body. Many of these people never feel at ease until death brings them the peace they could not find in a life they failed to understand or to which they lacked the wisdom to adjust.

In *The Meaning of Death* (the first book of its kind, published in 1959 by McGraw-Hill, edited by Herman Feifel, professor of psychiatry, University of Southern California, with contributions by eighteen noted authors, among them Carl Jung, Curt Richter of Johns Hopkins, Herbert Marcuse, professor of philosophy at Brandeis, Paul Tillich of Harvard, and psychiatrists, psychologists, psychobiologists), views and experiences of life and death were set forth. My contribution to this book was a chapter called "Personality Factors in Dying Patients," that grew out of a symposium on death and dying, sponsored by the American Psychological Association (in 1956), which in turn originated from a chapter in my first book entitled "Man Dies When He Wants to Die."

In "Personality Factors in Dying Patients," I compared the heart patient with patients who suffer or die from cancer, as I had observed them over many years. I described the cardiac patient as being an aggressive, driving individual, while the cancer patients, in their inner dynamics, were passive people who could not express hostility and struggled against feelings of depression. They eventually died from basic feelings of hopelessness, most of the time masked by a cheerful, pleasant facade.

In subsequent chapters of this book, papers by other scientists as well as myself shall give support to my theory that active hope is the motivation of life, while passive hope is a nihilistic or morbid, though unconscious, preoccupation with death. While genetic and environmental factors play a decisive role in the structure of a personality, a person's strive for wholesomeness and a creative way of life depends on the use and cultivation of inner active hope.

17

From a practical point of view special attention shall be given to the phenomenon of transference, that swift, unconscious interaction that takes place in any meeting of two people. We transfer to each other feelings and reactions that were originally associated with important figures in our lives, such as parents and siblings, and which psychodynamically lead to experiences of joy or concern, of anger and hopelessness. Because we pick up the positive or negative vibrations from each other, and also because we react specifically, these responses are decisive in close relationships.

In the physician-patient relationship transference plays a decisive role because the patient reacts to the emotional personality of the doctor, his or her warmth or coldness, a caring or matter-of-fact attitude, and the strength of hope or negativism he or she projects, more than to the words of reason the physician might be speaking.

In a crisis, when all the marvels of medical techniques fail, people who watch a life ebbing away, be they doctors, friends, or relatives, turn to hope. Reassuring one another, they use an old cliché: Where there is life, there is hope.

The psychodynamics of active versus passive hope and the effect of each on anyone's state of health inevitably leads to the question: Can negative people change their inner passivity to a new positive, assertive way of life? The answer is yes—if they want to understand themselves, their own emotional feelings and their reactions to other people, so that they can learn to control destructive behavior and replace it with new, healthy responses. Indeed, if people were not capable of changing, psychotherapy would never have come into existence.

If this book can inspire people to undertake the difficult task of recognizing and then changing negative reactions into positive ones then it was worth the effort of writing it. While I have no illusions that any change of an established pattern is less than hard work, I am, nevertheless, of the firm conviction that people can learn to turn existing inner negativism into a positive outlook on life, an outlook that inspires creativity and new ideas and goals that derive from the cultivation of active hope.

CHAPTER 1

Active Hope

IN THE COURSE of every human life there are times of crisis. There are traumatic events that cloud our vision and make even the bravest of us feel like giving up, like letting that precious gift that is life slip through our fingers. At such times nothing seems to matter. For that period, long or short, we cannot see a next step. For that period our minds draw a blank, our bodies feel drained, as if the last ounce of energy has oozed out. We feel lost or say we are depressed. But then, for the most part, we recover. We recover because in the deepest depth of our unconscious one small voice has not died. It could not be silenced because against all that to a numbed mind may seem futile, it has not abandoned hope.

The interplay of life and death is a constant drama that is being fed to us with the daily news. We may read about a famous newspaper columnist or a celebrated movie star who has died from an "accidental" overdose of sleeping pills combined with an intake of alcohol. The word *accidental* is often a euphemism for a deliberate or semiconscious suicide. At some crucial point many of these people have failed to make a healthy integration of the inner person they are with the outer person they project. Too often they have subscribed to an idealized image of extrinsic values, of charisma, glamour, or positions of power, while the ego has remained weak, intrinsic values neglected, and self-worth undeveloped. There are men and women who want to die at the peak of their glory rather than to decline into weak, hollow, histrionic failures. The childish pride of passive dreamers has prevented many of these people from adjusting to the merciless demands of reality, until they are overtaken by feelings of depression and hopelessness and then, in one way or another, die.

As a young medical assistant I responded to a call from the police to verify the death of an elderly lady whom I had seen some time earlier in the clinic of a nearby hospital. She had been a governess with a large family. Now, the youngest boy was leaving for college. She was not needed anymore. After thirty years of living in the United States, she had become estranged from the few remaining members of her family in her native Bavaria. Cleaning the window of her room she had fallen to her death. The detective, a kind man, inquired whether her death should be listed as an accident or suicide. Since I could not be certain, I replied that I would call it an accident, assuming that otherwise she might have difficulty being buried at a Catholic cemetery. Whether it was suicide or an accident, in my heart I knew that the old lady had felt lonely, useless, and despondent. Her real cause of death was hopelessness.

Self-Image and the Will to Live

While I am writing this chapter, I have been observing via the news media the slow dying of the eighty-seven-year-old Marshal Tito, the president of Yugoslavia. After his left leg was amputated (January 20, 1980) due to a spreading gangrene, he sank into a coma. Doctors gave out bulletins about his imminent death. After several days, there was an unexpected improvement. Doctors have often found that people, before they die, show signs of inexplicable improvement, displaying a clear mind and a stabilized physical condition. Then, a short while later, they die peacefully, aware of what is happening or in a coma. In Tito's case he showed a steady decline, suffering from kidney failure, pneumonia, internal bleeding. Yet he then attained a stabilized low point of survival which no one can really explain, clinging to life and the image of himself as a fighting hero. A team of doctors predicted his death to come within hours. Yet Tito lived on for months until, finally, on May 4, he died, after four months of illness.

What went on in the depth of Tito's mind, nobody knows. We may assume that, psychoanalytically, the loss of a limb represented an act of castration too traumatic for this macho type of man to accept, one that made him fight against the recommended operations. Perhaps this freedom fighter's self-image could not tolerate appearing to the outside world and his partisan followers as a cripple. The longer he could maintain a hero's image of a fighter the longer he could ward off the steady and inevitable decline into death.

When, about three decades ago, I wrote that a person dies when he or she wants to die, I was referring to that inner dialogue a man or a woman may have about the specific role they would want to play after their major battle has been fought and they are not needed anymore. "How will I appear in the eyes of the world?" a person may ask, "as the laws of nature demand a decline in my energies?" Pride and self-esteem play an important role. Some people grow in stature while others sink into a second childhood, which, I believe, has always existed on deeper, unconscious levels. How do we accept a life as an invalid, of powerlessness or insignificance, with the knowledge that a productive society does not have much toleration or empathy for the old or the poor? There comes a time for everybody when we must balance our inner budget, when we must measure energy versus activities or the knowledge that we still can produce, still have self-worth and still can arouse esteem in the eyes of the outside world. The decision that is fought in our deepest depth is not merely a cool, rational calculation but one of hope versus hopelessness.

A Reason to Fight: The Story of J.

Here is the story of a man who, at least for a little while, was in conflict over whether to live or to give up. It began with a phone call from this man, whom I shall call J.: "I am in Buffalo . . . the doctors say I had a heart attack." Always considerate, he, a friend and former patient, apologized for disturbing me. J.'s voice, generally forceful and jocular, sounded anxious and faint. His Spanish pride did not allow him to say outright: "I am in trouble. I need you." I answered, "I'll take the next plane."

When J. saw me in the hospital he became very emotional. A little tear was visible when he related what had happened. "I had been on a prolonged tour, working very hard," said J., a celebrated concert pianist. "I had given a concert that was difficult because of some disagreement with the conductor at a rehearsal before. That may have made me tense. Before going to bed I did not feel well. In the middle of the night I awoke with terrible pains in my chest. I took some tranquilizers. I kept checking my pulse all night long. Toward morning the pain had become unbearable. I then called the hotel doctor. My pulse ran very fast and irregular. I was sweating. My

E

rt kept on skipping beats. It terrified me. Each time I thought it
uld stop altogether.

"The doctor made a serious face. He insisted on calling an ambulance after he had given me a shot. After that all was in a haze. This
must be what people call shock. In the ambulance, and again when I
was wheeled into my room, I kept on saying to myself, 'That's
it—that's how a life ends.' "

Though in the twilight of semiconsciousness he rebelled against
being harassed by the barrage of questions by young, crisp interns.
" 'What previous illnesses have you had? Did you have a hernia? Or
allergies or an appendectomy?' I was too tired to fight them off. What
nonsense, to ask these questions at a time when I might die any
minute."

J. had a need to release pent-up hostility. An undercurrent of anger
began to displace his earlier indifference. He felt irritated by the
many people moving in and out of his room. There were nurses,
doctors, laboratory technicians—all of whom did not talk. This
increased his anxiety. "They just take your blood. They give you
shots. The refuse to tell you what they shoot into your veins. 'Routine,' they say. But when a young nurse, without embarrassment,
made the absurd request that I void into a flat bottle while laying in
bed, I exploded. I felt dehumanized and helpless. Must they treat you
like a Coca-Cola bottle on a conveyor belt?" he asked. "And mind you,
I was considered someone special, referred to as their 'famous
patient.' " J. had indeed gained fame by making movies that brought
music to millions.

J. was given an initial report since his concerts had to be canceled.
The chief cardiologist said J. had suffered a heart attack with
fibrillation and possible damage of the heart muscle. "You had better
count on staying in the hospital for at least four, possibly six weeks."
The doctor tried to cheer up his patient by singing an aria, which, in
the words of the patient, "made me feel like climbing the walls."

J. had always lived with muted aggression. Now there was the
heightened anxiety that he might die. The cardiologist's coldness did
little to alleviate his anguish and frustration. When I had met J. for
the first time, years back, he greeted me with the terse statement, "I
am from Valencia. We trust nobody." Now, he begged me, saying,
"Get me away from these kidnappers," as he called the doctors and, "I
don't want to be buried in Buffalo."

J. was in inner turmoil. He was both depressed and agitated, and
had been for some time. Tragically, earlier in life, he had lost his wife
and the woman who had helped him fight many battles in his career.

22

His depression had deepened after he lost his daughter and when a long and close personal relationship broke. Suddenly he felt lonely and discouraged. For a little while this strong and self-confident man felt that the world had become a hostile place, devoid of any meaning. His temporary withdrawal from people were signs of losing hope. As I saw it, his heart was more a target of all his frustrations and anger than an isolated physical illness. However, as is always the case, once constant inner stress has mounted to a point of damaging an organ, the threat to life becomes very real.

Anyone in a crisis, who has not fully given up on life, has a need to talk. Tragically, often there is no one these people can talk to. Many feel too embarrassed to show their emotions, especially anything that looks like weakness, like a situation they cannot handle. In J.'s case, fortunately, he trusted me. And yet he slid into a philosophical quandary to avoid talking about himself. Only in an outburst of anger could he reveal his true feelings. And he was building up anger that indicated a readiness to fight. He was far from giving up. Throughout his life J. was a man who could make a quick decision and then act. He was intolerant of mediocrity and hated dilettanteism. Being brutally critical of himself and others, he had anxieties about whether his illness would diminish the high standard of performance he demanded of himself. Until his alleged heart attack, J. was on the zenith of his physical and artistic power. He was then sixty-nine. "In my profession," he would say, "there are no excuses. How you play Carnegie Hall, that's all that matters."

At a time of momentary defeat, even a hardened soldier needs a word of reassurance; one word of encouragement may be all such a person needs to resume the battle. One sign that someone cares or believes may be all that is needed to trigger hope into mobilizing dormant positive forces and a renewed will to fight.

Now, a new complication arose. J.'s cancellation of the concerts prompted Lloyds of London, with whom he was insured for more than one million dollars, to send three specialists for additional evaluation. This new ordeal created an increase in anxiety. Suddenly the question of his career became of more concern to him than his fear of dying.

More lengthy tests had to be taken. The cardiologists invited me to their summing-up discussion and to a subsequent meeting in J.'s room. "We all agree," the senior cardiologist addressed J., "that you suffered a heart attack. As a consequence you will no longer be able to give concerts. You must not travel by air. Your own doctors will advise you further on your treatment. We are here only to assess what possible damage exists in accordance with the insurance policy you have with Lloyds. We shall promptly report our findings to our main office. They will contact your agent." As the three cardiologists were leaving, the spokesman turned again to J. and said, "We are sorry."

What followed was a stifling silence. First J. was numbed. Then his anger rose. He grimaced after the doctor. " 'We are sorry' . . . they kill you then say, 'We are sorry. . . .' " When we were alone he could not hold back his tears. He closed his eyes, then, probably to relieve the inner pain, his fingers began to play on an invisible keyboard across his bedcovers. Finally, he looked up. Calmly and with great sadness he said, "So that is the end. I had always wondered how it would feel when one's end comes."

In the absence of a strong family life, the blow to a dedicated man's work can indeed mean the end of his life. It takes imagination and strength to take stock of the possibilities and to consider new, more moderate goals. Until then J. had lived with a sense of immortality, but since the six cardiologists had presented the prospect of invalidism he had become vulnerable—a mortal. Practical self-discipline and self-worth supports a diminished power of hope. Nevertheless, it is a painful process to adjust to a diminishment of energy without grief.

In his late fifties J. had felt strong and had assumed a positive attitude toward growing old with the knowledge that he would continue to give concerts and fly all over the world. Now, not allowed to do either, he was deprived of the two pleasures that could prevent feelings of depression. Thus, the verdict of the doctors had a devastating effect and there was little anyone could say at such a moment.

Yet, as in any crisis, except when a wounded man or woman needs to be alone for a while, one must not allow an existing flow of communication to dry up. Steps must be taken to prevent rumination or regression. Trying to talk someone out of jumping out of a window is an attempt to bring that person out of a regressed state and back to a sense of reality. In their unconscious, people often test their own worth in the eyes of another by asking themselves if there is anyone in the world who cares. Once a patient told me that she stood outside on the ledge of her tenth-floor window. "The mind is faster than the thought. . . . I cannot do this to him." Although she was in a semiconscious state, she was aware of her dialogue. "He has put such effort in helping me." "At that," she said, "reality returned." She had not wanted to disappoint me. "I climbed back into my room to call you. . . ." Most people want to be saved.

Patients in a live-or-die mood have, for the most part, withdrawn into their own inner world. They are often not reachable by others. In their regressed mental state they have detached themselves from all that goes on around them, at least temporarily. One of our professors coined the term *autoplastic* disease picture to describe the picture some patients have about their illness and themselves. It means that these patients live in an isolated world they heavily defend against people, including friends and family, who attempt to penetrate the walls that separate them from the people they love. Love may hold them back from letting go and die.

Fortunately for J. and myself, his former ladyfriend had come at once and provided enormous moral support and sensible judgment. It was easier, therefore, for me to make J. aware that his case was neither unique nor as hopeless as he thought. His mind had to return to reality, for in a state of depression all looks black and pointless. The need then was to rouse him out of his morose mood and, instead of coddling, to get him to see that it was up to him to fight or to give up.

Sometimes patients play a desperate game with themselves and their doctor. Many behave like lost children who want to be talked out of throwing away their lives. They want someone else to make that decision for them. Or to have someone to blame for having been prevented from acting at that moment of "courage" in their search for attaining ultimate peace.

Once, a patient, a chronic complainer with deep fits of depression, turned against me aggressively and in an angry voice cried out how hopelessly trapped she felt, with no way out, though she was married to a loving and successful man. I said, "We always have a way out. We can become insane or we can destroy ourselves. Now, here, you attack me. If you can learn to use your energies usefully, you will not want to hurt others or yourself." When I failed to be provoked by her, she relaxed, cried a little, and spoke of her feelings of worthlessness. We now could talk rationally about what steps had to be taken for her to get well. People who commit suicide are mentally sick people. Those who are determined to commit suicide will not talk about it but do it quietly and effectively.

J. wanted no clinical double talk. He wanted a straight bottom-line statement about the illness and his chances. As a friend, I had no choice but to present the two alternatives to him. To accept the

25

findings of the doctors, which meant to give up his career and go into retirement, or disobey the doctors' advice, which meant to risk his life by having another, possibly fatal, heart attack.

Since a doctor must not give advice in a case as grave as that of J.'s, he can, if he so chooses, say what he would do. That is, of course, suggestive. But a doctor who has been in practice for many years develops an inner feeling about the human being who is the patient. Intuition is a mixture of unconscious knowledge about another person and the emotional vibrations he or she projects. It sends a message to our own brain of the feelings, needs, and fears of the other person. The physician then can choose his proper approach to a difficult situation.

Intuitively then, I knew that a man like J. might die not from a failure of his heart but from the slow disintegration of mind and body when condemned to inactivity. His unresolved inner anger and frustration would eventually wear out all his organs, including his heart, if he did not die in an acute cataclysm of inner rage first. Also to be considered was his intense hatred of hospital bureaucracy and impersonalness and being isolated from friends and his home. If he had to die, he wanted to die in his own bed.

In spite of his success in life J. had not, as is the case with many people, integrated his emotional personality with the power of his clear reasoning. A healthy integration should begin to take place in the teenage years, thus allowing a person to deal with conflict situations effectively. The better the integration, the stronger a person's dynamic strike force to cope with the adversities of life. This in turn helps people attain the goals they have set for themselves. The cultivation of an ongoing integrative power produces maturity and may lead to the highest degree of ability to cope with life, a process Jonas Salk has called "survival of the wisest."

Doctors know that there are times when even the healthiest person may have a tiny wish to die. Healthy people fall back on their inner strength and the active hope that allows a mind to mend a wound and to find alternative goals to embark on.

In J.'s case, the devastating statement of the doctors was a direct challenge to his basic will to live. Only he, as a man and a patient, had a right to make such a decision, not his doctors. His ladyfriend and I were in constant communication. She shared my views and, of course, said she would fly with him when he returned home. The next day J. decided to fly to New York accompanied by his life-long devoted friend.

A subsequent examination with a cardiologist friend of mine had a most surprising outcome. "It's unbelievable," said the specialist. "This man never had a coronary attack. He has a paroxysmal auricular fibrillation but no progressive [ST and T wave] changes to indicate myocardial infarction." He diagnosed the case as paroxysmal tachycardia.

The fibrillations continued and needed treatment. Without medication the rapid heartbeat would wear out his heart. However, the new cardiologist reassured J. that he saw no reason why he could not fly or, after proper rest, resume his career.

Before we leave J. to explore further the dynamics of hope, I must mention that almost twenty years later, shortly before his eightieth birthday, J. gave an inspiring concert at Lincoln Center's Avery Fisher Hall in New York City to an enthusiastic audience that rose to give him a standing ovation.

Making a Choice

Recent scientific studies seem to give us a clue to the puzzle of how it was possible that six heart specialists had seemingly erred, while another one came up with a different diagnosis—so different that it brought new hope into the life of the patient and with it an upsurging of his will to live.

It has been assumed that the 600,000 Americans who die each year from heart attacks had suffered these attacks as a result of arteriosclerotic changes in their arteries. In 70 to 75 percent of these cases where autopsies were performed, no blood clot was found in the coronary arteries. On the other hand, autopsies performed on marathon runners killed by automobiles while running showed, in four out of five cases severe arteriosclerotic changes. Furthermore, autopsies done on soldiers killed in Vietnam showed that 45 percent of these young men had already developed hardening of the arteries. Consequently, there is another element involved in the many heart attacks. Dr. Myron Prinzmetal, a noted cardiologist in California, assumed "spastic conditions" to be responsible for the chest pain or the heart attack which occurred because of an insufficient blood supply to the heart. It is an old theory that has been reinvented and backed up by a large number of autopsies. Other scientists have come up with similar observations. Significantly, *most heart attacks occur at rest—not during strenuous exercise,* a point that shall be explained in a later chapter and which proves that animals and men die from hopelessness and not from hard work. These observations have shown that death occurs in the diastole, the moment the heart rests. As proven in laboratory tests, animals "give up," as humans do by "something" that interferes with the automatic contraction of the heart, the systole, as if this something is giving an order, "Don't contract, don't go on, it's over, I have no hope left."

Chemical substances have been found to control the dilation or constriction of the arterial system, and intense stress or strong emotions trigger these chemical substances.

The case history of J. was presented as an example of how an individual may break down under prolonged, primarily emotional pressure, suffering anguish and mental depression with seemingly no way out. Until such a person can make a commitment to go on, help must come from the outside. Then, drawing on inner resources and a new, positive outlook on life, comes a new surge of hope, which sparks new decisions and determined action related to new goals.

Men and women who deny the existence of inner conflicts or who, by means of escapes, miss the chance to extricate themselves from a stalemate situation, thus causing wear and tear of body and mind, promote their unconscious wish to die. It seems that people must sometimes walk through the valley of suicidal fantasies before they shock themselves into reality and climb out of their pits to start on new and happier lives. There are people who have suffered from cancer and did not die but had a spontaneous healing of the illness. The same is true of an emotional crisis. Often a physical illness, such as pneumonia or a heart attack, may cover up a lingering deep-seated conflict or dissatisfaction with life, severe enough to challenge a weakened will to live in a person, and may move him or her toward life or death. Hope and will then become decisive factors for a sudden recovery or a surrender to death. People who cannot manage to arouse their own inner active hope will wither away or destroy themselves, either by a physical illness, by drugs, or by some seemingly innocent-looking accident.

While the decision about life is ours, the empathy of the physician often plays a decisive role. When I was a medical student, one of my professors, a man of international renown, stated in one of his lectures that in our profession of healing the sick, there might come a moment when all our knowledge and experience might fail us. If then ". . . we physicians," the professor said, "cannot instill any further hope in a patient who is sinking, we may just as well hand him over to the quacks." Indeed, at a time when a life hovers in the twilight zone of life and death, it is the power of hope that may carry a person through the crisis and point the direction toward life.

At such a time people may, on unconscious levels, review the full value of their lives, their past and what may be ahead of them. Sometimes I ask patients who may question their raison d'être: "If tomorrow was the last day of your life what would you say to yourself about how you have lived your life, and have you fulfilled yourself?"

Dr. Austin Kutscher, president of the Foundation of Thanatology and associate professor, Columbia Presbyterian Medical Center, has summed up his thoughts on life and death in the following way:

"Modern man has been led into confrontations with moral and ethical issues that confound the tasks of decision making and day-by-day living. The technology of contemporary medicine alone forces an acknowledgment of risk/benefit ratio factors which create dilemmas not only for those who are ill and dying but also for those who will survive. For who can really determine how and when death should come? Yet, when this is the quintessential question raised and at the very point that there seem to be no answers, one quality of the human condition offers a guideline—hope.

"From the nature of and the many kinds of hope, whether for patient and family before death or for survivors after the tragic event, the blending of these makes the whole greater than the sum of its parts. Four dimensions of hope are singled out here: the hope that springs from trust; the hope that is the mainspring of will; the hope that is realistic; and the hope that is nearly always therapeutic when it is offered with only the noblest motives of the mind and heart—the hope which should be denied no one.

"Thanatology, for some twenty or more years, has attempted to provide sensitive guidelines for care giving when a patient is afflicted with a life-threatening illness and for those times when family members must face an inevitable loss and emerge from its impact bereaved but—eventually—emotionally whole. Within its parameters, thanatology has explored such moral and ethical issues as are noted above—accepting their existence but attempting to mitigate and soften the trauma of both the facts and the issues.

"In thanatology, hope remains often mentioned but rarely pursued academically and clinically. A basic focus for civilized living should stress whatever maintains human dignity and personhood, whatever reinforces the positive in life even when nothing positive seems to exist any longer. What can be conceived of as more essential than the concept of hope when false promises exist side by side with the recognition of an individual's right to exercise free will and when we are led—often inappropriately—to questions that place the burden of decision making on the pragmatist rather than on the philosopher?

29

One need only consider two of the most pressing questions as illustrations of such a dilemma: Is euthanasia, or a direct action taken to terminate life when suffering becomes unbearable, acceptable? Is suicide, perhaps the prime example of the final exercise of an option offered by total free will, also acceptable? Such questions as these are raised here not to find answers but, rather, to introduce *hope* as an imperative element in life that transcends even scientific fact.

"Hope. At long last, in Dr. Hutschnecker's study, hope is elevated to a proper place in human existence. Hope must be an active force in every life, always offering a promise of fulfillment, involvement with living, and an expansion of life's horizons. By carefully assembling what can be hoped for and carefully avoiding false expectations, we can offer surcease from physical and mental suffering. For the dying and for the bereaved, hope brings a measure of comfort, a measure of personal growth, a measure of understanding, and even a measure of an acceptance of what is and what will be. Indeed, hope is the very essence that blesses human life, for now, for the future, and for all time."

Wise old family doctors knew that a crucial turning point was the height of an illness and knew how to give their patients the human support they needed. Self-assured young doctors may have every reason to rely on our vast arsenal of new miraculous drugs and technologies. But the practice of medicine is also an art. One facet of the art of healing is the knowledge of how to use and to instill in the patient the unique power of hope.

CHAPTER 2
Passive Hope

PASSIVE HOPE is the bread and wine of the poor. It is the beautiful fantasy world of children, of the oppressed, the fearful. And it is the pacifier of the bureaucrats, the vast army of employees who faithfully serve their surrogate father, the president or boss, in order to be taken care of and be rewarded by a gold watch, a pension, and the prospect of a rocking chair.

"Hope tells a flattering tale, delusive, vain, and hollow," writes one poet, a pessimist. But "hope springs eternal in the human breast," sings another poet, an optimist, evidently spirited by the wishful imagination of passive hope.

People who live on passive hope dream of riches and miracles and a good fairy to take them by the hand. It is their way of enduring the harshness of reality. While people with active hope use their strength and imagination to make their dreams come true, people with passive hope watch with admiration the pioneers building cities and bridges and hospitals and kindergartens, while they themselves never dare to spread their wings. Passive hope may indeed carry them through trials and hardships, but as a life philosophy it could one day, when it gives out, cause them to sink into depression. Even psychosomatic illnesses differ *in situ* and in etiology on the strength of whether a person is motivated by active or by passive hope.

People who utilize active hope will show the effect of stress in the "fighting organs," such as the heart, the circulatory system, the muscles and the joints, all of which are stimulated by adrenalin and other fighting hormones.

People who rely upon passive hope show their stress in organs that serve a peace economy, organs that turn food into energy, so it can be stored for fight or flight. These organs that show the wear and tear of stress are the stomach and the intestinal tract. Duodenal ulcer or ileitis can result in obesity, which is storing and not giving out. Obesity can also cause various illnesses of other organs. Whatever the specific agent that triggers the illness, it is psychodynamically seen in people who, in their deep emotional life, had been passive personalities.

Passive hope is basically an evasive, *laissez-faire* attitude. It becomes evident when people are compelled to take action or to make an important decision. Then many of these people become anxious, evasive, and show a tendency to withdraw. They tend to procrastinate or stall for time by saying, "I'll worry about it tomorrow. Or after a good night's sleep I may have a clearer mind to make the decision." Many react to a threatening situation with a fear-paralysis or even panic—when fear becomes terror—which makes them regress to the level of a helpless child. Since they lack the confidence to cope successfully with stress, they can't build self-esteem and, for the most part, have little or no self-worth. It is with envy that passive people look at others who seem to have no fear of climbing the highest mountain, of working indefatigably to conquer disease, to fly to the moon, and to meet the challenges that captivate the imagination of many. These are the ones who, when they fail, pick themselves up and begin again with the determination that comes from active hope.

Most passive people don't know or don't believe that they can learn to overcome the inhibitions that prevent them from growing up emotionally. And so they remain, for the most part, the way they are, the way they have been programmed to be. Positive people make a mountain to be crossed shrink into a hill; passive people turn that same hill back into a mountain.

Nowhere is the power of hope, be it positive or negative, more striking in its effect than at the bedside of a patient. Over and over doctors have witnessed changes in the course of a night. Patients in nearly hopeless conditions suddenly change for the better. The medical establishment has no scientific explanation for these seemingly miraculous improvements. And yet, if we think of J., our patient with the heart attack in the first chapter, it was the sudden surge of positive hope at a moment of deep depression that brought about his cure. Doctors have seen these cases. They know about them but because they are scientists most remain sceptical. But not all. Some believe in the healing power of hope.

The Healing Power of Hope

I think of an incident that occurred while I was writing this chapter. I went to visit a friend in the hospital and accidentally ran into the chief of surgery. I was eager to talk to him, for I had received a laboratory report regarding another friend who had just been operated on for a tumor.

The tumor was cancerous. His surgeon had called to ask me what to tell his very anxious patient, and also how to break the news to his patient's wife and children. I knew I was in for a rough time for the man could be persistent and would use pressure to make me confess the truth, as would the family. After some thought, I prepared two stories, one that sounded plausible enough for my friend, avoiding the term cancer unless he asked in a pointed manner, and another story for the family, telling them the full truth.

I asked the chief of surgery how he would handle such a situation. He answered with a story he had been told by Dr. Frank Leahy, then head of the famous Leahy Clinic in Boston. In a similar situation Dr. Leahy had decided to tell the truth to the family about a malignancy, but told them not to tell the patient. However, he thought it wise never to mention to the family that the cancer had invaded connective tissues, which gave the case a rather poor prognosis. Speaking about prognosis and self-healing of cancer, Dr. Leahy said, "How can anyone talk about a five-year waiting period and say that if there is no recurrence of cancer a patient can then be considered cured? The five years or ten years waiting . . . it's all nonsense."

The family in Dr. Leahy's story, especially the two sons, both Harvard graduates, insisted on telling their father the truth. There was a family meeting in Dr. Leahy's office. Finally, the mother raised her voice and addressing her sons, said emphatically: "I forbid you to say anything to your father other than all is well. I know your father. What you intend to say would destroy him." So, nothing was said. And the patient lived in good health and contentment for another twelve years, until he died from a heart attack.

I handled the situation with my friend and his family in exactly the same way. Since my early years as a physician, I had learned that taking away hope is, to most people, like pronouncing a death sentence. Their already hard-pressed will to live can be paralyzed and they may give up and die. In my friend's case he had been a heavy smoker, and the cancer had invaded his lungs, which is medically considered a *signum male ominis* (a bad or hopeless sign). Nevertheless, his wife took a strongly encouraging position. Her positive, reassuring attitude almost at once dispelled his gloomy mood and he did indeed show marked signs of improvement. But the disease had progressed too far. He had reached the same age as his father when he had died, a phenomenon that has always puzzled me and made me believe that we may actually mark our time of death and die by giving up the fight.

Another case comes to mind. The patient, in his late fifties, an ambassador of a foreign country, had asked about a thorough checkup to be sure that certain symptoms he was exhibiting were not due to cancer. I referred him to Memorial Hospital, one specializing in cancer and allied diseases. He called me a few days later, very disturbed. A brash young doctor had told him his condition was most likely due to a cancerous growth. Further examination proved the young doctor wrong. There was no malignancy. "How could this young doctor cold-bloodedly make a statement that almost destroyed me?" the ambassador, still shaken, demanded to know. "I understand a doctor must be truthful, but not overzealous, robbing a man of his hope, especially when the doctor is wrong!"

A pamphlet recently distributed by Hoffmann-La Roche, Inc. a pharmaceutical company, included an article entitled "Coping with Chronic and Catastrophic Illness." In it, the author writes, "An important recovery mechanism once the initial fear and disappointment subsides is the *mobilization of hope*. Patients in burn wards, for example, see others around them who are undergoing the same experience. One patient stated, 'I was pretty discouraged at first—didn't see how I'd get over it, but they [doctors and nurses] seemed to know. . . . You could see people getting better. . . .'"

The Hidden Cry for Help

Often hidden behind symptoms of a physical illness and a multitude of emotional problems, usually minimized or deliberately expressed in a most casual manner, is a tormented man or woman trying to conceal inner anguish. When encouraged to speak, such people may finally admit some of their fears or nightmares, speak of their despair, or may simply say that they feel discouraged or hopeless.

One such man had pleaded with me to see him in his home. He

could not rouse himself to come to the office. "My inner pressures," he said, "have become unbearable," Yet once I was there, the man seemed to have difficulty explaining why it was so important that I had come. Relieved by my presence he began to make conversation, evidently to minimize his anxiety. Suddenly he said, "Just look out of the window and see how beautiful Central Park looks with the first flowers of spring." I crossed over to the open window on the tenth floor of his Fifth Avenue apartment and as I was about to take in the spectacular view, something made me turn. I caught an irrational flicker in the man's dark blue eyes as he stared into space. A split-second passed. As I placed myself in front of the window, I asked, "Did you want to jump?" His answer was so direct, it was startling. "Yes. What is there left for me in life?" he replied in an almost inaudible voice. Why, then, did he call? Obviously, he wanted help. Obviously he had not lost all hope. But he was afraid or ashamed to ask for help.

This man, I learned, had just returned from Paris where he maintained an apartment. Over the past two years he had made three or four appointments, obviously to discuss some of his problems, only to cancel them just a day before sailing. "Now, I am at the end," he said. "I can't run anymore."

I looked at the patient. He was a tall, ruddy, silver-haired, distinguished-looking man in his late sixties. "I don't think anyone can help me," he said. Again, pride made him minimize his inner terror. "My closest friend insisted I call you." He paused. "You see . . . I have nothing to live for . . . no wife . . . no children. I had one daughter. She was killed in an accident a long time ago. . . . I can't go to church, for I have no belief in anything."

More and more, he began to speak as if the floodgates of a repressed, tortured mind had finally opened. It was like a confession. "I was reared an Episcopalian, but I lost my belief in God. Then I lost my joy in sex. What is there left when you grow old . . . booze, food, travel? I had the most rigid, puritanical upbringing. . . . Sex was the lure of the devil. Yes, a good education . . . but no preparation for life . . . or how to live with myself. . . ."

The patient spoke about his family, which had come from Scotland several generations ago. They made a great deal of money but human values were not taught. "Now, at the end of my life, I feel discouraged. . . . The hope I used to have is gone."

This man was like a child in his trust. His type of depression, called involutional melancholia, yields very effectively to a proper choice of psychotropic drugs. Indeed, in less than two months this patient felt better than he had in years. So affective was his transference to me that, as in the training process of a conditioned reflex, five or six repetitive meetings were sufficient to dispel any depressive mood. One day, his companion called from Florida saying it was an emergency. When I arrived there, the patient was relaxed. "What is it?" he asked. "Now that you are here for fifteen minutes, my depression is gone. I will be fine and confident." The name of the little wonder is Hope.

This patient lived for many more years. He found a female companion, a former nurse, who helped him dispel the heavy hours of loneliness and inspired him to resume his former life of traveling. He came for occasional visits until I learned, years later, that he had slipped in the bathroom in his Paris apartment and died from a concussion of the brain.

Another case is that of a housewife, an extraordinary, beautiful young woman. "I had everything," she said. "My father is the chairman of . . ." and she mentioned the name of one of the largest banks in America. "I am married. My husband is socially prominent and very attractive. He has a seat at the New York Stock Exchange. I have three beautiful children. I take care of them. I have a beautiful home in Darien, Connecticut. But comes Sunday, I can't get out of bed; I feel paralyzed. There seems to be no purpose. Life could go on without me. I feel down in the dumps. I have no energy. Though I take care of the home and my children, I am aware of how passive I am and I hate myself for it. None of the pills my family doctor gave me helped. And so my hope is at a low, low ebb. Then, at a moment of despair, my doctor sent me to you."

Another patient: "I lost my job when my boss retired. I came from the South. I was young and pretty and I thought I would conquer New York. I did get into a social whirl and I met some of the rich and the mighty.

"One of these men seemed understanding. He had just been divorced and I didn't know at first that he was a millionaire. We were married and then the yelling matches began. But after each fight, he was apologetic and covered me with jewels. He had exquisite taste and was very generous. However, when I was unruly, he took all my jewels away. Later, when we made up, he returned them with a new gem added. One day I had had it. I left him. He tried in every possible way to get me back. I refused. I left with no money and no settlement. It was my pride that would not let me be reasonable. I took a job as a secretary which paid just enough money to exist temporarily. Ten years have gone by. I have withdrawn from people.

I take my telephone off the hook. I watch TV programs until my eyes hurt. I always thought something good would happen. It hasn't. Now, I have hardly any money even to pay for this visit. Where did all my enthusiasm and my hope go?"

Another case: A young man, just thirty, had come to see me with great reluctance. His anxiety was evident. He was fidgety, shifting his position until finally he said, "I don't know why I am here. Maybe I am a little crazy but I am not a homosexual," he said. "Neither is my friend who finally convinced me to come here. We served together in Vietnam. And we talked a lot—about life and sex and everything. He is the only one I trust.

"My friend says I am crazy to work as a shipping clerk in a stockroom of a department store with my education and brain. I told him over and over that he was wrong. I have no brain, nothing extraordinary. I went to Princeton, okay, graduated *cum laude*—it was easy—and I did this just to get my parents off my back. They would like to brag about my 'working in the State Department' or having a business they would buy for me. I don't care. Money never interested me. If I had any real talent, I would have shown it by now. And to take anything from my parents? That's the last thing I would do. They buy everything. Even love."

Since he had talked about life with his friend I asked him, "How do you see life? Can you see any purpose, any place for yourself in society?" He thought for a long while. "These dreams I had, they're all kid-stuff. A farm. Maybe a ranch. A home, a wife, children. What can I give anyone? I am not a drifter because I believe a man must work for his living. You see, I would make an effort if I could believe in something in life. But all I have found are greed, hyprocrisy, and violence. Pompous old men talk about freedom and send their sons off to war to kill people who have never done anything to hurt anybody. We had to burn down their miserable huts—poor people, gentle people. Don't think. Just kill. It's an order. You follow orders. It's for freedom. It's for your country. They wanted to make me an officer because of Princeton, . . . I wanted to remain a private. When you get killed, what difference does it make what you are?

"And back home? The same rules. You follow orders. Instead of being a captain you become the vice-president of a company. That's more money. I don't need more money.

"I thought about this world. And about flying to the moon. And the United Nations. And what hope is there with all the hate, multiple warheads and nuclear death? There are a lot of eager beavers who go for big money and big cars and don't care about anything, but I think there must be something more to life, except I can't see it. I can't act happy if I feel the way I do about the future. And there are a lot of guys who feel the same way . . . I know."

What have all of these people in common: the rich man who wants to jump, the beautiful young housewife, the formerly wealthy secretary, the veteran? They are not poor socioeconomically, merely hampered by circumstances. They belong to the privileged. The economically poor living in misery may feel the unhappiness of these four people to be the result of self-pity or overindulgence. But from a point of positive hope, the privileged almost seem worse off than the poor. The socioeconomically deprived have the hope that if they could win in a lottery or could in some way make or inherit money, all would be well—a hope the rich no longer have.

What the people in these brief case histories have in common is a condition called mental depression. Except for the man who wanted to jump, their mental state of sadness is called reactive depression, because their loss of hope, or hopelessness, is the reaction to an intolerable situation they don't know how to change, because they don't even know what it is.

The beautiful housewife lives with a man she does not love. Her spirit, or ego, as we call it, was squashed by her parents. "And my husband was even more passive than I was. I think he was afraid of me. He tried to find little jobs to do to avoid talking to me." Both went through successful therapy but decided, since their marriage had no solid base, to separate. The secretary learned to understand her problems but instead of working them out decided to return to her hometown and friends. And the veteran? He made a spectacular adjustment. With the money from his trust fund he bought a farm, married, has children and feels that all his early years were like a bad dream. He calls himself a happy man and enjoys using his spare time to work on a project to help disadvantaged children.

People of passive hope suffer, although many know what they should do, they cannot rouse themselves to act. They are frozen. They put off a decision, or, sadly, settle for much less than they could accomplish.

Leaving Depression Behind: The First Steps

What can these unhappy people do? There are three things they can do if they want to become happier people. One is to try to understand the deeper causes for their fears and inhibition. The second is to write down, when their brains are clear, a program of how to act when they are confused. The third step is to seek professional help if they cannot do it by themselves. After all, most people cannot cure their physical illnesses by themselves and don't feel at all ashamed to call a doctor.

In a later chapter the cures for people who are motivated by passive hope or who have lost hope altogether shall be further outlined. With the resources at our disposal, psychology can help those *who want help* to participate in the great beautiful world that is available for those who make the effort.

Many, by trial and error, learn to pull themselves up by their own bootstraps. Others, frightened, confused, and insecure need professional help to encourage them to take the first fateful step toward the mainstream of life. No one in our day and age ought to go on existing without hope. Physicians the world over are dedicated to help those who ask for help. If we can learn to hope, we can learn to live. As Pliny the Elder said almost two thousand years ago, "Hope is the pillar that holds up the world."

CHAPTER 3

Losing Hope

J., THE PATIENT in our first chapter, recovered from the illness that struck his heart not only by his sheer force of will but also by the power of a new hope that sprang from the reassurance that he could recover. The realization of having escaped the oppressing pain of anticipatory annihilation produced the jubilation of just being alive, like shipwrecked people who after the rescue feel safe and grateful and eager to go on to greater creations.

That J.'s heart had become the target of his unbearable degree of stress was determined by the specific psychophysical structure of his personality. Another type of personality, as indicated earlier, might have reacted to similar pressures by suffering attacks on the respiratory system or the gastrointestinal tract.

Our patient's loss of hope was a frightening episode of short duration. One reason for his swift recovery was that he had always lived more or less compulsively and with the active hope necessary to accomplish what he wanted. This meant his energies were used toward moving forward, wasting little time indulging in rumination.

Another reason for his recovery was the awareness that he could possibly have become an invalid. This frightening prospect shocked him back to health and precipitated his resolve to be on guard against any regression.

Slipping into Despair

Many people may suffer similar attacks of intense anxiety mixed with debilitating feelings of depression. They may remain in a regressed state for a long period of time, because there may be nothing exciting enough ahead of them as a challenge, no will strong enough to penetrate the thick armor of inner isolation. The length and depth of a depression is often caused by a loss of hope for a happier, or at least more tolerable, life.

At a point when an anguished or battle-weary person begins to lose faith in his or her ability to succeed and is in doubt about the meaning of his or her existence, he or she is already in a state of mental depression. One of the advanced symptoms of depression is a diminishment of hope, which, if untreated, can lead to a deeper depression—the state of hopelessness. Before a person gives up on him- or herself, when there is still a connection with reality, an arousal of active hope by some joyful event or promise of happiness may turn the tide and produce a new optimistic outlook on what only a short while ago had seemed to be a lost cause. Hope can give an embattled person the courage to break a destructive entanglement before that entanglement can break the person. It is healthier to have an end with pain than to have a pain without an end.

Sometimes a few words of encouragement at the right time can stop a desperate person from sliding into a state of deep depression with suicidal ideation. One young man had the good sense to plead for help.

One night, many years ago, I received a long-distance phone call. There was a low, frightened voice on the other end of the phone. "You don't know me. . . . I am a student. . . . I am calling from out of town. . . . My roommate gave me your name. He said you treated his father and that you were nice." All this was said hastily, possibly for fear I might hang up. "It's important I talk to someone who would understand. I am having these terrible thoughts. . . . I am cracking up. . . . I am frightened. . . . I know my life is not worth very much. I don't know what it is. But if I fail my exams tomorrow, it surely will kill my parents. . . . then I could not face them and will kill myself. I don't want to do that . . . but what else can I do? Please, have patience . . . try to understand. . . . My parents are poor. They saved their money for years for me to go to college. They accepted me at Duke but what am I to do if I fail?"

The student's voice cracked. "Please, don't hang up. . . . I probably bore you. It's late. I know it's late. I know it's a terrible imposition. I don't know what came over me. I don't even have the money to pay you. . . . I feel so worthless . . . so like nothing . . . and then I thought if someone like you will say that I am not totally worthless . . . how stupid of me . . . you don't even know me . . . if you listen then I think maybe you care . . . then maybe I can make it."

I listened for nearly an hour to this young man's desperate outpouring of anguish and despair, asking only few questions and interjecting only a few remarks to the effect that everybody goes through a crisis like that and then, perhaps, never will again. Finally, his voice calmed down. "Thank you for listening, I will pull myself together. I promise when I come back to New York to come to see you! I want to pay you. I must know what happened to me that I lost control. Why I could get into such a state like cracking up and everything." I told him, all will be all right . . . to go to bed. He said good-night and thanked me.

Several months later this young man did come to see me. He wanted to work out his conflicts and he did. He graduated and is now a successful lawyer.

The acute fear to fail, the terror of being discovered weak or worthless, is a disturbing experience to anyone, at any age. It can trigger off a depression, especially among young people who are not as yet battle-hardened.

The young student who feared he might fail in his next day's examinations and the many other young people I have seen who consider their life worthless, so that they toy with the idea of throwing it away, are so often beautiful young people, physically strong, intellectually bright but inwardly alienated, lonely, and depressed. For the most part these young people have not been able to relate affectionally to another person in their home environment. They desperately need the reassurance that they are worthwhile or that someone cares or loves them. They dream of meeting someone they can share thoughts and feelings with, someone who has similar hopes of finding some meaning in life, of doing something worthwhile, perhaps of even building a happier world.

But these people are afraid. They are too often criticized, made fearful of a world they were told has no mercy for the weak. Thus, when their brain is at its peak of power to absorb knowledge and experience, they are wracked by doubts, conflicts, and fears.

Losing hope is a negative response to one or many unhappy demands of life. It denotes confusion and a not-caring attitude about life.

People who lose hope are passive people, disillusioned or dispirited enough to disregard warning signals that indicate they are moving into a depression or the dangerous zone of self-destructive tendencies. Those who have not quite given up can recognize their destructive trends. There is a change in their behavior. They may become sloppy, careless, and messy. They may not answer their phone. They may take unnecessary chances. When driving a car, they may race through red traffic lights or suddenly stop at a bar for an extra drink.

When we lose hope we often steer ourselves into disasters with unhesitating and almost somnambulistic directness, from which there may be no return. A good example may be the celebrated American rock singer Elvis Presley, who, like so many who achieve the peak of success, evidently lacked the maturity to develop inner values in order to set new meaningful goals for himself. Such a person may be drunk with success, surrounded by mobs and yet feel deperately lonely deep within.

Why We Give Up

The causes for self-destructive behavior are manifold, just as there are many different ways of self-destruction. Some people are driven by an irresistible morbid curiosity to seek out danger. Others need the thrill of playing Russian roulette and gamble away all they possess to dispel unbearable boredom, feelings of isolation, and inner deadness.

In a grown man there may be an adolescent Evel Knievel, driven by an urge to prove himself, to be noticed, even to the point of committing a misdeed to get attention. In the depths of such a person is an absence of self-worth. A man with self-worth does not throw away his life for a childish thrill or a neurotic compulsion.

There are many more people who feel driven by an insatiable hunger for power, money, or sexual conquests, causing them to move ever closer to the rim of an abyss. On deep emotional levels, these people suffer painful feelings of inferiority and alienation which they try desperately to hide or to cover up by putting their energies into acquiring material goods. They have no hope, because they failed to create a raison d'être for their existence. It is a "shitty world," said one of my patients, indicating that he got no respect from other people because he had no respect for himself.

We doctors cannot help but feel overwhelmed, sometimes, by the naiveté of some delightful, warm and talented individuals, who, despite their age, display the value judgments of children. Or we meet people who wander into any of their self-made traps—even signing their own death sentences—by way of uncontrollable greeds. These greeds, stronger than their will, might be a craving for money or sex, foods or hallucinatory drugs or alcohol, compulsive gambling, picking fights, creating court battles, family quarrels, all to release hostile impulses—all this because they lack the hope for a joyful and productive life. When warned, these people, as a rule, become defensive and react with denial or anger or with the defiance of adolescent children. People with no hope will pursue their reckless self-destructive life and end up, sooner or later, destroying themselves in one way or another.

Losing hope may be a slow-moving inner process triggered by failure, such as the breakup of a love affair, the loss of an important person, or the inability to relate to another human being; the traumatic impact of an awareness that—as some people put it—"I don't belong in this world." These events can lead to mental depression that exhibits symptoms that include outgoing people becoming meek, conservative behavior giving way to vulgarity, or polite manners being replaced by inappropriate behavior.

On the other hand, there may be a conscious awareness that hope is on the wane. It may leave a person feeling that he or she is losing control. Unfortunately, a person on a downhill trend continues to exist on a regressed level, thereby not consciously aware of drifting toward disaster.

Losing hope generally follows a crisis an individual could not resolve. All people go through crises. It is part of living. A decision to hang on or to let go of hope depends greatly on an understanding of ourselves in regard to the forces around us, our human interaction, and our socioeconomic structure, balanced by the strength or weakness of our ego.

Ages of Crises

Because life to many people is an enigma, they find certain periods more critical than others. The adolescent years are such a period. Not all young are prepared for adulthood. There is a natural need for independence, which causes a conflict of values between their own and those of their parents. The adolescent years are the years of inner integration. It is the period of a child's final adjustment to becoming the man or woman he or she wants to be, except that there is no such thing as absolute independence. We all carry within us values and

45

beliefs we absorbed in the home, and which were modified by institutions like school, religious training, and the interaction with our peers. These are the years we struggle for our own identity.

The middle years produce new crises. The realization that youth is gone demands a possible resetting of goals. Having failed to achieve earlier set goals causes anxiety and sometimes a diminishment of self-worth. The consciousness of "lost youth" is like any other psychological loss: It can cause a depression that may be shallow or deep, short or prolonged. With this depression come feelings of self-doubt and anxiety regarding future performance. It is a time for questioning the value of life coupled with a need to replace previously set goals with more mature ones.

The fifties are critical years for both men and women. In our youth-oriented society they cause anxieties for women who must cope with a fresh crop of younger competition each year. It is evident why many women dread the physical signs of aging more than men, except that nowadays, women are more career-oriented and less likely to be content with being mere seductive love-objects. Men on the other hand, who have careers they like, may be in less conflict and remain looking younger longer.

But in his middle years, a man reaches the peak of his work and now fears his decline. As in Ibsen's *The Master Builder,* he becomes compulsive to leave his mark by a need to create a masterwork, which in the Ibsen drama makes the builder climb to the top of his creation, to prove his youth, but then unconsciously fearing that his next work may show decline, "accidentally" slips and plunges to his death.

The woman, in her quest for youth, has given impetus to a powerful cosmetic industry as well as to plastic surgery or other methods of warding off those dreaded signs of aging. Women who have been creative usually remain more youthful. Having lived their lives with active hope, they have learned to be flexible and to adjust, thus remaining sensitive and more attractive by reducing anxieties. But the woman who lacks the inner glow that comes from having cultivated intrinsic values and has depended on potions and powders to maintain her youth lives with fear, and may lose hope when she feels herself slipping down the scale in a highly competitive and critical society. Depression follows as she gives up. Or we can put it the other way around and say that when she becomes depressed at the thought of aging she gives up and becomes hopeless.

A woman, who was to become a patient of mine, celebrated her fifty-first birthday a year after her husband, several years her senior, had died suddenly from a stroke. She had felt a mixture of grief and guilt at his death, the latter due to a sense of relief, which she tried very hard to conceal. She took great pains to appear as the mourning widow and to disperse any doubts that her marriage had not been one of exemplary happiness. Yet, she felt a surge of power as a result of her inheritance and a growing temptation to show off to her friends (both new ones and those of whom her husband had disapproved) through unbridled generosity. Her friends were only too ready to console her on cruises and fancy trips abroad. Although she had observed a conventional period of mourning, avoiding nightclubs and dancing, she gave private parties, including one on a chartered yacht cruising the Greek isles.

About a month before the first anniversary of her husband's death, she began to avoid her fun-loving friends, staying at home alone to conceal a growing melancholia. Her family doctor diagnosed her beginning depression as a vitamin deficiency and treated her with weekly injections. When her general condition declined, her family became disturbed and found another doctor who recognized her state of depression and treated her with medication and encouraged her to resume an active life. One day, in discussing her problem, the doctor used the term *mental* in connection with her melancholia and to reassure her she had no physical ailment. Angrily she left his office and refused to return, for she associated "mental" with "crazy." Further visits to this doctor would strengthen the fear in her mind of a possible abnormality.

It was at this point that the family asked me to see her. After two interviews she accepted without resistance my preliminary diagnosis of reactive depression as the result of her loss. I recommended that a registered nurse be hired to supervise the chemotherapy I prescribed. The drug (phenelzine sulfate, at the time the best available antidepressant) produced a startling initial improvement. The patient began to resume her social life and began planning a trip. But several months later she had regressed once again into a state of apathy, refusing to see any friends. When questioned she denied any sense of guilt. Nevertheless, her feelings of guilt and the need for self-punishment were so great that she was able to make only faint efforts to help herself to recover. In addition to her unconscious guilt, she felt shame and embarrassment at the prospect of meeting any friends who, she felt, would notice the loss of glamour and vivaciousness of her personality.

As conversations with the patient continued, I discovered she had been fiercely competitive with her husband and claimed it was her imagination and advice that were responsible for his success in

47

building a great fortune. While some of her ideas indeed had helped her husband to pursue his plans, she now felt that the respect that was shown to her was mostly due to the fact that she was a rich man's wife and that this respect was now fading. Feelings of insecurity and embarrassment were growing as was her unsettling realization that her impressive facade was a coverup for her self-doubts and passivity. Now, with her husband's position and moral support gone, she could no longer function.

Her family, to ease their own responsibilities, insisted upon having her transferred to an elegant and expensive, well-staffed sanitarium. Here she was able to live in a noncompetitive atmosphere where everybody was in the same boat, having difficulties coping effectively with the demands of the outside world. This woman recovered after prolonged treatment.

The clinical diagnosis of this patient, as it is for millions of people who seek psychiatric help, is that of depression—a mental state of sadness that seems to be on the rise.

When Hope Is Embattled

Psychiatrists define depression as a morbid sadness, a dejection or melancholy that must not be confused with grief. Grief is a realistic and appropriate reaction to an actual loss about which a person has full consciousness. Depression is a more subjective reaction to an event that was perhaps caused by the loss of a loved one or of one's security and self-esteem. It can lead to various degrees of feelings of futility according to the different degrees of maturity in people. Consequently depressions differ in depth, duration, and degree.

Some scientists consider depressions to be either genetic in origin or the result of a chemical imbalance. However, the majority of psychoanalytically oriented psychiatrists, who believe that unconscious motivations play a decisive role in human behavior, believe many depressions to be the result of a loss. (The exceptions are those depressions seen in psychotic disorders.) The loss can be immediate— the sudden death of a mate, as in the preceding case, or another close person. Or the loss can be expected or feared, as an anticipated death through illness or loss through divorce.

Depression also can be triggered by the loss of a possession, depending, of course, upon its value to the owner. This may be the loss of a home, of a job, of money and security. Or it may even be the loss of a faithful servant or beloved pet. Sometimes, the loss may have only sentimental value.

While failure and loss may depress some people, leaving them feeling deprived, they may cause others to mature. Life spares no one sorrow and fear about the future, but humans are built to meet challenges and hardships. We possess an amazing resiliency in coping with adversity. Many people emerge from a deeply unhappy experience much stronger, though not always wiser. Wisdom depends on insight and a clarity in objectively sizing up life situations, as well as an understanding of the reasons for failure. Wisdom comes by learning from experiences and integrating them into the scope of one's own value judgments.

Women are more prone to depression than men. The ratio is at least two to one, with some researchers believing it to be as high as three to one. Explanations range from hormone disturbances to heretofore repressed rebellion against the inferior role women have played in a male-dominated society. Women who have grown up with a depressed parent are more likely to become depressed later in life than those who came from homes with well-balanced parents. Even one well-functioning and mentally healthy parent reduces the chances of late-life depression. Interestingly enough, depressions can begin at a very early age, and have even been seen in six-month-old babies. These babies manifest their depressions by crying, sleep disturbances, and a failure to thrive. These are also colic babies. At first they display violent reactions, such as restlessness and banging their heads; then they show weakness and lie in their cribs motionless, eventually refusing to respond altogether.

Pavlov, perhaps our century's most precise scientist, demonstrated how deprived and restricted environmental factors produce inhibited and fearful behavior in dogs and in humans. Both react to prolonged stress by withdrawal and depression.

Often, a woman who is a homemaker may experience feelings of being trapped in an uninspiring setting. Lacking the incentive or imagination to use her energies creatively and meaningfully she becomes frustrated and bored. Boredom, a quiet surface state, always hides a conflict in which a person may indulge in wish-dreams, having fantasies of power and sex or just wanting to run away from a boring life. This brings no relief, and she gradually loses hope that anything will change. Childlike, she awaits help to come from without.

Repression of these rebellious thoughts or resentful submission to what she considers a life sentence in an uneventful routine also leads to loss of hope and to states of rebellion-repression-depression.

Some people may allow a painful or unrewarding relationship to continue out of a terrifying fear of loneliness that could result from a breakup of a long relationship. Said one woman, "After the loss of love I could not shake the paralyzing fear of being alone for the rest of my life."

Sex Roles and Depression

There are dangerous periods in the lives of men and women as a result of the different roles they play in a society as competitive and as youth-oriented as ours.

As stated earlier, women are more age-conscious than men. Healthy women want to maintain their femininity and desirability and enhance their attractiveness. For centuries men have been conditioned to be more aggressive and career-oriented than women. Thus they are able to discharge the greater part of their energies in work without worrying too much about aging. Only men who feel insecure about their masculinity, or men who are effeminate or homosexual worry about their looks. For the healthy man productive activity continues beyond retirement age. In recent years, and very much as a result of the feminist movement, more and more women are moving into careers. Yet comparatively few are feeling the sense of fulfillment they thought would go hand in hand with a job. In order to feel content a woman must have a sense of fulfillment as a sex partner, as well as a place in her home and the world she is living in.

To understand the role of women we first must appreciate the psychophysiological experience they go through as a result of simply being women. The onset of the menstrual cycle can be traumatic unless a woman is properly prepared. Sometimes complications occur, such as irregularities, pain and cramps that lead to anxiety about an expected menstruation. There often is a fear of pregnancy. There can be apprehension about bleeding, either too scanty or too heavy, being a sign of cancer.

There are pre- or postmenstrual blues, mostly due to a conscious, but more often unconscious, wish to have a baby, while at the same time not being "ready" for a pregnancy.

Other frequent problems that cause early depression relate to constitutional factors and the self-image young women have of themselves. They examine their bodies critically, detesting over- or underdeveloped breasts, being too skinny or too obese. They touch up their hair, their skin, the nose, or any particular part of the body on which they can blame their unhappiness.

I once treated a young woman who felt depressed because she had lost her father. But she blamed her great unhappiness on being cross-eyed. Fear of rejection by men caused her to withdraw and to feel the pain of loneliness.

She insisted upon and finally had plastic surgery performed. As it turned out, the operation was not successful. Her eye now looked too far out. Eventually she had another operation, which also did not satisfy her. When she became aware of the severe mental problems that kept her depressed, she was able to realize that her eyes had been a projection of her deep sense of discontent. Psychotherapy finally helped her to accept herself, to get married, and to have children.

The question of constitutional factors being responsible for a woman's personality has puzzled physicians for generations. One of my first research projects as an intern at the University Hospital in Berlin was a study of delayed menstrual cycles in young students and the possibility of this as a cause of depression. The study was to attempt to correlate constitutional characteristics, such as body build, height, the ratio of the measurement of hips, shoulders, and chest to the delayed onset of a menstrual period. Such an interrelationship exists. I assumed, according to the studies at that time, that the problems stemmed from a malfunctioning of the anterior lobe of the pituitary, the master gland at the base of the brain. I did not know then how important the psychodynamic interplay was in a person, how a young woman sees herself and what her self-evaluation is. Did she like or dislike herself? Was she happy or depressed? These factors via the hormone-glandular system could well contribute to disturbances of the menstrual cycle, though constitutional factors also play an important part.

Then, a woman must come to grips with her child-bearing potential. Pregnancy is a happy period for most women, because of natural glandular stimulation and the knowledge that they are creating a new life. Some woman may hope for a boy, others for a girl. Many indulge in fantasies happily attempting to predict characteristics of the new baby from each side of the family. Both parents may dream of a great future for their baby—perhaps one they wanted for themselves.

Few women are fully conscious of the almost godlike power they have in shaping the personality of a new life in their own images, whether for good or bad. But from a point of creativity and hope at its highest, pregnancy and birth are, for the most part, exhilarating and truly creative experiences.

The postpartum blues many women complain about result not really from hormonal changes in their bodies but, as this author believes, from the conflicts, anxieties, and responsibilities which surround their new roles as mothers.

The growing knowledge that babies can be badly damaged psychologically due to a lack of understanding has frightened many prospective mothers. If there is one problem facing a young mother, it is not motherhood as such, but a fear of her own inadequacy and inability to assume full responsibility for another life.

There are mothers who carry children they do not want—not because of rape—but because of the realization they do not love the father. Guilt can also be responsible in a case where a woman has married, not for love, but for a need to get out of a restrictive parental home or, perhaps, for what she feels a marriage will give her in wealth or social position.

Menopause is a much more critical time for many women. The gloomy anticipation of "old age" ahead feeds, perhaps an already existing anxiety, unfulfillment, or depression. In many cases menopausal symptoms often come as a result of less responsibility and more leisure time for which the woman has not prepared herself. Overabundant leisure often is more difficult to bear than too much work.

The problem facing men in their middle years is a constant self-assessment, which inevitably leads to these questions: Am I on the right track? Have I reached the goals I have set for myself when I laid the foundation for my hopes and dreams, for my accomplishments? Have I settled for less? Is this as far as I can go?

These questions become more pressing when a man is moving into his late forties and fears a physical decline, primarily in the area of effective sexual function. A man may suffer anguish or even a physical breakdown if he feels he has failed—even if in the eyes of society he may be considered a great success. A harsh self-condemnation or a neurotic fear of aging may cause many to sink into depressions that they will desperately try to conceal. And many depressions sail under the flag of physical illness.

Marriages, as we shall see later, have their own crises. There are periods of peaks and depressions, successes or failures, of hope soaring or hope waning.

Depressions bring a feeling of sadness about a loss and the fear of never regaining that which is lost: Protection and security in the young, youth in the aging woman, virility in the older man. These attitudes are understandable, but all reflect more or less immature attitudes toward life.

Causes and Symptoms of Depression

In the light of everyday experiences, there are several main causes for depression:

1. Failure in one's sexual functioning. In a woman, it is the inability to experience orgasm, and insecurity and confusion about her roles as a woman, wife, or mother. In a man, it is impotence or premature ejaculation or the inability to satisfy a woman, followed by a loss of self-respect.

2. Criticism and the risk of rejection, of failure, especially for someone who is exposed to public opinion and lacks an ego strong enough to maintain his or her self-esteem.

3. The lack of success in one's own eyes or in the eyes of the business world or in a profession or occupation measured by socio-economic factors. This is rooted in one's sense of inadequacy and/or fear of failure.

4. Sometimes success itself can bring about a depression in a person who feels guilty and basically unworthy and undeserving of praise or success.

5. Repressed inward aggression causing depressions are triggered by fear of losing love and protection or from outright cowardice to act when one knows one must.

When provoked, the body reacts with a natural impulse to strike back. But a rigid code of "proper" civilized behavior does not usually permit any expressions of rage and anger. To function effectively, we have to learn to apply a skillful diplomacy in negotiating a truce between our forces of healthy aggression and our often too harsh and too restrictive inhibitions or taboos. There is a safe area in between. Self-assertion means taking and defending a place in society according to one's ability and self-worth while respecting the needs of those for whom we are responsible and the rights of other human beings.

There are more symptoms that indicate the beginning of a depression. These symptoms may be subjective or objective. Some of the painful and morbid feelings are known only to the person who is depressed while others are evident to those around him or her.

Some of the most frequent early symptoms of people who are losing hope are:

1. Sleep disturbances. These can manifest themselves in difficulty in falling asleep or awakening too early. On the other hand sleep is a common means of escape. Depressed people may not wish to get up in the morning and may react to even slight adversities during the day by taking long naps. This group harbors a life-long depression, often

mixed with inner hostility they dare not release. Depressed people are the "night people," unconscious of and therefore defying the fear of death by staying awake for a great part of the night.

2. Constipation, frequent voiding during the night, and a variety of psychosomatic symptoms such as fatigue states and gastrointestinal or cardiovascular disturbances. Different people have different targets in their bodies, that is, organs that act up under stress. Psychosomatic illness often serves as a coverup for depression a person may not be able to face.

3. Behavioral changes. A woman who may always have taken great pride in her dress, hairstyle, and makeup may become negligent or untidy. A man who used to be well informed may stop reading books and newspapers. A change of life-style or a withdrawal from friends are signs of depression. So too may be a general loss of interest in life. Depressed people also lose their sense of joy and readiness to laugh. When deprived of a mental defense and suddenly faced with the cold facts of reality, a person may then feel naked and vulnerable.

4. Lessening of intellectual sharpness. This is a diminishing of the power of mental concentration to the point of both feeling and appearing dull. Unchecked, even the facial expression may become frozen and rigid and the eyes may seem lifeless. Depressed people may defend themselves in a way similar to that of insecure people, by assuming an air of arrogance, evasiveness, and an impenetrable unapproachability.

Fighting Depression

As with a physical illness, early detection of a depression will improve the chances for a cure. A depression is best fought by channeling aggression into controlled action. Instead of moving away from people we can make an effort to move toward them; we can use the telephone to communicate. (There is a need to talk, and confiding in someone we trust is helpful.) If we hear complaints from a person, that he or she has not received any social invitations lately, we may find that these people themselves have not cared to invite friends to their own home. The sharing of a meal helps to ban withdrawal. To share an area of interest can bring about a temporary emergence from a depressed state. Instead of ruminating alone, one can decide to go to a concert or to a movie. These counteractions to depression are helpful to stem a further loss of hope and bring about an upturn to a positive, dynamic hope.

The key word is *action*. The key philosophy, as Seneca, the Roman stoic, said, is to "take nature as your guide. . . . To live happily is to live naturally." We must use our bodies. We must walk or, if possible, run a mile a day. And above all, we must seek harmony of the intellectual, the emotional, and the physical person we are. We have needs in all these areas of living and they demand satisfaction. In order to become the man or the woman we wish to be, with all mental, socioeconomic, and psychosexual human needs, we must understand and, in the best way possible, aim to satisfy them.

There are many crossroads in life and many times when we may lose hope. But that does not mean that anyone has to remain in a slump of despondency. Nor must we remain passive and just wait and pray for a better day. We must not delay in climbing out of the pit into which we have fallen.

Once we recognize the causes of our self-defeats and then proceed to reconnect with an active life, we stop losing hope. Since life never stands still, we have already moved forward, a little bit, perhaps only one small step. And if we resist sliding back, which would be losing hope again, we will, with a little more courage, take the second step. Why? Because if depression is self-hate, its cure is self-love.

CHAPTER 4
Gaining Hope

NONE OF US is responsible for the color of our skin or the place of our birth or the environment into which we are born, but except for the very sick we are all responsible for the way we structure the most precious gifts given to us, our life and our intellect. America's distinctive Western culture gives dramatic evidence that regardless of one's background, if people believe in the basic goodness of mankind, they will be motivated to contribute to their society and most likely will succeed in the pursuit of their dreams. The confidence in themselves and the hope to realize these dreams has made many believe that the sky is the limit.

While there are many people who like what they are doing, there are probably more people who hate their work or hate to work at all.

Not all people know where they are going, nor why they are not succeeding. They may say that they just don't have any luck, or they may blame external conditions for inner failures. Unaware of their inner hostility, they are sloppy in their work, stretch their coffee breaks, and take advantage of every sick leave they can. In short, they want to take, not give. They want to be supported, because as one angry young man told me, "After all, I did not ask to be born."

This man would never have come to see me had it not been for the urging of his young wife, a former patient, who was threatening to leave him because of his anger and lack of cooperation. When he eventually did come, he was in a rebellious mood, his fists clenched, his demeanor alternating between arrogance and hostility. He was a most unenthusiastic patient. After our first session, I suggested a clinic and called the director to facilitate his acceptance. I learned later that while he was at the clinic he had an angry confrontation with one and then another psychiatrist and had expressed a wish to return to me.

This patient's wife pleaded with me to take her husband on as a patient in order to try to save their marriage. She was not sure whether she could or wanted to live with her husband but she wanted to spare no effort to try to make it work.

I agreed to work with this angry young man and proceeded to lay down some basic rules. He had to work or I would break off our treatment. Work meant he had to avoid escaping into superficial, convenient rationalizations and express fully and with honesty his feelings, regardless of how hostile and nasty they were. And they were nasty.

As is often the case, he saw in me an authority he hated, like his own mother. He also hated cops, was rude to waiters, cynical of politicians, but liked baseball players. The only motivation he had at first for continuing with me was the fear his wife might leave him. Her soft-natured personality suited his needs, though she became increasingly irritated by his uninvolved, hostile and, at times, provocative manner, which often led to fights. He admitted that he enjoyed these fights because they helped him release his simmering hostility.

There would have been little chance for this marriage to survive, if it were not for two reasons: First, the woman's self-control and hope that therapy would help her husband to improve; and second, the husband's increasing anxiety as his outer defenses began to crumble under the relentless demands in therapy to face reality. For instance, as he would enter the office, displaying his customary cockiness by ignoring my offered hand, I would question what he was covering up? Anger? Cowardice? Weakness? This forced him to examine the deeper motivations for his discourteous behavior. Similarly his looking away when extending a flabby handshake, the stiffness of his walk when entering my room, and a number of other signs of his hostile, uninvolved body language were challenged. The patient tolerated the candid interpretations, which he finally admitted were causing him pain and embarrassment. He was stymied in his use of aggression because of the fear of losing his wife and that I might terminate our treatments. When his more courteous behavior began to be noticed in his work and improved the relationship with his wife, he was encouraged to work harder. Now he discovered something he had never considered; that the poor self-image and the phony, somewhat pompous façade he had built for the outside world was to cover up the little angry boy he was. It was a long, hard struggle to help this man become a civilized, considerate person, with new values that went beyond his completely selfish needs.

Taking Control

Changing is hard work. Not changing is an acceptance of inner unworthiness and is self-destructive. The decision to change from being a passive person to becoming an active-aggressive one depends on keeping in mind, at all times, the nature of the defenses or inhibitions that hold us back from taking the first step toward shaping a new pattern of behavior. To delay taking that first step is to allow the continuation of the old, neurotic, self-defeating pattern. The victory over inertia—and the good feeling about oneself—begin with the second step we take, and then the third, and so on, toward a new course of growing up.

The process of maturing depends on four factors:
1. Clarity of new goals
2. Determination to work on ourselves
3. Guarding against and avoiding sliding back into an earlier neurotic state of regression
4. Resisting making compromises that lower our self-esteem; rather select those that continue to safeguard and build self-worth.

It is like tirelessly training for an Olympic game, except that while training the body may bring us satisfaction and fame, training the mind gives joy and meaning to life.

The following case is an example of a young man who changed his life in a comparatively short time because he was intellectually bright and very determined.

This patient was born in the lower East Side of New York City. He was physically frail, the youngest of four siblings. Being the smallest in his class, he was always at the mercy of bigger boys who delighted in beating him up. The home he grew up in was depressing; his parents were poor and, as he remembers, always quarreling about money. Money was an unattainable dream, a vain hope, and its lack a source of shame and discouragement. At one point he lost respect for his father, when he witnessed him striking his mother, and became very depressed. The ugly scene filled him with rage and helplessness, but strengthened the determination to study hard, in order to extricate himself from the gloom of his home environment. He made a promise to himself never to be poor again.

A part-time job enabled him to go to City College, which, at that time required no tuition. He majored in English. After he graduated, he succeeded in finding a job in the public relations department of one of the country's largest utility companies. He was a talented writer, who had a vivid imagination and a direct and pragmatic approach to a subject. He wrote good advertising copy and so his future seemed secure. But he was discontent. There was no challenge in his work. He saw little chance for progress in a large bureaucracy. Big jobs were given out to expensive and highly prestigious consulting firms. Because he lacked inner security and self-confidence, he did not dare to leave the company for fear of stopping his income. He was having nightmares about feeling disloyal to his company if he left it as well as about being unemployed. His lack of self-assertion caused him to hate himself for such cowardice.

His underlying depression was heightened by his inner isolation. Because he was small and thought himself unattractive, he was extremely shy with women. He felt paralyzed by a fear of being rejected, always asking himself why a woman would want to go out with him? He even questioned whether he had homosexual tendencies, though he felt repulsion when men in the subway accidentally touched him. He made a few attempts to date women but quickly withdrew from cultivating a relationship for fear he would bore a woman, who then would reject him. Finally, his loneliness became so intolerable and his feelings of hopelessness so deep that he had only two choices: suicide or seeking psychiatric help. It was at that moment that he called my office for an appointment.

When he first came, he said that he saw little sense in coming because he had analyzed himself and had come to the conclusion that his case was hopeless. Therapy could not make him grow taller or become better looking. He presented two other problems in relation to treatment. One was money. He had anxiety about spending money; he felt he should save. The other problem was the distance and the time he would lose, traveling two hours each way for a forty-five minute session, not even knowing whether it was worth it.

Like an angry child he was defensive, negative, and argumentative. He used his sardonic wit or cynical negativism as chief defenses against coming too close to a sensitive problem and tried to turn his superior intellect into a competitive battle with me. I finally had to stop him short by explaining that we were dealing with feelings and were not in an intellectual contest. What we were working on was his confused inner world. His self-analysis, he had to admit, was subjective and superficial, since he could not penetrate, by himself, the realm of his unconscious.

In a comparatively short time this patient gained great respect for psychotherapy as the only method to get through his defenses and into his weird inner world, his fears, and his sexual inhibitions. Except for an awareness of his superior intellect, the patient had lacked a clear image of himself. The one he had was distorted, because he was neither ugly nor really short. It was painful for him to realize how much he had emulated his own weak and insecure father. The explanation that such an emulation is a natural process every boy experiences only disturbed him more. As a result of this revelation, he now knew why he hated all that was weak and indecisive within himself. He needed to build a new identity, that of a secure masculine male and one he himself would respect.

A great difficulty with patients in therapy, even after a major breakthrough, is the application of their new knowledge. Some people take a daring first step that fits the building of a new image. Others have to wage a slow battle against a strongly defended pattern. The fear of failing and the fear of the unknown hold many people back from taking the action their intellect tells them they should take. But the fear of hurting a still overly sensitive ego makes many resist. There is the unconscious awareness of risking the opening up of old wounds.

My patient went through all the ups and downs of an awakening hope that he could possibly make his secret dreams come true. And one day he took action. He went to see his boss to offer his resignation. The boss was surprised and said that if it was a matter of money he would try to get a raise for him. But my patient remained firm, in spite of his two anxieties, money and a new job.

With his new self-confidence, he succeeded in getting a new job as an assistant editor with a national magazine.

This move became the turning point in his life. Psychologically, it meant turning conditioned passivity into assertive action. It also meant leaving fantasy living, moving along on passive hope, for embarking on more daring, positive actions. Psychodynamically, energies bound up in repressed anger were now being released and channeled toward building a new career and more human interaction, to create for himself a new, outgoing, enjoyable life-style.

The young man's ego grew stronger as he experienced, to his surprise, that in his new surroundings his opinions were respected. This bolstered his self-confidence. Carried by a momentum of success and a new hope for a happier future, he mustered enough courage to date a young woman. "I never would have dared to use any such aggressive approach before," he said during one of his last visits. He subsequently moved to Washington and wrote, some months later, that he was getting married. From a pessimistic outlook on life and little self-confidence, this man was well on his way to "gaining hope."

How to Change

Our attitudes toward life have all the nuances of a spectrum, ranging from hopeful to hopeless, from sadness to gladness. The same is true about our attitudes toward death, though the topic of death is still treated with evasion or denial. People who are convinced that the human instinct to survive is the strongest may have difficulty explaining the phenomenon of suicide, either the single act of self-destruction or the slow suicide resulting from self-destructive habits like smoking, drinking, or the use of addictive drugs.

Psychology teaches that even the sharpest intellect cannot explain the intrapsychic processes in terms of logic and pure reason. Feelings run their own course. They follow the pathways of conditioned responses set into motion by specific signals, such as tone of voice, physical attitudes, or even a smile. The responses to the millions of signals form a person's unconscious mental defense system. While their original need is to protect the fragile ego of the child, they can and do later on become a hindrance in our freedom to express feelings or take actions to release talents and potentials we have repressed.

Because we have learned to cover up genuine feelings, we may brush away early warning signals or fail to deal early with conflict situations. A continuous repression of hostility damages our bodily functionings and can lead to physical illness.

Every thinking person attempts to understand what makes him or her act the way they do. It may be called a kind of self-analysis. They may not reach the deepest depths of motivation and response but they may succeed well enough to become reasonably happy people. Others run into a variety of confusions about what they really want to get out of life. Or what their real potentials are. Because we lack objectivity, it is difficult to know whether we overrate or underestimate our talents or to know how good or bad our judgment is.

To live in a turbulent world with a fair amount of contentment demands the ability to make adjustments to the world with a minimal sacrifice of cherished ideals. Rigidity and lack of good judgment will not allow this, and this leads to conflict. The key is to be on the alert at all times to balance inner needs with the rules and laws of the outside world. Of course, we may want to take calculated risks. When Nietzsche said to live dangerously, he really meant to release fully our energies to avoid stagnation and death by inactivity. Peace of mind is not inaction. It comes from the use of our energies in satisfactorily fulfilling bodily needs for food and drink and sex and those needs produced by our imagination and inner desire to produce works of joy for ourselves or others. We may have a job, but we also like to paint or write, make love, go fishing or cook dinner, or share with friends the beauty of a sunset. Happiness comes from being in harmony with oneself or with another person in what we do and how we feel. We may have big dreams beyond our little pleasures. But fulfilling such dreams requires the positive hope that we can attain them and the sanity to begin with small and firm steps.

Sometimes I tell patients of an incident of rather minor importance to others but of significance to me. When I was a young doctor, I went to Switzerland on a skiing trip. Although I had learned to ski, I joined a morning class for medium to advanced skiers to train for a difficult hike high up in the mountains. One day, the instructor led five of our group to a steep cliff, ordering us to ski down to prepare us for possible emergencies. One look down made me think it was sheer madness to ski down that slope. I felt fear. I had sixty seconds to make a decision: ski or flee. Either go on that hike or quit.

When my turn came, I took the plunge and skied safely to the bottom.

The taking of a calculated risk on the ski slopes gave me a thrilling sense of freedom by overcoming fear. It also produced the exhilaration that comes from being in control of one's own body and mind. It was a lesson applicable to most conflict situations in life: Either fight or flight; either take action or give up fantasies of overestimating one's abilities.

Back from the Abyss: Jerry's Story

Here is an example of a young patient in the grips of utter hopelessness, struggling to reconnect with life. He was a young male student who contemplated suicide as his only way out of an intolerable existence. Different from the young man presented earlier, this patient had decided not to seek professional help because he considered himself beyond hope.

His uncle, a Texas physician, had telephoned me to talk about his nephew, who, the doctor said, was displaying symptoms of a deepening mental depression. He was morose and failing badly in his studies. The doctor thought it might be a good idea for his nephew to get psychiatric help but even better to get away from his parental home, which the doctor believed was contributing to his nephew's depression. He arranged for Jerry to accompany him on a trip to New York.

The patient, age nineteen, was a tall, heavyset adolescent, who still had a soft, round baby face. He wore his dark blond wavy hair long. He had deep blue eyes. He moved awkwardly and had clammy hands.

At our first meeting the student was overly friendly. His attitude revealed his great eagerness to please.

This is some of our dialogue:

"Do you know what kind of a doctor I am?"

He nodded. "Yes . . . a shrink."

"Did you want to come?"

"I wasn't sure," he said.

"If you weren't sure, what made you come?"

"Mostly to please my uncle. I like him a lot and respect him. But then, I was also a bit curious. At college we talk about shrinks. Some of the kids want to go, others think the Freudian stuff is for the birds. They say, 'We all are the brightest in the nation. So, we must know how to work things out by ourselves. To run to doctors just to gab is self-indulgent.' But my uncle believes in psychiatry. He's the only one in my family whose judgment I trust. He said, 'Just go there and talk about whatever comes to mind . . . and you will learn a lot.' Well, the good thing is he did not pressure. So, when he went East to attend a convention and invited me to come along, I said okay. I think he worries about me more than my own mother did. Sometimes he says funny things, like 'A person who is a stranger to himself will always try to be something he is not.' He must have meant me . . . or maybe my father. I didn't dare to ask."

"Ask me anything," he said bravely. "I'll answer all questions."

"What do you think is your greatest problem?" I asked.

Jerry was unsure, but he did know what was important or unimportant. "One problem I have," he said, "is that I am lazy. Sometimes

64

I think I could do something, but when I am about to start I get sleepy, I can't concentrate and then get very nervous. When I force myself it's worse. I get lost in a blur. A year ago, when my mother was still alive, I somehow could manage college. Now I am freaking out. Mother had great respect for education. Good manners and education . . . never mind happiness. I really want to go to college. I hate myself because I can't make it. What puzzles me is that everybody thinks I am so bright, but I know I can't concentrate for three minutes. Maybe there is something wrong with my brain that doesn't show. I think if a guy is fouled up genetically he has no chance. From what I read, not much can be done if your genes are all mixed up."

This young patient looked tortured. To keep him interested we talked at length about genetics in a general, scientific way. I was surprised at the knowledge he had in this field. He must have read a great deal for he showed a good understanding of DNA (deoxyribonucleic acid), the formula that determines all inherited characteristics. Jerry shared the belief of many people that our genetic code determines the way we are.

Scientists the world over have struggled with the problem of what part of human behavior is genetically predetermined and what is a result of conditioning. The latter deals with all the influences people have been exposed to, from the way they were picked up as babies to how they developed as a result of all that is perceived to be traumatic. In a last analysis it is love or hate or Freud's pain-pleasure principle that has shaped the personality.

The majority of psychiatrists today believe that a number of mental disorders, except those caused by brain damage, are the result of a chemical imbalance that affects the brain and its functioning. This is assumed to be particularly true in psychotic states. These mental disorders are of organic or emotional origin. They can cause breaks with reality or interfere with the ability to think, to interpret reality, to communicate, to behave appropriately in social situations and to display good, rational judgment. Psychopathic personalities cannot love, have no feelings of guilt, compassion, or concern for other human beings.

While our excursion into the theory of genetics and psychopathology seemed of great interest to Jerry, it was at this time, an escape into the realm of the intellect, which was less frightening to him than dealing with his own inner fears and conflicts. Theory, I told him, is important, but no more than a map of a territory. Theory, by itself, does not necessarily help people who are in the grips of an acute human conflict to function better. These people need support, need to be shown a way out of their inner jungle. They need to be reassured about their worth as human beings. Eventually they must learn to build up enough courage to walk by themselves toward set goals.

Psychotherapy, difficult and time-consuming as it may be, is, at the present time, the only method I know that allows doctors to objectively evaluate a patient's inner feelings, thoughts, and conflicts and relate these findings to the patient. Then he or she can begin to deal with their problems realistically. There are a variety of newer methods that claim to make a person function better. But underneath their scientific garb, most of them are mere techniques people can acquire, like soldiers behaving the way they were drilled.

The aim of therapy, then, is to help a person view the world the way it is, so that the patient can free him- or herself from neurotic enslavements and wasteful fantasies and ruminations. Beyond self-understanding, therapy helps to build self-worth, inner security, and the courage to use talents hidden deep within, which may be obscured by a person's lack of objective judgment.

What is needed most in a case like Jerry's is to establish a relationship of trust. Trust is a precondition to friendship. It is also the antechamber of love. Without trust no good work in psychotherapy can be accomplished. The first hurdle was overcome by this patient's transference of trust from his uncle to me. The feelings of friendship lifted some of Jerry's depression and he began to experience the first rays of hope.

After a few visits, Jerry said he had talked things over with his uncle and told him he wanted to stay in New York so he could work with me. His uncle had friends in the city, a family with whom Jerry could live.

After this decision, Jerry felt a great sense of relief. Suddenly he felt he was not alone anymore. But he felt good also because the decision was his own and not due to any pressure from his uncle. "Now I feel I can tell you everything," he said. "I must make a confession. A secret nobody knows about." Before coming to New York, he said, he had bought a gun, a German Luger, because he had learned they were the deadliest. "I know how to use it. I am a great shot." (The family often went on hunting trips over the border to Mexico.) Jerry was ready to blow his brains out when his uncle's phone call came through. "It was like telepathy, as if he had known in what serious trouble I was."

Jerry was disarmingly open. "When my uncle talked about a doctor in New York, I said to myself, well, I'll give that fellow a chance. I'll listen to what he has to say. The Luger can wait until I come back home."

Having made his confession, Jerry said that he felt better, as if he had broken through a barrier. This good feeling made him decide to come back as often as I would tell him. "I have my own money," he said. "At eighteen I was emancipated." After this decision Jerry's behavior changed. He acted as if he had become part of my office, chatting with my secretary and bringing her flowers. He tried to fill the void his mother's death had left with another, kinder woman.

Jerry's visits date back to 1966, when the war in Vietnam was raging. He worried greatly about being drafted. "It's not that I am a coward or that I don't want to go or that I am afraid of being killed. I would gladly give my life for my country. At this time, life means little to me. I told you about my gun. What worries me about going into the army is what would happen if I would be taken prisoner by the North Vietnamese. I am ashamed to admit it, but I am so afraid that under pressure or torture I would reveal everything. I know that I am weak. And I would give the enemy all the information, that is what I fear. I would betray my country. I don't want to be a traitor. Traitors should be shot. To be shot also doesn't bother me, but I have nightmares about the harm I could cause my country."

This statement, as honest as it was self-effacing, gave a clue to the weakness of Jerry's ego and how contemptuous he felt about himself. His self-image was that of a despicable, unworthy parasite. He said he had no character. "I am like a chameleon. . . . I try to be what people want me to be or say what they expect me to say. It's probably my strong need for approval or perhaps fear of mother's disapproval. I got whipped a lot."

Jerry described his father as a reserved gentleman whose behavior was always proper. "He has never shown any affection. He worshipped my mother. Whenever he thought I was displeasing her, he didn't ask questions. He just took off his belt and whipped me in great anger. At those moments I hated him. Later, I figured it all out. Father was a handsome but poor country boy. Mother was very rich and beautiful. Hers was the first family in town. She told her mother she wanted my father and that was that . . . nothing her own mother could do about it. And so, she got him. Mother was a real famous Southern belle. Then she began to drink. I saw her drunk and that hurt a lot. And then she began to entertain homosexuals. She said they were more gentle than real men. She helped them and their friends with money."

Jerry fell into a painful silence and then said, "I was sixteen. Mother had a special friend, a homosexual. One night, after drinking, she forced me to sleep with this man. I was frightened, embarrassed, disgusted, and angry. It was a trauma because I could never forget the incident or my shame and I thought if I become a homosexual it would please mother. I felt confused and depressed.

"I could never figure out why mother did this. Maybe she was unhappy. Maybe she was sexually frustrated. Maybe she hated men or she wanted to hurt father in some way. Father wasn't a very outgoing or giving man. He acted too proper. With people he was always quiet, never really ever laughed. I think he had no sense of humor. Or he did not dare to reveal himself. During my teenage years both of my parents were drinking heavily. Then mother died of cancer just about a year ago. It tore me apart. I will never get over her. I have tremendous guilt about having hurt her. I tried to be a good kid but it seemed I always did something wrong.

"When I was five years old I had a governess. One day mother said she was too close to me, so that governess was sent away. I was heartbroken. That woman was the only person who really loved me, and I loved her. Maybe I only imagined that mother loved me because I wanted it to be so. She never really had much time for me. She always seemed to be busy entertaining. She traveled a lot and always brought me a lot of toys.

"After she died, I bought my gun. I couldn't see any place for myself alone in this world, with father at the dinner table hardly saying a word. Now, with mother dead and my sister married the only one I feel close to is Uncle George. He is mother's brother."

One day Jerry came in and said, "I keep on making discoveries. Sometimes I lie and don't even know I am lying. For instance, when I said the other day I don't hate anybody, it's not true. Thinking about that, I discovered I can really hate. I didn't want to admit it to myself, because it is not right to hate. But I do hate my brother-in-law. I hate that bastard. . . . I could kill him without blinking an eyelash. He's a phony, riding around on the ranch my parents gave my sister, always with two loaded guns. I once asked him, 'Why do you need two guns.' He answered, 'In case of Communist aggression.' And this in the heart of Texas! Maybe he is more nuts than I. He treats my sister badly. He goes out all the time by himself, drinking and gambling. He keeps my sister pregnant all the time, so she can't leave him, and nobody says a word. I wonder about my family. Nobody ever says a word."

"Do you think people are against you?" I asked.

Jerry knew what this question meant. "I don't have a persecution complex," he replied, "though lately on hunting trips I have felt someone wanted to kill me. . . . I don't know who. Or why? I even had a dream about it. I have the sensation that someone behind me wants to kill me. It could be my father, perhaps my brother-in-law." He knew little about projection, perhaps wishing, in his unconscious, to kill his father for not having made his mother happy.

Since Jerry was under age, I wanted a release from his father to treat him. Jerry called his father, who, without difficulty, came to New York.

Jerry's father was a tall, slim, well-dressed Texan gentleman, laconic and critical. He wanted to know why his son needed treatment and what these treatments were. I told him that his son was depressed and suicidal, dating back a long time, and that his problems in school were caused by his mental depression and therefore he could not use his superior intellect.

"If this is so, how can that be cured?" he asked.

"We talk," I replied.

"You talk?" He repeated with utter disbelief. "You cure by just talking? Brainwashing," he said. "That I can understand and I don't approve of that."

"It's not brainwashing," I explained. "I don't tell patients what to do. I help them to find their own answers."

"I don't like psychiatry," Jerry's father said curtly. "I don't believe in it except for the really insane. They should be put away. Do you consider my son insane?"

"Of course not."

I tried to give a brief definition of neurotic behavior and mental illness. He listened stone-faced.

"I think people indulge themselves," he finally replied. "They don't work enough and are full of self-pity. These people don't help themselves. All they want to do is complain and be paid for it. I was raised a Southern Baptist. I believe in hard work and good old religion—that's all that is necessary and that's what Jerry and all these hippies need. He is too spoiled. He had it too good."

A few weeks later Jerry said his father was outraged that I had sent him a bill for his hour with me. He wouldn't pay because "You didn't do anything for him. You didn't examine him nor give him a prescription. It was only talk and for that he wouldn't pay."

For the first time in his life, Jerry took a stand. He didn't know what had happened to him, but he decided not to return home as his father had ordered, but to stay on in New York and to continue to see me. He was surprised by his new courage to tell this to his father by telephone, who, surprisingly, did not utter one word. Jerry decided to rent an apartment.

"My father knows it's my mother's money, so he can't say anything about how I spend it. My grandmother had set up a trust fund, so I can pay for my visits as well as my own apartment. Besides Uncle George's friends, I have a cousin who has just gotten married to a New York girl. Therefore, I won't be too alone.

"It wasn't only my uncle's influence that made me decide to stay in New York," he went on. "I am sorry about dad, but he doesn't know a thing about me. He didn't notice my deep depression nor that I was so desperate and alone that I wanted to kill myself. Now, I want to live. It's a matter of survival that made me decide to stay. Talking things out made me feel that perhaps I have a chance in life."

Jerry's absence of self-worth, his prolonged grief, his depression since his mother's death, motivated me to have new psychological testing done on Jerry. It was evident that even before the loss of his mother, he must have been depressed, perhaps since childhood.

Jerry's IQ was in the superior range, except that his striving for perfection and his tendency to get lost in picayune trifles was interfering with his performance. Another area of self-defeat, even to a point of becoming self-destructive, was his excessive dependency needs. When his mother died, Jerry lost an anchor, and all of his desperate attempts to seek greater closeness with his father failed.

A third, more serious problem was that Jerry was suffering from an underlying thought disorder that would break through occasionally and disrupt rational thought functioning. For example, I once asked him the meaning of the proverb "One swallow doesn't make a summer," and he replied, "Try to get as much out of something as you can or you won't have as much power."

When relaxed, Jerry proved to be well informed. He displayed excellent social judgment and awareness. He had a profound knowledge of European history and a high conceptual ability. He was competent mathematically and could handle manual material easily and in an organized, rapid manner. Projective testing, as defined by the American Psychiatric Association, are tests used as diagnostic tools, with the test material so structured that any response will reflect a projection of some aspect of the subject's underlying personality and psychopathology. In Jerry's case, they indicated a schizophrenic process of a paranoid type. Reality testing was poor. There was a lack of control and lack of objectivity. His character structure was obsessive-compulsive and he used a variety of mental defenses, such as intellectualizing and rationalization.

Jerry was ambivalent about almost everything. His paranoid defenses were projections and delusions. He had a preoccupation with good and evil and heaven and hell.

Jerry had strongly identified with his mother and therefore was confused about sexuality and his own masculinity. He felt badly that he did not have the lean body and small hips of his father. He did not control his weight because of self-gratification. He ate more because he felt he had no chance of becoming an attractive masculine male. He was terrified of homosexual tendencies and feared not being sexually adequate with women. Thus he avoided women for fear of being rejected and ridiculed. Some experiences with prostitutes and with one girl in college proved satisfactory. "When I am with a nice girl," he said, "I become insecure and extremely shy."

The conflict about sexuality is evident in the TAT (thematic apperception test). Cards that display vague situations are shown to a patient who must interpret their meanings. About one card Jerry said, "It is a boy sleeping and he's peaceful. His father is leaning over the bed, trying to touch him, but he can't. There's too much age difference [between them] and completely different characteristics." Of another card showing a rope, Jerry said, "A man is climbing a rope. He's in training. He is very strong. He doesn't like it but he's training to go to war. There is tension in his face. He gives the appearance of trying to see something but he can't because his eyes are closed."

In just these two cards, it was evident that Jerry had no communication with his father, who might have attempted to reach his son, but was unable to do so. They are too far apart, each having a different approach to life. Jerry identified with his aristocratic mother and rejected the lower-class background of his father, though Jerry admired his father and was hungry for his love.

The second card indicated that all his training to become strong was futile. The reference to closed eyes indicated that he couldn't see or understand reality.

Jerry's adjustment to life was difficult. His confused perception of reality, his deep sense of failure, his guilt about his conscious and unconscious sexual wishes, and his identification with his dead mother had deepened his feelings of hopelessness to a point that he wished to kill himself.

A few things were in Jerry's favor. Because of his dependency, he related rather quickly and warmly to me as he had done to his Uncle George. His uncle's support had played a good part in his positive attitude toward therapy. It was an enjoyable and novel experience for Jerry to speak freely, without fear of rejection or fear of being judged, or of losing the respect of another.

A number of outside events also proved helpful. Through his cousin, Jerry met a group of young people, mostly college students. He transferred to Columbia University, and though he had difficulty concentrating he did not give up. Active hope was now with him.

He loved life in New York, especially the freedom from "provincialism," by which he meant that he felt free to be himself and to do whatever he wanted. There was no fear of running into people he knew and with whom he had to make an effort to be liked and be on good behavior.

During therapy, Jerry blossomed. He displayed a sense of humor, a sign that his depression was diminishing. He met an airline hostess, slim, blue-eyed and blond. It became evident that she must have resembled Jerry's mother before she began to drink and destroy her beauty.

Jerry knew his family would object to the girl's background, assuming that she was impressed with Jerry's name and the social position of his family. My concern was Jerry's sexual insecurity. However, the girl evidently was an experienced young lady, who treated Jerry kindly and with respect and encouragement. He took her to his father's home for Easter.

The family at once considered the relationship a misalliance. Jerry, for the first time in his life, could admit that he was angry with his family's criticism, since they had provided very little love or concern for him. As he talked about it, he felt it mattered little that the girl was not as well educated nor as intellectually gifted as he, nor that she had had a few adventurous sexual episodes. What mattered was that somebody was there caring for him when he came home from classes. The girl had inner strength, something Jerry needed in his struggle to become a more mature young man. Indeed, he began to assert himself more and his studies improved. Jerry's genuine kindness and patience had a profound effect on the girl, who herself became interested in seeking help with a psychotherapist I recommended. It took several years of work before the relationship became a success story. They were married.

Jerry grew up emotionally. His mental problems diminished. He became increasingly aware of the signals that would lead to regressions. His thought disorder also disappeared and his span of concentration increased, as did his sense of security. In dealing with people he realized that he did not need to be loved by everybody but could maintain a more secure and pleasant relationship and avoid submissive behavior. He retained, however, a strong concern about the underdog, which years later, after he concluded his treatments with me and returned to Texas, he put into effect. Having sufficient means of his own, he took over a state agency for disadvantaged children, which he himself funded, and turned the agency into a model project.

The reason I have chosen Jerry's story is to demonstrate that a person with a serious mental health problem can fight his or her way out of a maze of confusion and depressions and overcome feelings of hopelessness and suicidal fantasies. While it is easier to work with younger people, anyone who is determined to change can, step by step, break a pattern and build a more contented life. It means building up or gaining hope.

Jerry's case may also serve as an example of what positive hope can do for many young or middle-aged people who have been living only half a life because of their crippling depression and their morbid belief that there is no way out for them. But as one young woman said, "If the pain of everyday living becomes unbearable and the hope goes down all the way, then you have no choice but to seek help or you will go under." The pain in growing up is child's play compared with the pain of being out of touch with life.

If the cases presented in this chapter seem like success stories, it is only because both young people worked with determination and an ever-stronger, growing, positive hope that they have a chance in life to find happiness. These people sought help and worked at it. Others could pull themselves up by their bootstraps against overwhelming odds. But whatever the case, whether help came from without or from within, active hope was the driving element that produced the change for the better in the people I have presented. Until the onset of the post-Freudian psychological revolution, the majority of people felt that they had no chance other than to follow a predestined course determined by their genetical code or their "conditioned" makeup, as it developed in the environment in which they had grown up.

In Summary: Three Steps for Creative Hope

The first step is the will to know oneself. This means a constant need to interpret one's reactions to conflict situations from without and from within, and then attempt to be objective about the quality of these feelings—whether we experience a sense of victory or defeat.

The second step is the detective work necessary to evaluate the feelings of other people in all areas of human interactions. It means, beyond trying to understand why we feel the way we do about others, trying to understand how others may feel about us and why others act the way they do. This may give us clues to the way we behave.

The third and decisive step is the actual process of changing. Once we recognize that we are self-destructive, self-indulgent, or overly aggressive, we must undertake that first significant step that will lead us out of confusion or a self-created prison. A second or third step, and so on, is like symbolically changing the structure of a building, replacing worn parts with new ones. Or, in regard to behavior, replacing bad habits with new, positive, healthy ones.

This third phase shows differences in "cures," that may range from feeling better about oneself to setting higher goals, and by a persistent pursuit eventually accomplishing them.

The dynamic force that is capable of changing unhappy lives into productive and happier ones is not accomplished by a mere desire of wanting to change but by a firm belief that we have the ability and will to carry through the work of self-improvement toward self-fulfillment. The force that generates the energies necessary for the wider scope of such work is triggered by the innate power of active hope.

Hope provides the impetus to begin. Hope encourages us through difficulties we encounter, and hope is the ultimate power that stirs our imagination to sculpt our life in accordance with the highest ideal we wish to accomplish.

CHAPTER 5

Love and Hope: Ariel's Story

This Is the Story of a Patient the Way She Wrote It:

I KNOW what despair is, I know what hopelessness is, I know the feeling of contemplating suicide. And I know what it takes to turn your life around and begin that steep climb back to life.

I am forty years old and for the first time in my life truly understand the full meaning of joy, love, and inner freedom. One year ago I married a man I deeply love and respect. It is my first marriage. I am also a successful career woman with a much-sought-after job in television. Yet four and half years ago I thought my life was over, that I had nothing to live for, that death couldn't be more painful than the despair and hopelessness I felt at having discovered that I had labored at ten years of unsuccessful therapy in treatment with a reputable Park Avenue psychiatrist.

The awareness was devastating, incomprehensible, nightmarish. It plunged me to the very depths of despair. I considered suicide. I didn't want to die, but life had become too painful. I lost hope feeling that at thirty-five time was against me in reversing my life. Although I didn't want to die, the cold reality of life was unbearable.

My analyst was retiring but had assured me that all was well and it was only a matter of time before I'd be a producer. When I asked him again and again "Why haven't I married?" he assured me that was only a matter of time and meeting the "right" man. He wished me well and gave me permission to "write occasionally," but only good news. After all, he was retiring and it would be too difficult to deal with bad news. I bent over to kiss him good-bye. His body tensed and he backed away extending his hand instead. That's how I remember him. After sobbing out my guts and agonizing over the most crucial years of my life in this man's office, all he could do was shake my hand. Detached, uninvolved, unemotional, as if we had just shook hands over a business transaction.

Within months of his retirement I suffered a series of nightmares and would break into crying spells for no apparent reason. Feeling that I might benefit from a session or two with a shrink I decided to interview several. Of course ten years had gone by since I had last done this, and I was now a worldly woman with a background in broadcast journalism. I set out to research the field. After narrowing the list to five, I arranged consultations. Approaching each interview with the cocky air of a "successful graduate," I could hardly absorb what they were saying.

A Jungian analyst interpreted my nightmares. Teenagers, violent and in rage, were throwing firecrackers in a crowded high-school auditorium. The room was explosive and there was no escape. There was fire everywhere. All the nightmares had to do with fire and violence. Her interpretation was that these teenagers represented repressed aspects of myself that had never been given the chance to develop. The fire wasn't destructive but symbolized spiritual rejuvenation. It represented a complete denial of my deepest feelings.

I trembled as I entered the second consultation with the Jungian analyst. She asked if I'd ever had an abortion; I had. She asked if my analyst had dealt with the abortion; he hadn't. She asked what my feelings were; I didn't have any and shrugged my shoulders. She stopped and looked at me in amazement. Then continued relentlessly attacking every aspect of my past treatment. She was confirming what the other shrinks were saying. That major conflicts had not been worked out. My head was reeling as I left her office. The truth of these sessions was creating a sense of shock in me. I was totally unprepared for what was happening. As the days went by I began plunging into a state of panic and despair. I felt that I was losing control of myself. I was trembling and shaking from the devastating impact of what this meant. I didn't feel I could function at my job. My entire world was collapsing.

Early one morning I called a friend to cancel a lunch appointment.

I didn't feel I could handle even the most casual of dates. Hearing my trembling voice she insisted we keep the appointment. I was a wreck. Carolyn said she'd never seen me so distraught. She thought I was ready to throw myself in front of a truck, and I almost was. I didn't want to go back to the Jungian analyst that afternoon. She had been too cruel in the force and pace at which she'd delivered the news to me. Carolyn said she had a dear friend who was an analyst and might see me. I knew his name because I had just finished reading two of his books, which I thought powerful and provocative. She arranged the appointment for the next day, but I didn't know if I'd last that long.

I had no idea that my life was about to be turned inside out and totally changed from the day I entered Dr. H.'s office.

He stirred me immediately. His provocative questions stung. I told him I must find out why I'd never married. He questioned me about my desire to be married, children, love, and the most basic of human emotions. I sensed a man who was compassionate, kind, highly intelligent, experienced, direct, confrontive, and strong. He intuitively knew how to rip away my defenses. Yet he left me with a feeling of hope. It was the first ray of hope in my dark tunnel of despair.

Although I kept returning I had not made a commitment with Dr. H. I was totally down on analysts and petrified of making another mistake. There was not the time nor money. I questioned my ability to choose an analyst. And so, for the first few weeks, I always had one foot out the door.

I felt utter fear and terror as he proceeded to tear away at my defenses. I was resistant even though I thought I wanted to change. I had no idea how laboriously painful the road to change would be. In my past therapy we simply talked about the past. I cried all the time and kept a box of Kleenex in my lap.

My experience in therapy had been that you talk about the past, cry a lot, and somehow in opening up old wounds one miraculously changes the unconscious and is cured. We never analyzed feelings. I had no idea how passive I had become.

My therapy with Dr. H. was totally different. We dealt only with feelings. In the beginning I tried to match intelligence. But he pointed out this was not an intelligence contest and it really didn't matter who was brighter. Here we deal only with feelings. But what did he mean? I actually went home and looked up *feelings* in the dictionary. I was that detached from my feelings.

By the third visit my usual pattern of placing the Kleenex in my lap and crying began. Dr. H. asked, "Do you still need this? Are you aware that you're whining?" I was stunned. Both my immigrant parents spent their lives whining and complaining about life. Now I was unconsciously imitating their most distasteful attribute. I was indulging in self-pity. It was such a great shock I never touched the Kleenex again. I became aware of my two voices, and could hear myself lapse into the whiny child routine.

Dr. H. was driving, confronting, and relentless. He was getting through my impenetrable defenses and into private worlds where no one had ever tread. I had to make a decision toward committing myself to therapy. My greatest fear was trusting my judgment. My instincts told me this doctor was right for me. And for the first time in my life I trusted my feelings and made the commitment.

Treatment was clouded by my fixation with time. Time overshadowed everything. I was thirty-five and wanted a husband and children. Yet the road ahead loomed like the Great Wall of China— endless, awesome, terrifying. Working out my problems would take too much time. I'd be too old to marry and have children. Fixated on time, I would become paralyzed with fear and plunge into periods of deep despair.

I discovered that I existed in two worlds. I had an inner life that felt hopelessness and despair and a glamorous facade developed for the outside world. That facade was an act. So much so that at night I would collapse in exhaustion. To the outside world I was an ambitious, competitive career woman. Glamorous and carefree. Dramatically I floated in and out of rooms imitating stars on television. I relied on my presence and looks for everything. I was bright and intellectual, repressing my feelings. Since I had a demanding job, I could submerge myself in work and travel. But the escape value of success no longer gave me the high it once did. I was terribly lonely and the loneliness and lack of roots couldn't be replaced by the glamour of the job, the romantic flings, the endless cocktail parties, and the trips to exotic lands. Walking home on a Friday night to an empty apartment or through the park alone on a magnificent Sunday stirred feelings of overwhelming sadness.

I saw the shallowness of my world. No longer able to justify the self-indulgence of the carefree life, the running and constant traveling, the endless line of lovers now only bored me. The parties and conversation that I once found either amusing or stimulating now left me discontent and magnified my aloneness. The giddiness riding the merry-go-round meant nothing. My life had no roots and no purpose. To avoid reality I had thrown myself into work and the drive for power. I had quit teaching art to pursue a career in television and had absorbed its image. The facade shattered, and as it crumbled I was left staring at the waste and emptiness of my life. During that period, at the urging of Dr. H., I started writing.

I lived my life dreaming of exquisite joy,
Of happiness and sweet children calling momma,
I lived my life in pain, suffering and never knowing why,
I lived my life crying, lips painted orange with a big smile,
I lived my life through others, looking for answers.
Can my eyes find the strength to open on another day?
Can I go home and hide in my cell and close my moist
    eyes and dream of kisses, of love, of sailing far away?
Must I always be on parade, hair painted yellow?
Will no one love me in my sadness?
Fear, cold fear! That old, ugly distorted woman,
Stay out of my garden, my soul, my fears!
I must open my window, open the bars—
My body yearns for life!

Filled with fear and the terror of the unknown, I had no choice but to risk the unknown. To risk meant a chance for hope. To stand still meant death. Yet I panicked at the bottom being pulled out from under me. I thought I would fall into a bottomless pit and ferociously defended the very values I sought to be free from. The old shoe might be miserable, but it was known and familiar. As Dr. H. would talk about the need to break old patterns to find the inner freedom I was seeking, I would listen, yet not really understand what he was talking about. I clung desperately to what I knew, even if it was sick or neurotic.

Every time Dr. H. suggested we talk about men, I avoided the subject. My previous shrink had made me feel that talking about men was like "true confessions time." He always said there was much more to life than just getting married. Consequently, I refused to talk about men and would freeze at the suggestion. Instead, we started talking about mother.

Talking about mother would enrage me. Each session left me drained. I never felt that she loved me. I was an annoyance to her. I had no memories of mother holding or kissing me. I would have nightmares as a very young child forcing her to comfort me. Motherhood did not come naturally to her. She was a teacher but never had

* * *   79

the time to help me with my homework. She downgraded my intelligence. I could be a secretary when I grew up. Why should she suffer the financial burden, when I wasn't smart enough to go to college.

As a young child I began drawing, and started private art lessons when I was six. I was musically inclined, and began piano lessons when I was eight. I was a natural athlete and the leader of school teams. In high school I was placed in several honor classes. But without mother's love I was left with the feeling that there must be something wrong with me, otherwise she would love me. No matter what talents I showed as an artist or what other honors I received, achievement was clouded by my impression that there must be something wrong with me. My lack of self-worth was the single most destructive force in my life. It drove me to try to please mother in everything I did. Without understanding this deep motivation, my entire life was ruled by its compulsion.

I wanted to be an artist but mother said I had to earn a living. Artists couldn't take care of themselves and they—my parents— wouldn't help me. No, I couldn't go to college to major in art. When the chairman of the art department at school found out, he asked to see my parents. He apparently told them I was the most talented art student he ever had. This had enough impact that my parents relented enough to at least permit me to go to college, but with the stipulation that I become an art teacher. The college had to be close to New York and if it was in Manhattan I would have to live at home. I was not free to choose my career nor my college. The rage and anger was brewing from that time on and was to become like a virus in its never-ending revenge.

Although I taught art I refused to marry. From what I'd seen at home marriage only symbolized misery and bondage. I had not seen love, giving, or spontaneous joy. A career and travel was much more alluring, but unheard of for a woman twenty years ago. I began traveling extensively, but never lived abroad for long periods because I was still afraid of the ultimate rejection of mother. I was still looking for her approval. As I taught, my anger at yielding to this control festered, until finally, after eight years, it exploded and I quit to start over again in a new career. I really did not know what I wanted to do, but it would be my choice this time. I pursued a career in television, unaware of the still-present drive to prove my worth to mother. Subconsciously she was still in control. I was in therapy at the time with my former shrink, but he thought a career in television was exciting and we never examined my real motivation. Mother had become the "Power Supreme."

In therapy with Dr. H. we dissected motivations, and I became acutely aware of the control I had surrendered to my mother through this compulsion. The examples were plentiful and painful. I couldn't stand hearing this and kept asking if there wasn't another way. Dr. H. replied, "There is no other way." And so we continued. At one point Dr. H. stopped and looked at me for a long time. He slowly said, "You are a very angry woman; you have no idea how angry you really are." I didn't. The anger was too intense and, fearing its violence, through the years I had buried it as deeply as I could. Now I was coming in touch with a volcano of anger. All the years of self-denial were opening up. All the years of repressing joy, spontaneity, laughter, sexual curiosity, dreams, and hope. The years denying me the full expression of my total development as a woman; all repressed and buried. The anger was so intense and volatile I was afraid of my deepest inclination. I wanted to kill my own mother.

My unconscious was under assault, and as it yielded its feelings I struggled to find a way to vent the rage before it erupted in uncontrollable violence. Dr. H. said, "A nucleus of hate is like a live virus that can spread and would ultimately destroy both of us." I had to understand how to deal with this powerful and terrifying emotion. Intellectually I knew there had to be a way, and with the insight of Dr. H. we started to dig deeper and deeper into motivation, this time hers.

My mother was an intensely angry and unsatisfied woman. She was a pessimist and a defeatist. She never gave love or affection and I wondered if she ever had the capacity to love. She denied her femininity and never took care of herself. She repressed any sexual feelings she might have had. She was judgmental and critical. The only pleasant thoughts I have of her is when she was with her sisters and friends. She was a Dr. Jekyll and Mr. Hyde. From screaming at me, the phone would ring and she would turn into the sweetest, funniest, most amusing person. I was always bewildered at the transformation. By others she was loved. She was the life of the party. She must have resented marrying my father. It was an arranged marriage and the love that was absent was never found. I, as the first child, was the symbol of her imprisonment and confinement.

When I was a young child my mother and I were complete opposites, which drove her mad. Her world was ruled by fear, mine by adventure and curiosity. Where she was unattractive, overweight, and clumsy, I was beautiful, thin and graceful. Where she was not creative, I was talented and imaginative. The seeds for a love/hate relationship were there from the time I breathed my first breath, and even that she denied me. The most dramatic incident I recall is contracting whooping cough as a kid. She couldn't stand the coughing and would scream at me to stop. I had to stifle the coughing, and that inhibition symbolized how I faced every obstacle in the years thereafter. The repression caused anger, which was further fueled by her total denial of my individuality. Consequently, development of my inner resources was impossible. I grew up defiantly, yet subconsciously remained the little helpless child hoping for mother's love.

Through the years I absorbed her anger, her fears, and her inability to deal with life assertively. I was becoming her, my most hated enemy. A woman I held no respect for. I couldn't stand hearing this. I was in pain. I couldn't stand therapy. Stop! I can't bear this. And again Dr. H. said, "There is no other way. You must understand who you are, and who she is, so that you can separate the two, so that she cannot destroy you or hold any power over you." I wrote during that time:

> Where is Ariel the woman and Ariel the child? Interwoven, they must be torn apart. The loving Ariel from the ugly Ariel. Torn from her, the ugly, the master of torture. I must find love with myself first. Then no one can rob me of love. No one can hurt me. No one can destroy me. I'm terrified of life. Terrified of being alone. Yet who is this inner voice that pushed me beyond my limits? It is Ariel. The strong Ariel. The soul that cries, let me love, let me breathe, LET ME BE.

I was realizing that my mother brainwashed me to believe never to expect happiness, love, or anything but a compromise marriage. Why should life be better to me than it was to her. Be satisfied with what little you have. That was her conditioning and she brainwashed me to think the same way. In my deepest being I knew that meant death and total destruction.

> On my thirty-eighth birthday I wrote: An empty job with no purpose other than to prove, mother, I can be successful. Mission accomplished. Making money with no inner satisfaction. No roots, no lover, no children. What then do I have that no one can rob me of? What can give me self-gratification and a sense of purpose? My own work. My artistic vision of the world. My art.

82

I called that a new beginning. I was crossing the bridge from hate to love, and shedding mother's values for my own. Love of myself and my inner talents and resources. I was finding my own strength. Learning to trust my own judgment. Learning to think for myself, and learning to take a stand. But the periods of depression would still throw me into black states of despair and hopelessness. The difference was the periods were shorter and I knew I would come out of them. I was aware that during regressions I would become a little child and look at the world with fear and terror, feeling that I would never see hope again. I had to consciously make an effort to realize I was regressed so that I could pull myself out.

At one point Dr. H. said that I reminded him of a rough-cut jewel. I could hardly believe what he was saying. Was I really the person he thought I was? No, as he gets to know me he'll find out that mother was right after all. I had that little self-worth. What kept me going during these most painful years was his confidence. He was driving me on to break the destructiveness, the despair, and the panic. To let go of the little helpless child and to develop into a mature, strong, and independent woman was a constant struggle.

I feared the unknown so deeply that I was clinging furiously to the past, and to the sick values I came to free myself from. I had little concept of the word *freedom*. It was still an enigma to me. I clung to the negative self-image and the glamorous outer image.

Everytime the suggestion came up that we talk about men I would feel terror and resist. Although the purpose of seeking help was to discover the reason why I never married I was filled with fear at uncovering the truth. All my relationships with men had been unfulfilling. I was petrified of being close to a man.

Although I had not been involved for a long time, I didn't really understand why. We talked about trust and the deep sense of betrayal I felt from my retired shrink. How could he, a respectable Park Avenue shrink, let me waste the ten most crucial years of my life? How could a responsible person of his profession avoid making me confront my innermost conflicts? And who was I to question the giant authority figure? The rage became violent as I understood his indifference and inadequacy. I was angry at myself and at him for the wasted and destructive years. Trust was now a most difficult thing.

Understanding men had to begin with understanding the first man in my life, my father. I remember him as being an enigma, because he was remote, uncommunicative, unaffectionate. He had been very handsome and always smartly dressed, yet I remember him as weak and unprotective. My first memory of him was seeing him sobbing and telling mother he didn't want to die. I had peeked in the bedroom and saw father in bed, forlorn. If he died who would protect us? Would he abandon us? I was angry to see my strong father crying. He should be comforting all of us. When he recovered he started working long and tedious hours, and when he came home mother only tormented him. Although he fought her he never protected me from her wrath. But he was also a kind, gentle, and generous man, who never really hurt my brother and me. He just wasn't there for me. I didn't understand men. They made me feel uncomfortable. "My father was a phantom, a crier, a ghost of a man." And I was at a loss in dealing with them.

As we continued to probe my feelings the stress tore at me and I developed breathing problems reminiscent of my whooping cough as a young child. There were sessions I couldn't stop wheezing or catch my breath; others where I arrived hyperventilating and had to calm down before I could speak. I was dragging myself to work and to therapy and taking Valium and antihistamines to stay in control. My resistance got worse as we started exploring my feelings about two abortions. One when I was twenty-five and another five years later.

In ten years of therapy we never talked about the abortions. I was not encouraged to talk about my feelings, even though the reason I had sought out a therapist was to unravel problems arising in my first serious relationship with a man. That first doctor encouraged me to forget the trauma as quickly as possible and go on with living. I was so devastated by the abortion, I could only get through it by mustering every ounce of self-control, and turning to steel. I buried the trauma in the deepest recesses of my mind but the poison spilled out and I developed asthma in my late twenties.

While on vacation I met a very attractive lawyer. We dated for six months and I, being twenty-five, thought I was ready for marriage and a family. I unconsciously fantasized a child and acted out the fantasy by getting pregnant. I assumed he would marry me. But reality struck like lightning. He informed me that he had no intentions of marrying me or anybody else. He loved his freedom. In fact, since he felt I was partially to blame, he expected me to pay for half of the abortion, which to him was the only solution. I couldn't believe the nightmare I was in. I felt as though someone had thrown a poison arrow at my heart. I was lost, in a state of shock, bewildered. I couldn't go to my parents, they would have thrown me out. I was living with two roommates in a cold, impersonal upper East Side apartment. I had nowhere to turn and was alone. Really alone. Abortions were illegal at that time, and in addition to being terrified I felt like a common criminal. Would I die in the hands of a butcher? Is this the fairy tale little girls dream of that comes back to mock you with the cruel realities of life? My roommate helped me find a doctor, and I dragged myself to the gallows not knowing if I would live or die.

From the time I told him I was pregnant to the time of the wretched operation I saw my boyfriend just once. He had disappeared. He showed up to take me to the doctor's office and then took the next plane to Florida for a two-week vacation, calling me once during that time. I despised him for his cruelty, selfishness, coldness, and total lack of compassion. He abandoned me at the most crucial point in my life, yet he fully intended the relationship to go on. I buried the trauma. And in burying the nightmare I buried my hope for a child and marriage. The crisis confirmed the image I had of men . . . weak, unprotective, who in the end will use you and abandon you. From that time on I never trusted a man nor allowed anyone to get really close. The second abortion totally buried the last glimmer of hope for marriage and a family.

I started setting myself to be a self-reliant career woman and left teaching to pursue a career in broadcasting. I dated and traveled and threw myself into work. I had long- and short-term relationships, but I was no longer there. By the second abortion I was buried so deep that I didn't know who I was. I was building a wall that would be impenetrable, protecting me from the world I never understood and didn't know how to deal with.

> Killed, denied life by a mother who never mourned. By a woman too frightened to love. Too frightened to fight. My poor souls. I would have loved you. Forgive me. Pity me, my lack of courage.

For me to climb the steep road back to life I had to come to terms with the two most powerful forces in me—love and rage. My life had been shadowed by anger and hate. Yet the hate was like a live virus that spreads and destroys. I knew that to work toward happiness I would have to choose between the two most powerful forces. Love represented life and creative energies. Anger destroys and leads to death. I could hold on to the anger for the rest of my life and become a very bitter woman, or I could lean toward the love I yearned for. For me to choose love as the major force in my life I first had to find that love in myself, and for myself. I needed to find my own roots and inner strength so that I could be proud of who I was. I had to shed the power of my mother.

It was time for action and time for a move in my life. Dr. H.'s philosophy was that life is now, you cure depression with action. And I was depressed in the tiny, dark, one-room apartment I was living in. I had moved there after quitting teaching because I had no money as I started over again in a new career. My parents refused to help and wanted to see me fail because I defied them by leaving teaching.

The room was too small for a studio, so when I moved in I packed up my paints and put away my easel. There were bars on the windows but still I was robbed shortly after moving in. That meant to protect myself I had to seal up the one remaining window. For the seven years I lived there I felt like a caged-in animal.

> There is no sun, no air,
> Only bars
> Bars to block intruders or to block me
>   from the world outside.

When Dr. H. and I talked about moving I kept replying "I can't move, I don't have the money." We had many discussions and I kept insisting that I had no money to move. I didn't want to take a subsidy from my parents, even though they had finally offered because they feared for my life in this vandalized apartment.

My fear of money was connected to my fear of losing power and independence and having to return to a mocking, smug mother. Thus I was chained to that dark tomb. My lack of self-worth reinforced that was all I deserved.

Dr. H. insisted. "You must move. From a point of building self-worth you must move. You must dynamically replace unworthiness with a solid cornerstone of self-worth. Accept the money and move. Do it on doctor's orders."

I didn't want to accept the money and be dependent on them. Yet I was sick at living in a cell. Making the move was a tormenting decision. I put aside my pride and decided to accept the subsidy.

As I looked for a new apartment I approached it as the beginning of a new life. I would move across town to a new neighborhood and new start. I wanted an apartment that would be bathed in sunlight and fresh air, and would be large enough for a studio, because I wanted to go back to painting after a seven-year exile.

I found an apartment with a spectacular view of the river and boat basin that dominated each room. It had a separate bedroom and large eat-in kitchen. The open, sunlit, airy space made me feel like I was living in Greece. I was full of hope and inspiration after nearly a year of total despair. Living there filled me with such joy that I felt propelled forward and intensified my therapy. I started going three times a week. I also started drawing and painting. I woke up with the freshness of the river and the traffic of boats. Coming home I anticipated magnificent sunsets that would wash the walls with their flaming colors. I felt so motivated and full of hope that I was determined to create a home surrounded with love and beauty. There would be nothing destructive here in my "first home." This home would be totally my creation. The interior design, the colors, the paintings, and the friends and lovers I would choose to have. I gave up old lovers that represented dead-end relationships.

> I feel like a giant octopus, coiled and hidden from the world, frightened to be uncovered. But each tentacle is being severed, discarded, and the yearning . . . the lost sadness, is leaving. It is being replaced by love.

During that first year I went through a series of major changes. Three of the insights I gained are described in the following passages I wrote during that year.

> I am frightened as hell at what's emerging. A frightened, sad, lonely child is my body and it is out to destroy me. I can't go back and I can't seem to move forward. I am hanging between two bridges, the ocean below and this state of anxiety, of facing more is driving me mad. I must find peace with myself. I must break these chains. I must reach solid ground. Courage. There is no turning back.

> I have crossed the bridge. I did not fall. I did not drown. I did not go insane. I came out of the panic to safety, and the safety is inside myself. I will save myself. I have been on the edge of the cliff and I made the passage to the other side. And that was within me and I never knew it. I NO LONGER FEEL TORMENT.

> Light is coming back into my life. I understand the fear now. I have confronted the worst. I can stand up to fear. I found the courage to live through the nightmares of my

inner life, and have chosen not to die. And I can conquer the worst through my willpower and my mind.

The new joy of having a beautiful apartment and painting again gave me inspiration to work even harder. Positive and enlightening growth experiences were building my new foundation. Love was a new thing for me. I had made a positive transference to Dr. H. . . . two years from the time I first entered his office. On a plane to Chicago I wrote him:

> I love my new doctor. He has been the only person to give me hope. I love him for his genuine concern and compassion. For his belief that I am a worthwhile woman with many beautiful qualities that he had brought out in me. I love him for his honesty, for his not trying to deceive me. He has *forced* me to see my life. He has held up a mirror for me. You know the worst about me and I feel love and affection from you. You make me appreciate myself.

We had developed a close working relationship in which I was feeling love and trust for a man, and that was a unique experience. During those years Dr. H. had made me confront things I wanted to leave buried. Although he was kind and compassionate, he was driving toward the truth and would not allow me to stray off course. This relentless pursuit was what eventually led to my most powerful and volatile breakthrough. It was a breakthrough that reached the very depth of my being, touched every raw nerve, sensation, feeling and thought I'd ever had. It changed my life completely. I found true inner strength and would never again be the frightened child.

Months before I had met a fabulous man. We met at a bus stop while I was on my way to work. We seemed to have an instant rapport and that led to months of dating. The closer we became the greater my fear became. The greater my fear the greater my conflict. Getting close to David was bringing all my fears to the surface.

I wanted to flee and leave both my doctor and my boyfriend, but neither would allow me to escape. After talking theory all these years I was about to be tested. I was in a terrible state of anxiety headed for a collision course.

We were in a restaurant and I couldn't stop coughing. My face got red and my body was sweating. I couldn't control my cough and wanted to run out the door because people had started to look at me. David looked worried and disturbed. I wanted to flee. But he wouldn't let me. And the cough continued. It continued throughout the night and into the next day. By that night my breathing was extremely heavy and I couldn't catch my breath.

I was in a panic as I labored to get air into my lungs. I got so bad that David had me breathe into a paper bag. What was happening to me? I felt like a junkie. I went into the bathroom and closed the door and lay on the cold tile floor. I tried to calm myself down. But I just rocked back and forth crying as I labored to breathe.

Like a smoldering volcano that had been dormant for years, I was repressing inner rage and anger that was erupting in a shattering explosion. All the poisonous gases that had been destroying me for so many years were being released. The fury of the explosion ripped at every raw nerve and turned my guts inside out. It was becoming my struggle for survival. From such an eruption one either succumbs and is destroyed or emerges victorious.

For two horrible endless days this fight for breath continued. By the third day I was so desperate and panicked I called Dr. H. Instead of consoling and calming me he was confrontive and attacking. He called me a coward and told me I was absolutely destroying my relationship with David. At that moment I despised my doctor. He was the enemy. He had no compassion. He had turned against me. I left his office feeling abandoned by the one person I had trusted. That night I collapsed and had to be taken to a hospital emergency room.

Safe inside the walls of the hospital I could find refuge away from my doctor and away from David. I was entering a long pitch-black tunnel, full of traps and dangers. Inside were all the hidden fears, nightmares, rejections, abandonments and failures . . . the repressed traumas of a lifetime. The tunnel had two exits. On one end was mother. She was in the darkest recesses of the tunnel, standing in darkness, surrounded by death. In the other end of the tunnel was my doctor, surrounded by sunlight . . . holding up hope, and offering it to me for just one more giant footstep if I could find the strength.

And there I was, the frightened little five-year-old child frozen in fear. Should I dare to believe my doctor?

Maybe he had overestimated me. And there was mother, smug, full of evil, but offering the misery of the past. I wouldn't have to take any chances by retreating to the confines of her womb. And there was my doctor forcing me to fight, to break the passive pattern I had followed for a lifetime. I knew that following my doctor meant a chance for a new life. He represented hope. To retreat to mother meant instant death. I thought a great deal about dying. I thought about the powerful influence mother had over me. How I'd been brainwashed to believe I'd never marry. How she made me turn away from my inner resources and give up the one thing I loved most, my art. I thought about her negative pessimistic attitude toward life. How fearful she was, and how fearful she made me. How she convinced me of her own unworthiness by never loving me. I was certain that if I allowed a man to get close to me, he'd discover all the awful things that mother knew and he'd leave me. I also thought about hope and love. I thought about fighting. I knew that to choose life meant to take risks, with no guarantees. To choose the fight meant taking chances and risking the possibility of rejection. I thought about being alone and the pain of that loneliness. I thought about Dr. H. and how wonderful he made me feel about myself. I thought about marriage and a family.

I would wake in the middle of the night trembling with fear. What if I were old and alone and sick in this big impersonal city. Who would take care of me? Who would grieve if I died? How had I given of myself to anyone that they would mourn my loss?

And I thought about my dreams and how they had all been fantasies. I let go of my real dreams when I was twenty-five years old. I lived with fantasy and never admitted to myself that I felt no hope of ever achieving my dreams. Somewhere during that inner journey through that tunnel I realized I didn't want to die. That became clearer every day. I did not want to die. I did not want to become my mother. She represented misery and death. I knew that if I chose life I had to fight. It meant breaking the strongest patterns of a lifetime. Fighting meant gambling, trusting, opening up, giving, risking loss and abandonment. But it was the only way. I wanted to live. I wanted to follow the sunlit exit out of the tunnel.

My doctor had come to visit me. The visit was strained because I was angry at him. But he left me with some very powerful thoughts. He said this was the turning point of my life. That I lacked clarity but in time would realize that a major breakthrough had occurred. He said he saw a strength in me that I was not yet in touch with. He left and I didn't tell him if I'd ever be back. I was still furious with him. But his comments stayed with me.

I chose to live and to accept all the dangers that that meant. That decision was reinforced each day.

> I never never wanted to die. In the darkest of moments I
> prayed for light and the courage to go on.

The decision was made. I was on the journey to hope, and to freedom. I buried the frightened child in the hospital because she was ill-equipped to deal with life. I had no need for her anymore. Mother lost her power. I took it away from her.

It was a glorious spring day when I left the hospital. I left it alone. Unencumbered. Free of ghosts and feeling better about myself than I ever had. I felt fortified by my new-found strength. I had found a new respect for myself. I felt a determination and commitment to work out my life. I wanted to share my life with someone. I didn't know if it would be David. I did know that I wouldn't stop until I'd achieved my dream. I had found active hope. That would never leave me. I returned to treatment with Dr. H.

That was two years ago. I still look back on that crisis as the major turning point of my life. I worked out a wonderful relationship with David. We got married a year later. My wedding day was a day of tremendous inner victory. I felt triumphant in the war I had waged and in the courage I had shown. I had indeed grown into that strong, mature, independent woman. I am finding greater inner joy and freedom than I ever dreamed was possible. Each morning I wake up feeling loved and happy. I'll be eternally thankful that Dr. H. had the courage of his convictions and the belief in me to push me toward that last giant step. Had he given me a sugar pill I never would have done it. All my life people had promised me everything would be all right. My former shrink gave me sugar pills and I got nowhere. Dr. H. had pushed me over the last hurdle when I didn't think I could do it. And in that he gave me my life. Few would have had the courage. Few would have been as dedicated and as driving. He kept saying it was the only way whenever I begged for an easier solution. He was right. It was the only way. And in the victory of inner freedom I no longer have the need for tranquilizers nor allergy shots. Repressed anger has been released and I no longer have the need for drugs nor do I have the physical ailments that accompany stress.

All the love that was repressed flows out in abundance. Through the year I have found solid roots. I feel a sense of peace and inner fulfillment I never knew existed. Approaching our future and dreams together is tremendously exciting as David and I plan on having a child and creating a home full of love. A home that will inspire inner freedom and stimulate creativity. These feelings are still very new to me and I am just starting to appreciate what freedom represents. It took six months to fully comprehend that I am actually married and that it is not a fantasy. David is there when I wake up in the morning and I feel comfortable with the thought that he will be there for the rest of my life.

Recently I came into Dr. H.'s office with an air of super confidence, as if all was in the bag and all my major problems were solved. Dr. H. was quiet and then said, "Your therapy is not finished until one more problem is solved."

"I thought I had solved all major problems."

"A most important one remains to be solved," he said.

"Which one?"

"Mother."

"We spent hours and hours on mother," I said.

"That was to prove that all your motivations had come from one source: to prove mother wrong. None was really your own."

That was a blow.

"What is there to work out?" I said.

"To make peace with mother."

"My tormentor?"

"She gave you life. . . . Now you'll have to grow up, and when you feel free and strong within, you'll see mother and tell her why you feel the way you did, that you wanted to love her . . . how you felt she turned you away. . . . Now that you feel independent and don't have to prove anything, you would like to be friends with her. Only then will you be truly free."

I have made peace with mother this year. In making peace with her I feel tranquil within. I no longer have the need to punish her. I simply feel sorry for her.

I plan to leave broadcasting to convert a childhood dream into reality. I have made a commitment to myself to go back to my first love . . . painting. As the time approaches anxieties arise. But it is tempered against the power of commitment and the inner strength to accomplish my goals. I returned to the source of my inner resources, to develop a talent that has never let me rest.

At forty years old I feel the most exciting part of my life is just beginning. I am filled with anticipation and excitement. All was worth it for the joy I now have.

ARIEL SUTIN
July 1980

CHAPTER 6
Death from Hopelessness

FEAR AND SUPERSTITION kill hope. The loss of hope can kill a person. The psychodynamics of fear, strong enough to cause a human or animal to send a message from the brain to the heart to stop its next beat, comes from a signal of utter hopelessness. The short circuit in the brain may read, "It is futile. No more torture. Give up."

Bob was seventeen, an exuberant, strapping six-foot-three-inch senior in high school He was eagerly looking forward to fall when he would leave home for college. There were no financial worries since his outstanding performance as a high-school quarterback and an all-around athlete had guaranteed him a full football scholarship to his state college.

On this particular Friday evening he was celebrating those things teenagers celebrate—no school the next day, a pretty girlfriend, a good grade on his math test earlier that day—with a boisterous group of friends, who were eager to share with him the enjoyment of the Florida spring evening by dancing to rock records and sipping an occasional beer.

Bob left the party to run to his house for extra records. Barefoot, he cut through a neighboring vacant lot to save time. Suddenly he stopped, in amazement then in horror, as he first heard then saw the Florida diamondback rattler strike his unprotected foot.

Hearing his terrified yells, his friends came quickly. An ambulance was called, the snake was killed. Bob was taken swiftly to a nearby hospital.

The next morning Bob was dead.

An autopsy proved nothing unusual. The death certificate read, "Cause of death: snake bite."

A patient of mine, a young and eager newspaperwoman, wondered why a seventeen-year-old boy in the peak of physical health, with no record of any previous ailments, should die from the bite of a particular snake which she had heard was, as a rule, not lethal? She decided to investigate further and learned that during that year only three people in the entire United States had died as a result of rattlesnake bites. These people were all over fifty years of age and they most likely were less vigorous than our high-school boy.

She queried the doctor in the hospital who had filled out the death certificate. Her persuasive charm made the doctor finally admit— and this in the strictest of confidence—that he had written the cause of death out of consideration for the feelings of the boy's grieving parents. "Bob died from fear," said the doctor. The boy had been told that rattlesnake bites were lethal. The terror and paralysis of fear caused him to lose all hope and simply give up. Hopelessness had killed Bob.

An even more dramatic case that demonstrates the destructive power of hopelessness and the paralysis of the will is that of a young woman. In 1947 the president of the General Assembly of the United Nations was a Brazilian, and many of his countrymen came to visit the wonder city of New York. Some of them came to consult me. One of the visitors was a woman about thirty-two years old, who had been born in Germany and had married a rich Brazilian businessman. The young woman's problem was of a minor nature. Some years later I received a cable from her husband saying his wife was seriously ill. He asked me to recommend the best specialist in the United States to confirm or deny a diagnosis of a lymphosarcoma, a malignant tumor of lymphatic tissue. The choice was between two authorities, one in Boston and one in New York.

My former patient decided on New York. Together we saw the specialist who was affiliated with Memorial Hospital. After extensive examinations and tests, he confirmed the provisional diagnosis of a lymphosarcoma. The tumor was located in the mediastinum, the area in the chest between the left and the right lungs. It was inoperable. The patient related well to her new doctor and he helped her to accept his treatment of a series of heavy doses of radiation.

The young woman improved markedly. She left for Rio, but was advised to return in six months. However, she returned to New York sooner than scheduled because of a variety of disturbing new symptoms. Before seeing her cancer specialist, she came to visit me, admitting how dejected and very frightened she was. She became even more depressed when her doctor insisted she return to the hospital. She asked me whether she should accept the doctor's advice or take a plane back to Rio and let fate decide the outcome of her illness. With persuasion on my part and great reluctance on hers, she again checked into Memorial Hospital. New tests were made, after which she accepted, with little opposition, another series of radiation treatments.

Again, the patient reacted quickly and favorably to the radiation therapy. Initially she showed some remission of her symptoms but was advised that she had to be under constant observation and therefore should not return to Brazil.

The patient did not object to this, a decision that surprised her husband, who feared that the doctor's suggestion would greatly lower his wife's morale.

The patient, who was a very attractive and elegant woman, now demanded that her husband rent a large apartment on Park Avenue, so that she could entertain her diplomatic friends as well as a rich, international, swinging crowd. She was very demanding in this, while her husband, a serious businessman, was perturbed about his wife's new recklessness and costly life-style. Because he knew how seriously ill she was, he did not dare oppose her openly and asked me to intercede for him. When I did talk to her about it, she displayed great charm to me but said her husband was jealous and stingy.

The relationship between the much older husband and his younger wife was not a very good one. There was little communication between them. She was a very emotional, sensitive woman with rather superficial values. She had a sharp, slightly sarcastic wit, which she used to tease men. Nevertheless, she professed to have utter trust in me, stating that I had become her only source of moral support.

Her prognosis was not very good. Soon, she did not have enough energy to go out or give the great parties she had planned. She became more and more depressed, asking me to visit her, first in the hospital and later on, a few times, in her new home. Then, one Saturday afternoon she telephoned. She sounded desperate and begged me to see her.

When I arrived she was apprehensive and slightly agitated. She looked thin and very pale. Finally, as if using extra strength to pull herself together, she said, "I am very much troubled and I would like to tell you something if you promise not to laugh."

She now became very serious. "I know I am going to die," she said. "Don't console me. . . . I don't want to waste time. . . . I need your advice. . . . I am very desperate. . . ."

She struggled for a beginning, then began to speak to me in German rather than in English. "Now, about my illness . . . please have patience . . . it goes back to an experience I had quite a bit over a year ago. In our house in Rio we have many servants. On this particular day . . . a Friday, which I remember so well . . . I was talking to a houseboy. He had been extremely rude and disobedient, so I scolded him sharply and dismissed him. Before he left, he turned and handed me something, saying, 'With this I put a curse on you. You will become sick but nothing can save you. You will die. . . .' I chased him out and laughed and threw away the object. However, I felt a peculiar sensation in my hand for a while, but I dismissed the incident. After all, I am not superstitious and don't believe in that voodoo nonsense practiced by primitive blacks in the interior of Brazil. I cannot accept a relationship between the houseboy's threat and my illness," she said. "But on the other hand, I have heard that some people who believe in this black magic have died.

"Anyway, after two weeks or so, I had vague symptoms of something being wrong. My doctor thought at first that I was coming down with the flu. I had always been healthy, so, he thought it would pass in a few days. Instead, I began to feel worse. Tests were conducted but no sign of illness could be found. I did not feel really sick but I did not feel well either. My energy used to be unlimited. I could dance through a night, but now I began to tire easily and became more and more irritable. I have a beautiful child. A boy. I love him but I began to be impatient with him.

"Months went by. I did not improve. I saw all the famous specialists in Brazil, even a psychiatrist, but I didn't want to talk to him about the quarrels with my husband or my sex life. How could that have anything to do with the way I felt? I was just physically sick.

"Nearly six months went by when one young specialist became suspicious of something in my chest. After a number of X-rays, he talked to my husband, who became very upset but no one told me a thing. Now other specialists began to concentrate on these X-rays, comparing new films with earlier ones. Everybody was so serious. Finally, my husband called you. He had gotten the names of a few specialists in the States he thought you would know.

"We came to New York. They tried to hide the nature of my illness, but a patient knows. My specialist was a very kind man who said it was nothing serious . . . only a few lymph glands were enlarged, and some X-ray treatment would take care of that. The rest you know. Some improvement. Back to Brazil. Back to New York. And my horrible stay at Memorial Hospital. Every child knows it is a cancer hospital.

"This then is my question. I know what I have. I don't know the exact name of my illness, but I know I am going to die. I keep on thinking of that houseboy. Is it medically possible that a curse could cause a malignant growth? But that is only one question. The real question is, would you think it's crazy for me to go to the interior of Brazil, where I have heard about a chief medicine man who has a great power to remove every curse? I know how you doctors feel about that kind of thing. That's why I asked you not to laugh or just dismiss it as hocus-pocus. But is it not possible that such a medicine man might be able to remove the curse and make me well? After all, you doctors can't cure me."

She paused, waiting for a reply. I looked at the intense face of the woman. The "curse" had become too deeply rooted in her mind to be simply brushed away. She was on the mentally regressed level of a frightened and confused child. Therefore logic would not reach her, nor could her questions be laughed away.

I had come to question this woman's mental stability. I sensed her deep inner conflict, her feeling that she was trapped in an unhappy marriage, unable to leave her husband because of her dependency on him.

Rage, anger, and anxiety were deeply repressed, as were her guilt feelings about her parents, who perished in the Holocaust in Germany and whom she could have saved. She had briefly mentioned this fact but avoided talking about it in any depth. She had built an enormously strong defense of denial, finding escape and security in a fast, active social life. She greatly enjoyed her acceptance by a discriminating society and knew that it was her beauty and her husband's money that had made her eligible.

These things went through my mind in the minute or so I had before giving my answer. Finally, I said, "Never mind what we doctors think about a curse or voodoo. . . . My answer to your main question is go . . . go and see the chief medicine man and have your curse removed."

She was not prepared for this answer from a doctor and fell silent. I now watched her reaction, her facial expression of inner torment. I waited for her response. What would she do? Would she go? It was a test. How much will to live did she have? How strong was her hope that she could be saved? Finally, I said, "Think about it. . . . Don't feel ashamed and don't consider it an act of cowardice if you decide to have your curse removed. Anyway, ask me anything more you wish to know." She remained silent. She seemed very exhausted. Her confession had stirred her and evidently drained her of whatever energy she had. I took her thin hand and said, "Call me anytime you feel you want to talk more about this."

Later on I talked to her husband, who thought the idea to go into the interior of Brazil was absurd, especially in light of her weakened condition. But he would go along with it, just as he had satisfied so many of her whims. I did not relate her confession to the surgeon, but continued to see her from time to time, observing her slow process of disintegration. I felt she would not pursue the only course her obsessed mind saw as a cure. Having lost all hope she regressed from a state of discouragement to one of complete hopelessness, which blackened her mood and paralyzed her actions. After the doctors said her condition was terminal and that nothing more could be done, her husband took her back to Brazil while she was still able to travel.

Months went by. Then her husband sent me the announcement of her death. Later that same year he came to visit me, to talk about his wife. He displayed grief and guilt but also some anger about her reckless and self-destructive way of life. However, his overriding feeling was the pain of loss and a deep love he had for his wife. He had known her since she was a little girl, and told me about his courtship, marriage, and life with her. His need to talk was great and he sobbed as he talked about her.

With hesitancy he finally asked, "Do you, as a doctor, really believe that seeing the medicine man could have saved my wife's life?"

"No one can give a precise answer to your question," I replied. "Medically, the answer would have to be 'probably not.' However an obsessed mind, one under a spell, can react to signals just as people do in states of hypnosis, with a sudden revival of hope and a new will to live.

"I cannot say your wife would be alive today . . . neither can I say she would have died."

Giving Up

The mysticism of voodoo death has aroused the curiosity of several researchers. Perhaps the most outstanding was Walter B. Cannon, professor of physiology at Harvard University. In an article called "Voodoo Death," published in the *American Anthropologist* (April-June 1942, volume 49), Cannon wrote that people, when subjected to spells of sorcery or black magic, may be brought to death. Natives in South America, Africa, Australia, New Zealand and Haiti display this phenomenon ". . . so extraordinary and so foreign to the experience of civilized people that it seems incredible."

In 1587, Soares de Sousa observed instances of death among Tupinamba Indians. Death was induced by fright when people were condemned and sentenced by a so-called medicine man.

In 1906 Leonard described hardened Hausa soldiers dying steadily because they believed themselves to be bewitched. Dr. S. M. Lambert of the Western Pacific Health Service of the Rockefeller Foundation wrote down the experience of Dr. P. S. Clarke, who has seen evidence of death from fear. One day, a Kanaka came to the New Queensland Hospital in Australia and told him he was going to die within a few days because a spell had been put upon him and nothing could be done to counteract it. Dr. Clarke called the foreman of the Kanakas to the hospital to reassure the man. The foreman leaned over saying, "Yes, doctor, close him up, he die." And the next day at 11:00 A.M. he did indeed die.

What is the cause of the demise? Dr. Cannon believed that the death was due to a persistent activity of the adrenocortical (hormone) system.

Studies done by Dr. Curt Richter, professor of psychobiology, Phipps Psychiatric Clinic, Johns Hopkins Medical School, Baltimore, give us a more precise scientific explanation of the physiology of *death due to hopelessness*. In a chapter called "The Phenomenon of Unexplained Sudden Death in Animals and Man," Dr. Richter writes that his interest in this study grew out of a series of chance observations on the behavior of the common laboratory rat.

As part of a pilot experiment, Dr. Richter wished to study the effects of a high salt intake in rats. In order to keep food particles from falling into the rats' urine, he trimmed the whiskers of three rats with electric clippers. "Almost at once one of the three rats began to behave in a very peculiar way," he observed. "It incessantly pushed its nose into the corners of the cage with corkscrewing motions. The next morning it was dead." A careful autopsy showed no cause of death.

Two years later he studied the effects of stress on swimming rats. Again their whiskers were trimmed and they were put in jars of water. In order to prevent the rats from resting, jets kept the water in constant turbulent motion. The first rat swam around excitedly on the surface for a few seconds, dived to the bottom obviously searching for an avenue of escape, then swam below the surface until it suddenly stopped swimming and died. An autopsy revealed no sign of drowning. Another rat exhibited a similar behavior and also died within minutes. The third rat swam on for hours.

It appeared that the loss of the whiskers—and the resulting deprivation of one of its chief sources of sensory contact with the outside world—constitutes a stress great enough to end the rat's life. When further observations showed some wild rats with their whiskers intact died in the same mysterious manner, the researcher assumed that he was dealing with a more general phenomenon of unexplained sudden death.

Influenced by Dr. Cannon's studies of sudden death, Dr. Richter looked first for signs of sympathetic stimulation, that is, tachycardia and death in the systole—the moment the heart contracts. To establish this point the researchers attached fine wires to the rats to record their heartbeats while in the swimming tests. The studies showed that the rats did not die from exhaustion. Nor did death occur during the systole; it came, instead, during the diastole, when the heart rests. *The rats died from hopelessness.* They gave up. When the surviving rats were removed from the turbulent jar, then later put back, they did not die but continued to swim. *Now they had hope they would be saved*—a state we may call passive hope. The conclusion of Dr. Richter's study was that *rats as well as human beings die from a reaction of hopelessness.*

Sudden death may depend on emotional reactions to restraint or confinement. Shrews die when restrained or when exposed to sudden noises. Mice can die in response to handling. Larger wild animals can die within a few minutes when restrained. Wild birds can die in the hands of bird banders during the banding.

Instant death in humans has been reported under different conditions and different ages. Death as a result of fright or at the sight of blood or a hypodermic needle has been observed. In most cases autopsies revealed no organic causes.

Each year coroners' reports show a fair percentage of unaccountable sudden deaths. People may die *after* but not overtly from suicide attempts when the skin was hardly scratched or after having taken a few aspirin tablets.

Hopelessness as a cause of death has intrigued me for many years. As far back as 1959, the *Ohio State Medical Journal* published a paper of mine entitled "Health and Wholeness." Subtitles were: "The Heart Patient, The Cancer Patient, *and Hopelessness as Cause of Death*" (my italics). Richter's findings gave scientific support to my own clinical observations that in a crisis or when overcome by feelings of utter hopelessness, human beings can die by some "inner decision" to give up. Indeed, many people die, not necessarily from physical exhaustion or battle fatigue, but by an firm inner belief they have no chance at all for survival. At that moment of a peak experience of intolerable stress, they abandon the fight and let go of that mystical force that is life. The desperate need of the moment blunting every rational thought is the cessation of pain. Men can experience extraordinary pain as long as there is a glimmer of hope. The trigger then to give up fighting the pain and misery is hopelessness. Psychodynamically hopeless human beings welcome rather than resist a total regression, which is a return to the womb—symbolically Mother Earth or death.

Approximately 94,000 United States servicemen were taken prisoner in the European theater during World War II. A study of those prisoners showed that most were imprisoned for an average of ten months and less than one percent died. In contrast, in the Pacific theater of war, approximately 25,000 Americans were imprisoned, remaining confined for an average of three years. They were tortured, threatened, abused, and humiliated. About one-third of these men died. During the Korean War, about 6,000 soldiers were captured by the North Koreans and, here again, approximately one-third died. The cause of death in many instances was not clear, and references were made to "give-up-itis." States of demoralization, despair, humiliation, and a sense of futility caused apathetic, listless, states of mind. The men refused food or drink and stared into space, resulting in a gradual decline of vitality that ended in death.

"Give-up-itis" was seen in soldiers in the Vietnam War. The reference here is not made to prisoners of war but to widespread drug abuse of American soldiers due to feelings of hopelessness. They did not die physically but it can be said that a part of them died when they cut themselves off from active life.

An entirely different type of "give-up-itis" is one that is so strongly masked that it easily escapes detection. It is considered an unquestionably organic, that is, nonneurotic, disease. I refer to America's number-one killer, heart disease.

Hope and hopelessness play a major part in a patient's attitude toward his illness, though that interrelationship has not been greatly studied.

In a discussion with Dr. Christiaan Barnard, the South African heart surgeon, I asked what he felt caused tissue rejection in his patients with transplanted hearts. The rejection of the new hearts caused complications and ultimate death. His answer was that of most medical doctors: The body's natural defense system fights off the "foreign intruder" so successfully that it ultimately leads to death. In other words, it is a biochemical process.

While this theory may have merit I believe there is a far more basic cause of death. We often find a person unconsciously singling out an organ—in this case the heart—as a target for a release of aggressive energies creating prolonged stress. Without relaxation of this stress, the person damages his or her heart, sometimes so badly that its functioning is severely limited. This kind of self-destruction is an expression of that person's total personality and inner wish to let go of life. More than any other organ, it is the heart that gives the evidence of being worn out because of an inability to relax. A person may have set a goal higher than the strength it takes to reach it.

Dr. Barnard and other surgeons may interpret tissue rejection to be a pure biochemical process, but even if this could be proven by more precise scientific criteria, it would not be the full story of a person's heart at a moment when it ceases to beat.

For instance, when a middle-aged man dies from a heart attack his death can be considered premature. Death is described by some pathologists as natural when all organs wear out evenly and at a harmonious rate, as in old age. Hope or hopelessness play a paramount role in an inner decision to go on or to give up.

In the summer of 1976 I was asked to present a deposition paper for the symposium of the Foundation of Thanatology (the study of death) in conjunction with the Department of Psychiatry of Columbia University. The title was "Psychosocial Aspects of the Life-Threatened Cardiovascular Patient," printed in the *Archives of the Foundation of Thanatology* (volume 6, number 1, 1976). The following is an excerpt from it:

"If life, in the words of Herbert Spencer, is a 'continual adjustment of internal relations to external relations,' we find the cardiovascular patient engaged in a relentless struggle of his inner hostile-aggressive feelings against the external psychosocial demands of his group and his own set of values. This type of patient is conditioned to meet the challenges of life by fight rather than flight and by a relentless need to excel in order for the world to consider him worthy of love. Early experiences of rejection cause him to compensate for his feelings of vulnerability or insignificance by setting extraordinary goals for himself, and by pursuing difficult tasks to attain the recognition he craves. Striving for positions of power, status, and money does not allow him to relax, not to be overly concerned about intrinsic values that would help him to mature, and to relate affectionately to another human being.

"In his studies of hypertension, at the Chicago Institute of Psychoanalysis, Franz Alexander had found that most of these patients

> as children were prone to attacks or rage and to be aggressive. Then, at some point, a change of attitude had taken place. . . . Unable to assert himself, the aggressive child then becomes overly compliant. . . .

"Compliance in the hostile-aggressive person, who may eventually become a cardiovascular patient, is the mask that covers the fire that burns within. Pride and ambition stir and he can never allow himself to appear weak. He is like the captain on the bridge who never sleeps. Or the politician whose deeds must stand out and at all times attest to his brilliance, his magnificence, and his human concern for others.

"Different from the mentally depressed and suicidal individual, the cardiovascular patient is psychodynamically a person who chooses to die with his boots on. It is not society that makes continual demands on this patient. It is his interpretation of what he believes society demands of him that feeds on inner aggressive drives. It is his autoplastic disease picture—the picture he has of himself in relation to his illness—that is causing the difficulties these patients create for other people, primarily their families, their friends, and their physicians.

"The psychosocial aspects of the life-threatened cardiovascular patient then must be considered in the light of his specific psychodynamic functioning and his established reaction pattern. His inner will and emphasis on the heroic, namely to die at the peak of power rather than to go on with a prospect of vegetating, is a decisive factor to the outcome of the illness. These are patients who will say, 'Doc . . . give it to me straight' and, as a rule, will not settle for a promise to be taken care of. Their ultimate meaning of life is achievement, for on it depends their feeling of worthiness to be loved. *Whenever there is a break of this hope,* the life-threatened cardiovascular patient will turn his aggression against himself and must then be considered a potential suicide."

Incidentally, in a book scheduled to be published in 1980 by Columbia University Press, under the title *Psychosocial Aspects of Cardiovascular Disease: The Patient, the Family and the Staff,* by James

Reiffel, et al, editors, the introduction to Part II, "The Cardiovascular Patient," is a condensation of the above paper.

In Summary: The Tragedy of No Hope

Hopelessness is a state of a painfully sad existence in which there is little or no expectation of a return to an active and enjoyable life. It expresses an unconscious wish to return to the womb, a return that promises freedom from fear or stress, anguish or passion, and to welcome death as a deliverer from the deeply buried hates and the intolerable self-image of worthlessness.

Giving up one's battle for life is a person's invitation to a premature death by processes of mental and/or physical disintegration. The longer the state of hopelessness, the greater the alienation of the individual's inner world and the world around him.

Hopelessness can be the plea of a helpless child, too ashamed and embarrassed to ask for help. Yet medical help can produce the hope necessary to return to life for those who are not convinced they wish to die.

CHAPTER 7

Hope and the Aged

INFIRMITY. LAMENTING. Perhaps an old man or woman's little tear for a paradise lost. Most of the people who feel sad about getting old are people who have failed to face up to reality. They have lived in fantasy, perhaps with anxiety, and have seen their lives slip by, unable to grasp and hold time and so, against all reason, hope for a better tomorrow. But reality punches holes into their make-believe world of dreams, for deep down they are aware of the fallacy of expecting the next day to bring them less pain or freedom from the despair of today.

The sober realization that their bodily strength is declining and the awareness of the deteriorating sharpness of their mind is one of the causes of an apparent increase of depressions in the aged. Even the courageous, those who with pride and vigor continue to work, cannot escape feeling the burden of their responsibilities weighing heavier, their hope growing thinner, their anxieties increasing, and other signs of old age encroaching. In a mood of wry humor many may concur with the French cynic who called old age "a tyrant who forbids upon the pain of death, all the pleasures of youth."

Many old people who share the gloom of various poets about the loss of one more hour of glory might lack the awareness that they may have been self-indulgent throughout life, lamenting whenever they had to experience the loss of an hour of pleasure or a ball they could not attend. As the facade of their glamour wears thin, the true personality emerges. Those who have given receive, and those who could not give with their heart may end up alone or abandoned.

So many may enter their later years looking back at their lives with too many regrets—and forward with only little hope. No one is spared that day of self-judgment when they fade out of the limelight and realize that they have to live with themselves, their sparse resources, and the best self-image they have been able to create. Self-condemnation unopposed can lead to illness and depression.

The Frailties of Aging

Many people who grow old have good reason to be sad. They have weathered tragedies and losses and, while they try to grow old with dignity, their bodies may become frail and their minds despairing. Older people who suffer from depression often isolate themselves because their pride does not allow them to be seen by friends and others as someone who has become weak or frail or someone to be pitied. They suffer needlessly; old age is not a plague. It can be an age of wisdom, of veneration and self-fulfillment.

People who have not mentally prepared themselves for their later years are, for the most part, people who have lived with a hope that one day Lady Luck might come with a letter saying that they have won a lottery or a free trip around the world. They are eager to grasp any hand that reaches out rather than to defend their integrity by using, in whatever small way they can, their creative energies. Thus many people grow old before they grow up only to watch with anxiety the castles they had built in the air swallowed up by thickening clouds.

Then there is the torturer: vanity. Many people, men and women, study with horror the wrinkles in their face. With another face-lift to conceal the loss of their beauty they might beat aging for a few years. If it makes people feel good, why not? A famous Hollywood star had great moral apprehension. "It's a fake," she said. "My Yankee background does not allow me to be phony or dishonest." Yet she needed a good-looking face to get better parts in movies she still made. We had a talk. "Do you use lipstick and makeup?" I asked. She nodded. "Then, what is the difference? It is a difference in degree only, not in principle." And all went well.

But many people don't have a career to fall back on. They may not like themselves and thus expect others not to like them. Many women feel ashamed to go out for fear of being seen wrinkled. So they stay in hiding. Some rationalize that a stormy outside world is for the young and has neither patience nor reverence for the old.

Old age paints in stark color the character: the kind, the loving, the angry, and the not giving. Then, there are many old people who are shy and don't know how to ask for help. They need to be encouraged, for physicians have learned how to be of help to those who are sad, hopeless, and depressed. Most depressions can be cured.

One patient, a gentle septuagenarian, may speak for many when she answered my question as to why she had finally come to see me professionally. "I had hoped you could perhaps help me to put into my golden years a little silver . . . or maybe tell me, what I can do to chase away those black thoughts of suicide." This patient wanted to hope but was not certain that her life of "quiet desperation" could be changed. "It's probably too late anyway," she said, "but I thought I would try." She had reasoned that her unhappiness was just one of the misfortunes in life; nothing anyone could do much about. Her golden years had painfully increased inner feelings of loneliness and alienation, both of which had become almost intolerable.

This woman had been married for forty years to a man with whom, she said, there was nothing much to share, because "he lived a very selfish and superficial life." He was a mama's boy and in the habit of leaving all responsibilities to her. She described her husband as being overly critical and demanding, constantly finding faults with her and never missing out on an opportunity to belittle her. "I had little self-esteem to begin with and so it always hurts again. I came to America straight from a cowbarn, with no schooling. I terribly missed not having had an education. But there was never time. I worked long hours as a domestic, because I was brought up to be very conscientious and thorough. I wanted to learn and so I went, whenever I could, to the public library. I even studied the philosophers because I hated being so uneducated."

At her second visit six months later, she reported feeling better, as now her husband had been under treatment. But a more important reason for feeling better, she said, was that she had learned that a great part of her depression had come from repressing her deep-seated anger—anger against her husband and anger against herself—for having been always so meek and submissive, and for having swallowed her husband's humiliating attacks without saying a word. During her first visit, she had written down a few principles, especially on how to become more self-assertive without risking ugly confrontations. She was surprised that her husband reacted to her gentle but firm self-assertion by showing more respect for her. She

107

was wise enough to use her better understanding cautiously, slowly extending it in other areas of human interaction. And she was healthy enough to turn a hopeless situation in her marriage that previously "had made my heart sick" into one of new moderate hope by teaching herself how to cope with her husband and other stress situations. At the same rate as her self-confidence grew, her depressions lessened. She realized that the change had come by having opened a door that led her out of the prison in which she had lived. In psychodynamic terms her happier life had come by having embarked more effectively and more satisfactorily on the road to active hope.

This patient made herself a happier woman because all along she had tried to fight her depression actively, though not effectively enough. Therefore her depression was not very deep. It had not corroded her basic optimistic nature, nor reached a state of lasting hopelessness.

Responding to Depression

Many people fear the term *depression,* associating it with a possible incurable psychiatric disorder. There is also a fear of putting a burden on friends or of losing them. Consequently, they mask their inner sadness and despair by a variety of physical complaints, like fatigue, loss of appetite, sleep disturbances, and other symptoms. These symptoms, of course, are not conscious, willful reactions but the results of inner psychophysical stress. Another device depressed people use to cover up mood swings or withdrawal from people is to blame discouragement on outer causes, such as worry about the economic depression or about the threatening political crisis. These are often real and justifiable fears of seeing their little bit of money being reduced in value or perhaps even wiped out altogether by galloping inflation.

Depressions in the aged have become an increasing mental and emotional problem. Or, perhaps, as a result of studies on a worldwide scale, the causes of depressions and the rapid improvements by chemotherapy has made physicians more aware of this disabling illness. Many depressions in the past, and possibly still today, sail under different flags of physical ailments or nervous conditions. One has only to listen to the commercials on TV to realize how widespread these nervous symptoms are, for example, take N or S for insomnia, X and Y for constipation, or this and that compound or vitamins for vigor, etc.

In an article I wrote for *Vogue* magazine (and which I have updated for this book), I said, "There are 20,000 successful suicides in the United States every year. If we consider the unknown number of unsuccessful attempts and the masked suicides listed as accidents, we can at best only estimate the multitude of people who, consciously or unconsciously, felt driven by some inner power to destroy themselves. Adding to this uncertain figure the despondent, the chronically sad, and the legions of people who by means of alcohol, nicotine, and drug abuse cut short their lives, we are overwhelmed not only by the staggering figure itself but by the diffident question of how such a widespread morbid trend in our society tallies with man's allegedly indomitable will to live.

"What force is it that drives man to ruin his health, to cripple his ability to function, or to annihilate that precious force we call life? In almost every act of self-destructive behavior, the illness that exists in depth is medically described as depression.

"So acute and widespread has this problem become in recent years that it has moved into the limelight of intense psychiatric investigation.

"A clear distinction must be made between neurotic and psychotic depressions. Psychotically depressed patients are the more seriously mentally sick. They are the wretched human beings who used to fill the mental hospitals, where they had been sent by their physicians or families to wither away.

"A significant step toward a cure of heretofore hopeless cases of depression took place before World War II with the introduction of electric shock therapy and insulin shock treatment, but progress of more fundamental depth has resulted from our growing understanding of the dynamics of the human mind, of psychotherapy, and the enormous advances in the field of chemotherapy, especially during the past two decades. This has produced a variety of effective antidepressant drugs capable of restoring many people to useful and pleasant lives.

"We are concerned here not with the serious depressions of the estimated six million to eight million people who, every year, require psychiatric help, but with those depressions we may call "normal," since *all people experience a depressed mood at one time or another in their lives.*

"Why, for reasons often unknown to themselves, do people slide into a state of depression, and what can they do to pull themselves out of it? Let us examine why with some people depressions last a few days or weeks and with others it takes a longer time for the morbid symptoms to disappear. When a person cannot shake off a depression, when such a state lingers on for several months or longer, then we are dealing with a more serious emotional illness.

"Depressions are universal experiences and not necessarily caused by our highly civilized society. The Romans referred to this low, listless state simply as *taedium vitae*—tiredness of life. The more sophisticated French call a depression a *maladie sans maladie.* Hippocrates came closer to our scientific understanding of depression. He explained health and illness as a matter of the four "temperaments," due to various mixtures of the body fluids (today we would name these fluids hormones or other chemical body products). Hippocrates believed that melancholics, the large group of people who feel sad and dejected, suffered from too much black bile. He compared the melancholics with the cholerics—the ever angry—who behaved in a hostile-aggressive manner due, perhaps, to an abundance of too freely flowing green bile.

"As to the higher rate of depression in women, it seems to me that men, more than women, spend their aggression in their work and derive a sense of security from a home managed by a woman. Even if women work, they still run a house, care about their children; even if they have help, they still carry the responsibility of the home and cannot relax in the way a man does, who too often pursues his own interests at home, which irritates his wife and usually makes her feel 'left out.'

"There are, moreover, events most women share, though not all women become depressed by them. One is childbirth, another is menopause. The postpartum blues of many women are, I believe, partially due to their personality type. They may be among the restless, the quickly irritated temperaments; but more are the melancholics who find life a joyless and tormenting business one has to endure. Whatever the personality, too many women, it seems, are ill-prepared for motherhood and are fearful of failure, of assuming the responsibility for a new life. *Women who wish to escape the frightening demands of reality are prone to depression,* while happy women, women who enjoy pregnancy, are unlikely to become depressed.

"We have talked earlier about the postpartum blues due to the fact that not all women genuinely love the man whose child they have carried and now have to bring up. The aggressive or choleric woman may want the child, but she may also want her independence and a career or a life that is less restricting. We are not born with maturity, we have to develop it.

"Menopause, we have said, is difficult for most women, because they associate it as an advanced sign of old age and therefore it becomes a frequent cause of depression. In my intern years, I treated many women for menopausal complaints, a known syndrome of hot flashes, sweating, insomnia, and depression, and I shot them full of estrogen. They felt better; perhaps it was the attention and the hope of prolonging youth. But as I watched them I got the mental picture of all those women dreading, as if forced by nature, to walk through a gate above which big letters read 'Old Age.' Regardless of the vast armory of cosmetic marvels, including plastic surgery, the onset of menopause is traumatic and anticipated with anxiety.

"Of course, this gloomy anticipation is fed by inner anxiety and feelings of unfulfillment. Women who are in tune with life are less fearful. Indeed, women can and do retain a youthful look and an attractiveness that comes from inner harmony. *An angry woman cannot retain her beauty.* There are beautiful faces, cold and without lines, looking like Greek statues, but they are statues and not women. I dare say that they have not given of themselves, nor have they really enjoyed the abandonment of feelings that a woman has when she is in love and that grows and deepens when a woman has the capacity to love.

"Another period of crisis and depression is the mid-thirties. The child-bearing period has come to an end, not physiologically, of course, but culturally. Healthy women have their children young. Nature has set for them the task of reproducing. Having fulfilled their destiny, women, unless they can sublimate their creativity in a way that has meaning, may feel useless, ineffectual, and become depressed.

"In the forever-game women play for the attention of men, the mid-thirties are years of anxiety, increased by a sharper battle of competition. And yet, it is true that *women can be more magnetic and seductive in their middle years than many of their younger rivals.* There can be an attractiveness that comes with ripeness, and a command of subtly projecting an individual style that is alluringly feminine.

"In depressions . . . there is a sadness about a loss and the fear of never regaining what has been lost—protection and security in the young, youth in the aging. . . . Both attitudes are understandable and both reflect an immature attitude toward life. The young woman must make efforts to discover a meaning for her life. The older woman has to adjust to where she is in life, and she must give her life some direction if she wishes to avoid moods of depression.

"A sensitive area that causes depression is one's sexual functioning. In a woman it is the inability to experience orgasm and the insecurity or confusion about her role as a woman, as a wife, or as a mother. In the male, it is impotence.

"Everyone is exposed to criticism and runs the risk of rejection, failure, and depression—especially someone who is in the public eye. Artists are constantly open to verdicts of censure and rejection. Annihilating criticism may cause a depression of short duration for one person, but may be deep and paralyzing for another.

"We say it is a matter of personality. What we mean to say is that one person possesses enough self-confidence and ego-strength to absorb a blow while another withdraws from a world that is unkind and does not understand him or her. In the first case we assume the person is sound and honest and capable of admitting inadequacy. In the second, we are probably dealing with a neurotic, not very stable individual. Such a person may live in fantasy and be megalomaniacal about him- or herself, displaying a daring facade to cover up deeper feelings of inferiority. People of this type are likely to sink into deep depression and may stay in it, since there is little incentive for them to take up a battle that may again end in failure.

"Not failure but success may set off depression in an entirely different type of personality, one who feels guilty and basically unworthy. For example: An actress in her early thirties came to see me because she was deeply depressed. She had made a name for herself in Hollywood but, as she said contemptuously, in B-pictures only. She felt wounded, discouraged, and unwanted. Her movie career had come to an end.

"The woman's personal life was also in a state of disaster. Her marriage had just ended in divorce. 'He was a nice boy,' she said, 'but he did not want a woman, he wanted a mommy.' She married him because she was lonely and he was attractive and amusing. But, actually, she felt flattered that someone wanted her so badly. She blamed herself for her poor judgment, insisting that the whole thing had been her fault, and she therefore did not ask for any alimony.

"At the time of her divorce she did not know she was pregnant. In New York when she discovered this, she required a curettage. This experience depressed her greatly. Although she had been ambivalent about having children, the loss of the child filled her with deep guilt and regret, but she knew she could not take care of a child at the time, with no job, no money, and no husband.

"During her first interview in my office, fighting off tears, she displayed a disarming honesty and helplessness. She had never felt as confused, as lost; and she was embarrassed about asking for help.

As for her future, she had only a very vague plan of trying to find a small restaurant where she could sing just to eat.

"In spite of her misery she carried herself straight and with dignity. Yet, when questioned, she had a distorted and self-condemning picture of herself. 'People always said that I was beautiful, but I never really believed it.' Yet she was a beautiful woman, blond, slim, with the wide-eyed openness of a child.

"A year later her great opportunity came. She had worked hard and had developed more confidence and poise than ever before. But she was frightened: 'Will I make it, or lose a chance that may never come again?' She controlled her fear and her often rising anger during all of the rough and merciless auditions, and succeeded in getting the leading role in a Broadway musical. Opening night was a triumph; the critics made her a star.

"After three weeks of living in an exalted state close to unreality, she telephoned one night. Her jubilation was gone. Her small voice and her crying indicated that she was depressed. That evening she had been told that her performances had become so bad she was jeopardizing the show. She was still dumbfounded when she resumed her therapy. In her state of regression she was bewildered as to what had happened. She gave all sorts of reasons, one being that she was not used to the demands of playing on Broadway. She found acting the same part every night boring.

"The deeper reason for her failure was linked to her mother. When she was a girl, she dreamed of doing something extraordinary to win her mother's approval. Her mother had never praised her and, while the girl had felt immense rage and anger about it, she felt driven by a compulsive need to win, for once, her mother's applause.

"Why did she fail? Her mother had always favored her older brother. And yet she had paid for all the dancing and singing lessons during the girl's adolescence because she considered her daughter awkward and clumsy and thought that dancing and singing would make it easier for her to find a nice, well-to-do husband.

"Her mother's negative attitude became evident when her daughter's Hollywood career began to decline. She wrote letters pleading with her daughter to give up 'that circus life' and come home. 'I had to convince her—just for once—that I was worthy of her love.'

"My patient's success in the theater was therefore not an act of pure creativity of love but an act of vengeance for which she was using creativity. Consequently, after having proven her point, she lacked further motivation. The depression came as the result of a deep feeling of disappointment and anger and guilt. She felt betrayed. The love she craved never came. The difficult lesson she had to learn was to replace her neurotic drives with new goals and new values to develop a sense of self-worth.

"Depressions are triggered not only by loss. The greater number are caused by an inability to express hostility. It is aggression turned against the self.

"When provoked, the body reacts with a natural impulse to strike back. It is fight or flight. But when a rigid code of 'proper' civilized behavior does not permit any acting out of rage or anger or disagreement with another, the instinctive forces of aggression become an explosive and destructive or paralyzing force within.

"Our conscience, its greater part hidden in the unconscious, retains an almighty veto power over what the instincts desire and the ego may want. We all have to exercise control in order to live in an organized society. And we all have to negotiate between what is desirable and what is realistically possible or safe. In that way we make decisions. Control, then, is a necessity. Overinhibition becomes a destructive force that flattens out the remarkable potentials of one's ego and straitjackets inner freedom. To function effectively, we have to learn more or less skillful diplomacy in negotiating between our forces of healthy aggression and our often too harsh and too restrictive taboos. There is a safe area in between. Within the given framework of our civilized society, there is ample room for an enjoyable and creative life. Self-assertion means to take one's place in society according to one's ability, and to respect the rights of others. It means to speak one's mind, without fear and without resorting to pressure or force.

"There are subjective and objective signs of depression. Some of the painful and morbid feelings are known only to the person who is depressed. Other symptoms are evident to people around him.

"Depressions that appear some time after a traumatic impact, or become deeper, relate to changes within the personality, often accompanied by a loss of hope. To a person under such a depression life becomes meaningless, to the point of confessing he or she would be better off dead than alive. Recurring suicidal fantasies must be taken seriously, because a person in a prolonged state of depression is capable of acting out a destructive impulse.

"We have mentioned in an earlier chapter various symptoms of depression like constipation, frequent voiding during the night, and a variety of psychosomatic symptoms, such as fatigue states and gastrointestinal or cardiovascular disturbances.

"Unless depression is successfully masked, family and friends have no difficulty in detecting changes. A heretofore fastidious woman may become sloppy in her way of dressing or of making up or of wearing her hair. There may be a general loss of interest or a change in life-style or a withdrawal from friends. Depressed people lose their sense of joy and their readiness to laugh.

"Sleep is a common known means of escape. Depressed people may not want to get up in the morning and may react to even slight adversities during the day by taking long naps.

"Depressed people may defend themselves by an air of unapproachability. They create an atmosphere of an impenetrable void or condensed boredom so that no one can get through to them.

"Having stated that all people may become depressed at one time or another, let us draw a conclusion about the causes of depression. It is almost self-evident that we can stem a depression if we recognize the symptoms early enough and if we decide to do something about it. Unfortunately, there are people who think we become better human beings through suffering and, unfortunately, there are martyrs who use suffering as a means of making others feel guilty. These people wallow in their misery and depression, but if we discount these neurotic people and if we accept the belief that everyone is entitled to enjoy his existence and productivity, then let us pull out the weeds of depression before they grow deeper roots.

"A depression is best fought by channeling aggression into controlled action. We call this process sublimation. Instead of taking a nap, we can take a walk. Instead of withdrawing into solitude, we can decide to give a party. Instead of moving away from people, we can make an effort to move toward people; use the telephone to communicate, visit someone. Instead of ruminating we can go to a concert or to a movie. There are endless things we can do even if initially it is an immense and at times frightening effort. But action is the best weapon to fight a depression, and joy one of the best medicines to prevent a relapse.

"We may wish to die for a moment when we lose someone we have loved deeply, a mate or a friend, or even money. Mourning must be limited in time. To prolong grief is a sweet-bitter self-indulging neurotic reaction that can turn into sickness. As healthy humans we must replace a loss. A beloved human being cannot be replaced as simply as a house. But we cannot live in a void; we must not—as Lot's wife did—look back. Whatever the season of life, it offers different joys—if we care to turn our eyes outward, if we avoid self-pity and self-torture. When depressed, we must take a small step at a time and two steps the next day."

Life, after all, is a constant adjustment of inner conditions to outer conditions, set by the demands of life, it also requires the ability to accept inevitable and painful experiences, those of aging and of losing people we love. Longevity and a joyful disposition then depends on maintaining inner balance and a constant cultivation of active hope.

Because mental defenses can effectively cover up feelings of self-hate, of poor self-esteem, and of crippling inferiority, many people are not aware of the deeper causes of their discontent and failure and, consequently, are helpless to stem a growing depression.

Many people cannot love. This is a simple and cruel reality. Many people cannot give of themselves, also a cruel reality. Many of these people can love a dog or a cat or a bird but they cannot love another human being. Neither can they display genuine affection. Said one woman, whose gentleman-friend had taken her on a vacation, "I love him in my own way," and only God and she must have known what that meant. Her friend took a suite so as not to embarrass her. And he showed great patience by not touching her. She was a bright and beautiful lady. When he finally took her to bed, she did not fight him off but was angry and spent the rest of their vacation by turning her back to him—a typical action of immature women who say "love me but don't touch me."

The man broke off the relationship. The woman said she felt sad about it but could not break out of her shell. At times she would write to her former friend: "I love you in my own way." She was a depressed lady.

This woman represents many unhappy people, overcontrolled, fearful to trust, and too inhibited to admit even liking another person. They are self-centered, narcissistic, isolated, and cannot love humanity. And if in a family or friendship relationship they feel obliged to give, it will be out of a sense of obligation or a code of good manners but not with their heart. Consequently these people remain uninvolved, alienated, and depressed regardless of how well they try to conceal this.

Another area of depression mixed with anxiety in older people is, as stated before, their constant fear of losing their physical attractiveness. This is particularly true with women. It is not merely vanity that makes them spend millions of dollars on what are, for the most part, worthless creams and lotions to fight off all the various signs of aging. In a youth-oriented society for women to grow old means to run the risk of being ignored or to lose their chance to attract men.

116

Women need to be loved. They need to hear it. When a woman feels that men don't pay any attention anymore, she feels old and tends to be depressed. Women can deny the need to be loved. Said a superstar on national television: "What about love? I love my children and I love my work . . . everything else, forget it. Work, that is all that matters. That is an ally that never betrays you."

Deep down, men and women never cease to play the boy-girl game, the need to be liked, to be noticed and, in fantasy, to imagine themselves still desirable as a love object by the other.

"To defy power which seems omnipotent; To love and bear; to hope till Hope creates from his own wreck the thing it contemplates." These thoughts of hope expressed by Shelley can be a beacon of light in the darkness of depression if we, as individuals, don't want to give up on life. Once in the grips of a depression we must seek help or learn to help ourselves. A depression, as stated so often before, is a loss of hope that can be either of short duration or long-lived. It depends on a person's positive or negative involvement with life. People who enjoy their misery will be like beggars who are at the lowest point on a scale of self-worth. They live off the sweat of other people's work—take food and money—the way children expect to be taken care of. Consequently, there is no incentive to change their passive state.

People with some self-esteem will struggle to help themselves, regardless of age. When lost in a heavy fog, it is not weakness to ask for directions. When depressed, it is false pride not to open up to a friend, to a member of one's family, or to a physician one trusts, rather than to wither away. Prolonged states of deep sadness or depression that causes acute paralysis of thought and by waiting too long makes us sink deeper into a state of discouragement requires professional help.

The depression in older people has primarily three sources. One is *senility,* which clinically relates to the infirmities of old age, primarily the diminished functions of the brain, caused by a dying-off of brain cells. A second cause is *arteriosclerosis,* the degenerative and thickening of the walls of the arteries that produces a diminished blood and oxygen supply to the brain, as it does to all the organs of the body. Nicotine, alcohol, drugs, overeating and metabolic disturbances lead to brain damage, because the hardened arteries cannot supply the brain cells with sufficient oxygen.

The third cause of depression is due to a *chemical imbalance of the brain metabolism, or psychotic depressive reactions.* Scientific research over the past two decades has brought new hope to these heretofore

117

difficult or even dangerous conditions. Psychotropic drugs can prevent the very highs and lows that occur in these patients and help them maintain states of balanced functioning.

The reactive depression in old age differs from that in the younger years. Aging people run a greater chance of feeling discouragement or futility due to the inescapable knowledge that they are coming closer to the end of their lives. Another source of discouragement is the experience that people of their age group have begun to die out. Depressions occur after the loss of a mate or a close member of a family; the loss of sexuality or the anticipation of such a loss. Hypochondriacs may have an increased fear of sudden death or of some grave illness. These depressions manifest themselves by morbid thoughts and withdrawals from people or activities. Many of these symptoms are of neurotic nature and can be helped greatly by supportive psychotherapy or psychotropic drugs.

Sometimes talking to someone who will listen unhurriedly and with empathy can help a frightened man or woman overcome the terrifying emanations from their own inner, and at times irrational, fear. We all have the choice to live or die. The in-between is sickness. We can choose to crawl out of a suffocating cave and leave its imaginary safety and begin to breathe fresh air and turn our eyes outward. There is something we can do to give our day some meaning. All it takes is one decision. But to say, as one depressed patient put it, "If I can't paint as Michelangelo, I won't even start," is to avoid facing the realities of existence.

Coming to Terms with Aging

To narrow the gap of an alienation from life we must begin by using our energies in some constructive way, regardless of how small or how little it may be in the eyes of the world. Everybody has learned something from past experiences in life and if we ourselves cannot pull it together, then we must find a mechanic who can, one who is willing to help remove a roadblock. The rationale that all is futile is just as cynical as a son's attack on his father by saying he did not ask to be born. It is a sign of a depressed mind. It is a mental illness that has grown out of a virulent hate that has extinguished a normal and healthy will to live.

Many older people have realistic fears and suffer pain. I have come to admire the quiet courage of many of these people and the dignity with which they live, neither wanting to complain nor bother anyone but rather go on until, like a candle, their lives expire.

How do the elderly retain their sanity knowing that every day they come one day closer to death?

All people will have to come to terms with aging in one way or another if they want to live without fear. All rational people will take into account that slow and inevitable decline of energy and bodily functioning, as did Queen Juliana of Holland when she abdicated her throne on her seventieth birthday, saying she must give way to her younger daughter.

Thinking people do think of their end, though they may not dwell on it. They prepare a last will. They determine where they want to be buried or cremated. But before that, they plan some sort of existence they may wish to lead once they no longer have to respond to an alarm clock or to the responsibilities of a business or a job or a profession.

Some people use humor as a defense against the grim reality of dying or the infirmities of aging. Years back I heard Noel Baker, the 1959 Nobel Peace Prize winner, tell this little story: "Walking," he said, "I met the former British Prime Minister Clement Attlee, who was in very poor health." Asked Noel Baker: "Mr. Prime Minister, how do you feel? Wherepon Attlee replied, 'When I consider the alternative, I must say very well.' " This response is similar to the one received by one doctor who asked a long-retired colleague about his health, and was answered, "I feel like twenty . . . for half an hour." Or an old soldier meeting his long-lost army buddy: "Remember the saltpeter they fed us during the war to quiet our sex drive?" he asked. "I remember." "Well, it's just beginning to take effect."

Some people play hide and seek with themselves. As long as they can make themselves see only what they want to see, they can stretch their life of escape a long way.

A friend told me a remark of her uncle, a musician in his nineties. "When I take the bus," said the man, "I pay the full fare. I don't want the half-price because I don't want anyone to think that I am a senior citizen."

Before World War II the fate of most older people was in a deplorable state unless they belonged to an upper socioeconomic class and could afford comfort and friends. My professor in psychiatry told us students how his professor handled his duty of inspecting the state mental hospital once a month. The patients had to assemble in a semimilitary fashion. His checkup consisted of addressing these patients by asking, "Are you all still nuts?" And knowing that there was no cure, or answer, would write his report: "Condition unchanged."

Now, since people live longer and are better able to protect themselves economically, the relatively new medical specialty of geriatrics has developed, and is well equipped to deal with the problems of the aged. There is a huge new industry that caters to the needs of senior citizens. Homes and condominiums are being built that provide companionship and entertainment for the elderly. They have sprung up in all the larger communities of the United States, providing privileges and consideration to preserve the senior citizens' often embattled sense of dignity. The southern part of Florida has become senior citizen country on a gigantic scale, with simple to luxurious hotellike accommodations. Here the elderly, in addition to food and shelter, obtain medical care and a chance to form friendships built on a common need, a most effective agent to prevent depressions.

In their later years, men and women sometimes regress emotionally into adolescentlike behavior, such as flirtatiousness, half-embarrassed datings, rivalries, jealousies—in brief, a playing out of their basic pattern of social and mental games with perhaps a revival of faded macho masculinity or earlier seductive feminine lure. Sexual needs and fantasies never cease in people until they die, except in the depressed. The loss of sexual interest is often one of the advance symptoms of depression.

Qualms of the elderly to admit their age is often a neurotic obstacle to entering a senior citizen's home. This behavior can cause many people to suffer from loneliness and depression. Independent people who possess a strong sense of pride will simply fight what they see as the return to an organized childhood nursery. I remember the plight of a middle-aged lady I treated. Her mother had died and her widowed father played on his daughter's grief and guilt, demanding more of her time than she could give. She needed to be guided on how to present to her father, firmly and without tears, the concept that it would be best for him to live in a home with other people. She was forewarned not to weaken when he would pressure her by a display of hurt feelings, of rejection, of being kicked out now when he was old and useless. Daughter and father finally reached an agreement to look at a few homes and to select one where he would stay for a couple of weeks on a trial basis, with the option to return home in case he felt unhappy.

The first week he called every day to say how terrible the place was but that he would live up to his promise. After three weeks he wanted to leave, although he had become friendly with another man with whom he shared many interests, one of which was playing cards. "But," said the father to the daughter, "I can't stay at that terrible place any longer. . . . The man I play cards with is cheating and has a terrible character."

The daughter took the father home. During the next few days he became quieter and quieter. After a week, he said, "The man I had complained about, actually he was not that bad and maybe he wasn't even cheating." The following week he wanted to be taken back to the place. He was missing the companionship.

"Body and mind, like man and wife, do not always agree to die together," said Charles Caleb Colton. Aging processes may differ with different people. Some people keep on training their bodies or keeping their minds active, so that they retain their mind-body functioning until a very old age. Some neglect their bodies by a lack of activities, overweight, or other destructive habits. Others take care of themselves, remain productive and cultivate friendships or hobbies and as a result live longer with more enjoyment.

Thinkers, writers, painters, and other people feel an inner need to create goals for themselves, sometimes a kind of a mission they wish to fulfill. It is active hope that proves to be supportive for these people who can go on with the business of living and the joy of producing with little outward sign of declining vitality. And here we see the positive and negative mind, people who have something to contribute go on because they have a reason to live. People who have nothing to contribute and have lived a frivolous or superficial life—who have always depended on others and always cleverly managed to find people who would take care of them—eventually fade out and die. If this does not happen prematurely, then it occurs in an angry-depressed state, leaving life, in Shakespeare's words, by "signifying nothing."

George Bernard Shaw was ninety-four when he wrote a last memo about "the will to live," saying that, rationally, "I ought to blow out my brains, but I don't and won't. . . ." "I ought to clear out, my bolt being shot and overshot." He decided to die a "natural" death. And so he did. He died from an accident, falling from a tree, which, in the light of his last written words, appears less accidental and more like an inner decision to let go at a moment of "carelessness." Perhaps a preoccupation with death makes one cease to fight back, like the rats in the Richter experiment that stopped their still-healthy hearts in the diastole, the moment of rest.

Ivan Petrovich Pavlov, the discover of the conditioned reflex, and this century's greatest physiologist, was eighty years old when he wrote a moving paper in which he stated his *raison d'être* for entering the field of psychiatry. (His concepts of mental illness are still the basis of the psychiatry that is being practiced in the Soviet Union and the other Iron Curtain countries. This author, in 1959, visited the Pavlov Institute, a rare grant to foreign scientists.) Pavlov died at eighty-six, saying "Let's go, hurry," fell over and was dead.

Johann Wolfgang von Goethe, Germany's greatest poet, lived productively until eighty-three; Pablo Picasso until ninety-one; Arthur Rubinstein, the pianist, at ninety, still gives concerts.

Large is the list of creative men and women who have lived long and productive lives because they kept their brain cells exercised. Perhaps even more significantly, they created within themselves some reason for continuing their existence, rather than resting on old laurels. These creative older people have a dignity about themselves that commands respect. And these people deal with reality productively and positively. Passive people are more likely to fear and to complain.

Adjusted older people, for the most part, try to be useful, to be thoughtful of others, and to be patient. They have fought their battles with life and have made peace with themselves. Those who have grown up with self-worth have cultivated concern for their fellow man and love for mankind. Many of these old people have beautiful faces because, for the most part, they avoided hate, anger, or cynicism, all of which helped not only to prevent excessive wear and tear, but helped them utilize their energies creatively. They belong to the group of people who had dreams that were realistic and visions that were conceived and nourished by dynamic hope. Their beliefs, ideas and inner urges to create, besides giving them satisfaction and a constant build-up of self-esteem, also fulfilled another need—that of making a contribution to the world they live in and, through their work, to be in touch with the rest of humanity.

These older people's forms of expression be it artistic, scientific, literary, farming, or carrying on their trade or business, if done with the positive belief of its value, builds self-worth because of its usefulness to themselves and others. The more one gives of oneself the greater the gratification and self-worth.

The great thinkers or talents we remember, have accomplished what they did because they continued to cultivate their minds to be productive. A productive mind is a mind in harmony. *To live a productive life means to struggle with a thought but not quarrel with a neighbor.* Aggressive energy goes into the labor of chiseling the rawness of a rock into an image that reflects the spirit of humanity and the unending wonders of nature that are reflected in human life itself. And it is this creative drive that renews itself in the minds of men and women. Though they may grow old in years, they remain young in the strength of their ideas, thoughts, and the width of their productive horizon, until the last substance of life in the aged has been burned out and they go to sleep, at peace with themselves and with a world they have loved and to which they have known when to say good-bye.

Mankind owes to the child
the best it has to give.
—U.N. Declaration

Chapter 8
Hope and Childhood

"As the twig is bent the tree inclines," said Vergil, the prince of the ancient Latin poets. Hope develops early. The way the child is picked up and held leads to its first positive or negative responses to life.

It was just before World War II, while working at the clinic of New York's Lenox Hill Hospital, that a young psychologist presented a film on the life of a baby for all the staff members.

There were pictures of the delivery followed by the first breast feeding. The camera focused on the face of the baby's mother. It was thin, tense, and evidently frightened by the experience. Her arms and fingers, with which she was holding the baby, were stiff, as if avoiding too close a contact. The camera showed the baby's mouth frantically snapping for the nipple, while the mother, made even more nervous by the infant's restlessness, made no attempt to help the baby until it finally found the nipple and then began to suck eagerly. (Incidentally, some babies revenge themselves for their prolonged hunger pain by biting their mother's nipple with their still-toothless jaws, a very first expression of an infant's aggression and hostility.)

The camera moved on to a next bed. A nurse was handing a baby to a full-faced Rubenesque woman who was smiling in happy anticipation, stretching out her arms to pick up her child. At once she embraced it lovingly while her fingers were gently pushing her nipple into the mouth of the hungry infant. It was the inspiring picture of mother and child, an eternal symbol of unconditional love.

The movie camera switched back to the first baby. Still there was no suggestion of close intimacy. Neither mother nor baby were relaxed.

The psychologist kept on filming scenes of the maturing child, first every day, then every week, and later on every month for a number of years. He picked out scenes to record significant reactions during the various stages of the child's development.

At age three there was already clear evidence that this child had learned to be afraid. There was a scene in New York's Central Park. Children were using a slide. Since it was a silent film the viewer could not hear the children's shrieks of joy. Now, it was our child's turn. The mother stopped the child from climbing up the small ladder to the slide and took out a towel she had brought along to wipe clean the handlebars of the slide, impressing on the child the danger of contact and fear of germs. The child's face lacked the excitement and spontaneity of the other children.

Another scene: The child's age must have been four. She was in the kitchen climbing on a chair to pick up a glass. As she stepped down the glass fell and broke. There was terror in the child's face. Her body seemed to freeze for a moment, then she began to pick up the pieces. As she realized that she could not put them together nor hide the evidence of the accident she stood for a while, dejected, a picture of utter confusion. Then she broke out in tears and left the kitchen to tell her mother what had happened. Her fear was pervasive. The onlooker was left with the spectacle of a tiny human's feelings of misery, helplessness, and fear. In this case it was evident already which way the twig had been bent. Whatever would follow is a matter of speculation.

Fostering Hope

Although the point has recently been disputed, the brain of a newly born baby is a blank. It begins to imprint signals. This means that a specific event produces a specific response which, by repetition, forms a pattern the child takes into adulthood. Pavlov proved the making of behavior scientifically. He rang a bell each time he was feeding a dog. After a number of times he found that the dog would salivate at the sound of the bell even when no food was given. Repetition of the experiment, the ringing of the bell, which could be replaced by another signal in association with food, would produce a specific psychophysiological reaction, salivation. Pavlov called this process a conditioned relfex. The bell, or its substitute, becomes a signal imprinted in the brain of the animal. The human infant with its larger brain develops an even larger system of signals with specific responses. Thus, a child's basic behavior is formed.

Going back to the first feeding of the two babies, the conditioning of the first infant suggests tension and anxiety about hunger, food, and comfort. Most likely there will remain a state of tension: When will I get my food, or how will it be given or served? And since it cannot be assumed that the nervous mother will change into a relaxed and giving woman, the response to the first baby's feeding will be strengthened in its association with restlessness and irritability about food. Feeding will become a source of anxiety. When do we eat? Where do we eat? Later on in a restaurant such a person might be very impatient with a waiter who is too slow or too indifferent in serving the dinner.

The second baby, on the other hand, is most likely to be at ease, because he has no doubt about getting his food. He can therefore be relaxed and anticipate with pleasure the serving of a good meal, like his mother served him willingly her warm milk. That person might become a gourmet, expanding on the enjoyment of an intake of food. There is, in this type of a person, the added, unconscious, erotic pleasure of his sensitized lips touching the eroticized fullness of his mother's breast. Since this infant's mother displayed joy and physical closeness, the person this infant might later on become would tend to be trusting, secure, feeling confident that his needs would be fulfilled, that he would be loved. People who begin life with this kind of security are people who enjoy the touch of another person or who symbolically can love and embrace other people or mankind as a whole. Even in times of economic depression these people may have concern but no real fear of going hungry.

The first child will most likely grow up to be a person with anxiety and passive hope, perhaps dreaming of a better life than that with mother, who did not prepare her well for life. Or, she may maintain feelings of deprivation and grow up with discontent and anger and take by force what mother had not been able to give her willingly. Or there might develop feelings of unworthiness because mother did not care much. Another frequent response to deprivation may be to use all an individual's cunning and intelligence to gain power and to buy love or to impress on a mother an image of power or to build one's own image of worth to be loved by the world.

The second child will, in all likelihood, move throughout life with the optimism or positive hope that somehow all will work out well. Since he received freely he may tend to give freely. Having less anxiety than the first child, he might pursue his goals with less anxiety and also less anticipation of failure. And if he fails, he will begin again: Whatever he does he has the basic motivation that he can finish what he starts.

This then is the beginning of hope. Like a tiny fountainhead, hope may grow into a river, symbolic for the structure of our personality in which energy is channeled into a positive or negative direction. Whether we grow up with active or passive hope depends on the positive or negative forces that affect us at our first responses to life.

The Neurotic Child

Because of the importance to know ourselves and how we can go about healing ourselves from possible irrational fears, angers, reactions of violent impulses or depressions, let us look at our human development from another psychodynamic point of view we call neurotic.

William E. Sorrel, former professor of psychiatry, Yeshiva University, describes neurosis as being essentially a disturbance in human relations. Although it starts with a disturbance in relationship to others, it soon becomes a disturbance in relationship to oneself.

The foundation of all neuroses begins in childhood, through an unfavorable psychological environment. As the individual grows older, the neurosis becomes more complex. It has a purpose. Just as a toothache's purpose is to make an individual aware of some pathological condition of the tooth, the purpose of a neurosis is to *achieve certain unconscious goals* in one's life. *Therefore there is a strong resistance to give up this (neurotic) purpose.*

In a psychiatric or psychoanalytic practice we may sometimes question who is the patient—the parent or the child? Also, while children start out loving their parents, it is only later that they begin to judge them.

Dr. Sorrel believes there are few problem children. We (the parents or their surrogates) malign some children by calling them problem

128

children when some conditions should be called problems *of* children. (Often the child's problem is a parent.)

The child has a natural feeling of omnipotence. He feels that everybody loves him, that "I am the best." This egocentric attitude changes as he ages. But the neurotic still feels that way when he is an adult and therefore is unable to take defeat and rejection. He goes into a depression after he has a clash with reality.

The neurotic child is dominated by fear and anxiety. At the root of his behavior is a deep sense of inadequacy. Unaware of himself, he may say, "I can't take it anymore." Sorell compares attitudes toward life with the feeling of a good swimmer to whom it does not matter how deep the water is. To the insecure and unstable the very thought of deep water leads to emotional confusion and anxiety.

Because of prolonged schooling and thus prolonged dependency, Dr. Sorell points out these four major problems of children:

Deprivation: absent parents, divorced or detached parents
Rejection: an unloved or unwanted child, a male preference
Exploitation: parents want the child to grow up quickly; to put demands of achievement or other burdens on the child
Overprotection: depriving the child from gaining feelings of independence or of growing up emotionally. A mother might say: "Take your coat, it's going to rain and you will get a cold"

Learning from Living

While parents are responsible for initiating neuroses, our culture demands and perpetuates them. The system tends to praise a mother who has borne six or more children rather than for the way they are being brought up or turn out.

Since a child emulates the parents—a boy the father, a girl the mother—the growing-up children take into adulthood the peaceful positive or the disturbing negative atmosphere that was pervasive in a home. *Thus active hope or passive hope develops.*

The child feels he is living, after all, in a world of giants, and he is only a little fellow. The fear of how to get along in a frightening and confusing world causes the child to go the safe way, to imitate his parents, though it may lead him astray. Wise and loving parents will assist the child to become independent and to learn to distinguish healthy values from neurotic ones.

Dr. Sorrel's paper, "On Neurosis," which he read at the 1980 convention of the American Association of Psychoanalytic Physicians, concluded with this observation. "Several years ago, I had the pleasure of being an American Delegate to the International Congress on Mental Health held in England, and from there a group of other psychiatrists and I went on to half a dozen other countries in a psychiatric survey. What we saw and heard made us quite convinced that we shall never have a peaceful social world as long as we have anxious and neurotic children, who later grow up to be our leaders."

Whether we believe it or not, Dr. Sorell's summary read: Children *learn* what they *live*.

If a child lives with criticism, he learns to condemn.
If a child lives with hostility, he learns to fight.
If a child lives with fear, he learns to be apprehensive.
If a child lives with pity, he learns to feel sorry.
If a child lives with ridicule, he learns to be shy.
If a child lives with jealousy, he learns to feel guilty.
If a child lives with tolerance, he learns to be patient.
If a child lives with encouragement, he learns to feel confident.
If a child lives with praise, he learns to be appreciative.
If a child lives with acceptance, he learns to love.
If a child lives with approval, he learns to like himself.
If a child lives with recognition, he learns it is good to have a goal.
If a child lives with honesty, he learns what truth is.
If a child lives with fairness, he learns justice.
If a child lives with security, he learns to have faith about himself and those about him.
If a child lives with friendliness, he learns the world is a nice place in which to live.

This interjection of the various influences in a child's early years is meant to make us aware of why we have become the person we are, of whether we have felt wanted, loved, or unloved. Or that our parents never understood our needs. Whatever the case, we need not go through life blaming them for our troubles. They gave us life and a brain which we can use to gain self-awareness as a first step toward building our very own identity. "We must learn to think," is what I am in a habit of telling my patients. "Use your brain. Get an understanding of yourself and your world. Instead of whining, try to adjust. Instead of claiming to be tired or bored mobilize the energies that lie dormant. And instead of fearing an emotional involvement, dare to fall in love." As stated so often before, work at turning passive hope into the dynamic hope with which to structure and cultivate new creative goals for yourself. Only they hold the promise of giving you a sense of joy and fulfillment. We must never forget that it is, after all, our life that is at stake.

Building Active Hope

Now that we understand how our own type of hope has developed, we can decide how to go about building strong active hope. The first lesson is to recognize that it is *our* choice to live a happy or a miserable life, to be healthy or to nurture sickness. The second lesson is to recognize, every day, that the power of our signal system remains intact throughout life and thus triggers off set conditioned responses. Recognizing this fact, we must learn that we, and only we, as individual people, have the power to fight to defend our neurotic responses, or to break them by daring to restructure our lives. Doctors don't cure a signal, they cure a response, one that is still childish or destructive. "Why do we behave the way we do?" must be our question. Always. Do we have the will to first recognize and then change our response? Or do we wish to hide behind excuses and nourish, like a bad gardener, the weeds of our neuroses? We may feel determined enough to do the work of changing ourselves. Or, if we are confused and weak—and it is not shameful to admit this—we should seek professional help. The work of changing is hard work because it demands that we must be aware every minute of the day how destructive our move, or the action we are about to undertake, may be, and then apply control, much as the child has learned not to act out. We have the obsessive-compulsive person who, unless he acts out his compromise, experiences tensions. If a surgeon breaks a bone to reset it straight there is pain, followed by painful exercises in order to learn to walk again. So it is with the practice of new healthy responses to old signals.

Shaping Our Children

Let's assume the girl mentioned earlier in this chapter who showed neurotic behavior because of her rigid and distant mother had been a boy who had sexual fantasies and desires for physical closeness with his mother but repressed them forcefully for fear that his father might discover these thoughts. He now may remain psychosexually "fixated" on his mother. The boy may not mature emotionally or sexually. He may look for a mother substitute and marry an older woman. Or he may be sexually attracted to women he despises and uses for sexual satisfaction but without any display of affection. In his search for closeness he may run from woman to woman, or he may be afraid of getting emotionally involved with a woman for fear she may "close in on him." If he does marry, such a man may read or do some work and push his wife away when she puts her arms around him, not knowing why he is angry, while she also does not know why he is angry and hurting or rejecting her.

The image of the father can play a strong compensating role. If the boy's father is strong and kind, the boy will emulate him and might have an easier time in adjusting to normal sexuality. However, if the father is cold, cruel and distant, they boy cannot build a distinct identity and will remain aloof. Fearing women and being confused about the male role, such a boy may remain weak and withdrawn and turn to homosexuality to avoid deep involvement and adult responsibility for another human being. This is a life for which Tennessee Williams, the American playwright, suggests a compromise, as he does in his play *Small Craft Warnings,* that half a life is better than none.

The fixation of a boy on his mother can produce three sexual images: One to find one's sexual ideal; another to revere one's mother as a saint while having sex with a whore; and the third, to court women in order to live out the thrill of conquest and then torture them in many little ways or by outright acts of sexual sadism.

The fixation of a girl on her father displays similar dynamics— those of closeness, of fear, of hate, of dislike, of loss of respect, and at the same time, a need for the affection of a father who may be unable or unwilling to give to the little girl the love and security she needs to grow up. Such was the case with the following patient.

As a little girl this patient had pulled her hair out in fits of despair, having received no love from her mother, who was too immature, too introverted, and could not love, nor from her father, who was in constant turmoil because of his own discontent and severe emotional problems. At age ten, she spent a year and half at one of the best psychiatric hospitals in New York but was unable to develop any trust or closeness with any of the doctors, nurses, or the social workers. All this girl was wishing for was to die. When I saw her she was in her late twenties, an attractive young woman who was most difficult, angry, oppositional (she had to contradict whatever was said) and, if interrupted for a question or to make a point, would react with an attack of rage and uncontrollable screaming that had to run its course like a hurricane until rational awareness returned.

It was not easy to retain patience and eventually guide her out of her inflexible fixation. She eventually could relate to me positively, and as I was listening to her description of her daily pains and crises it was evident that she had a remarkable writing talent, which hopefully she would be using professionally one day, after she had made a healthy adjustment to life.

Whether a girl is arrested in her emotional growth because of her fixation on her father—or on her mother if she is the stronger parent—later on in life the child in the grown person will act out all phases of unresolved childhood conflicts on a love partner. The same is true in the son-mother relationship. This acting out becomes a frequent source of marital battles or incompatibilities.

Here is an example: A young man came for help because his wife wanted a divorce. He was thirty-one years old, tall, well-mannered, and very passive. He had most attractive features, a gift from his mother, who had been an aspiring Hollywood actress. The father was a known writer. His parents were divorced when he was six years old.

Since his mother was preoccupied with furthering her career, she did not have too much time for her young son. One dreadful memory came back to him one day as he told me about his childhood. He recalled many hours he spent in a dark closet, locked in by his mother, so that her suitors should not become aware that she had a son, which would belie her age. My patient had "forgotten" the dreadful hours in the dark closet, and was aware of the destructive effect these incarcerations had on his mind. Besides feelings of being unloved, his mother's actions meant a denial of his existence. "I am not worthy to be alive," was his final summing up of his mother's attitude toward him. "Why then did she fight for custody?" said this patient bitterly. "Probably because it was the 'right' thing to do."

The woman he had married was as glamorous as his mother. My patient never knew that he had been depressed as long as he could remember. His passivity and distrust of women created tensions in their marriage, because the wife, a passive personality, expected guidance and strength my patient could not provide. Both people had lived in fantasy. Because they were so very attractive they were a delight to many people in social settings. They acted out their roles until one day the wife said she was leaving. He then decided to come for professional help.

It was too late to save that marriage because it had no foundation in reality. It had been a fantasy for both. When I saw the wife—a striking-looking young lady—she spoke the language of the women's lib movement: freedom, independence. She did not really know what these words meant. Having no direction, she got into a social whirl of the then-chic Studio 54. My patient, a sincere and kind man, tried to reevaluate his existing values, to gain an understanding of himself and the life his parents had failed to give him, not because they were ungiving people but because of their ignorance about human values and the needs of a child.

Another young man, age twenty-one, came to see me while he was still in college. This young patient, a victim of a broken home, was also a victim of the drug cult of the early seventies. His early years were years of chaos, of being torn between two battling parents. His father, insecure as a man, was ambivalent toward his son, loving at one time, cold and indifferent at others. The boy lived with the father for a few years, then with the mother until sent away to a boarding school. He lacked the permanence of a secure home and never had any real sense of belonging.

The mother followed her own career. She, more than the boy's father, lacked emotional security, though she did her utmost to take care of her son. She loved the boy and the boy loved her, except that he felt helpless, angry, and frustrated when she went through periods of depression, which frightened him. He wanted her there when he needed her. The mother lavished gifts on him and then was critical when the boy developed an expensive taste for quality men's wear.

He had no difficulties scholastically but was anxious outside of the physical environment of school. To travel by car or train caused him unbearable anxiety and he panicked at the thought of flying to see his mother in California. His panics, states of sudden, irrational fear combined with little breaks with reality as to time or the place he was in or was going to, filled him with terror. "I spin out for thirty seconds," he said. These states caused in him a fear of "going insane—going berserk—losing all sensibilities—" At age five he was lost in a department store. He still had a fear of elevators, an anxiety "to be forgotten there." A year later his parents were divorced. All was so traumatic that he could not remember how he felt. At age thirteen he was shipped off to boarding school. "I could have become a kid in trouble. Most kids were on drugs." He too used some drugs, but not to excess.

The beginning of his states of panic went back to age fifteen, when he took marijuana and mescalin, an alkaloid that has narcotic properties and causes hallucinations and convulsions. This was on a rooftop in Princeton. It was the history of a young man searching for an identity and ways of escaping his fits of depression and his constant anxiety. His self-worth was nil, except that he had a strong belief that he could succeed as a composer.

Though he was initially reluctant to come to see me, he began to feel better, which is often the case with people who come for therapy because they feel that finally they are doing something about their problems and also because they feel they are not alone anymore, coping with the frightening anticipation of panic attacks.

But because of money problems, this patient's visits were sporadic. His father objected to his treatments and his mother was financially not able to help very much. He had great ups and downs. He eagerly picked up my suggestion to write down his feelings. Writing notes about one's feelings of depression is therapeutic and very helpful. Describing the thoughts and fears patients may have in their regressed state diminishes intense self-involvement because writing is an intellectual process and demands a return to reality, even if this return is not a completely free and rational function.

Here are some excerpts from this patient's notes:

Sunday

Another weekend gone by; it has now been thirteen weeks of living in this constant fear and panic. I am so goddamn sick and tired of all this continual bullshit. Angry as hell, and now, at this moment, I feel inclined to lay the blame on someone or something, in effect, I'm through taking the responsibility for it. I am very aware that this notion in itself is an unhealthy approach—but damn it, no matter what I try, or what I set out to do or accomplish, I make what seems to be no progress. WHY? I am sick of even trying to search for answers and justifications, pass it off on some psychological reason. . . . Enough is enough. Why the fuck do I have to live this way? What did I do to deserve this way of life?

Friday night I went to some cocktail party with Elizabeth and Jani. I was very genuinely scared going there; on the walk over to Sixty-eighth Street, there were a few very, very anxious moments. Okay . . . I got there, I am nervous but the fact is I got there without any major incident. But I cannot relax, and I'm watching the clock, waiting to leave. We leave what amounts to be a terrible party, walk home, someone suggests a movie, I become very anxious and nix that idea, we get home and I am very nervous and anxious.

Saturday, I wake up, feel pretty good; am at a point where I am more on top of my problem—We go to dinner to a restaurant that has been something of a bother—When we have gone recently, I would refuse to eat out of fear that the food is poisoned. I just watch everyone else eat. Well, I ended up eating pretty well, and made it through dinner without any great panics. We later went to Trax, and I had a fairly even, uneven night—Basically no different from any nights there in the past thirteen weeks. We took the limousine down to Possible Twenty, I had a beer there, then we dropped

George off in the limo at the Carlyle Hotel, and took the car back to Trax. We left the club around 3:00 A.M., stopped at the Carnegie Deli for a sandwich to go, and arrived at our building around 3:30 A.M. The doorman was not there to let us in so we had to bang on the glass to attract his attention. We were outside waiting and banging for about ten minutes, then he arrives to let us in. . . . During those moments waiting to be let in, I became extremely anxious and fearful, feeling really trapped in a bizarre way. I could not get into my apartment building. What a strange twist on an old theme. When I go into our apartment, I did not become suddenly at ease; rather the waiting outside the building had impressed me in such a way as to make me feel unsettled outside, as well as inside. That my apartment was no longer a safe refuge. All my goddamn security blankets are being destroyed. I am so scared, so alone, and now, nothing seems to comfort me. It is such a helpless futile situation.

Today, Sunday, I am a mess. I kept waking up every two hours out of dreams last night. Elizabeth and friends talk about going to the movies. Fourteen weeks ago, the thought of going to a movie was no problem. I gladly would go. But now it is a new ball game. I am terrified of going. I walked to the drugstore to get cigarettes—I almost fell into a full-scale panic.

ENOUGH IS ENOUGH. I DON'T WANT TO HEAR FUCKING EXPLANATIONS ANYMORE. I want to know the truth. Is this shit going to last forever, because if it is I want no more part of it. I would rather just be through with my life—It would be better for me and for everyone else concerned. Where the fuck are my mother and my father—they really don't give a shit. How can I help myself??? I don't have any answers. I'm sorry to face this, but I really think this is permanent. I just don't know what I could do to change.
Friday

I am beginning to realize the importance of self-worth, and how extraordinarily helpful this concept can be to my betterment. Yes, indeed it would be good if I could gain a certain amount of confidence through my work and my creative abilities. However, I am not certain that this accomplishment would be a complete and secure cure. I believe the problem and the cure to be more simple, and by the same token, complex.

Besides having an extremely low estimation of my worth and a serious deficiency in confidence, what I seem to really lack is a true ability to believe and respect myself, to like/love myself. Why is it that I really hate myself so deeply, have such a completely, low level of self-respect??? With that question, I can immediately come up with one explanation. While my mother has always told me of her love for me, of how important I've been to her, I suffered through her constant, though petty, criticism. Whether it be my clothes, my hair, my education, my music, my voice—Name it, she has at one

*time or another, found it necessary to criticize me, all in the hope of getting
better at whatever it is she has in mind.*

*Therefore, I was brought up by a highly critical mother, critical of me, but
even more important, critical of herself. Growing up, I watched her fall
apart over broken love relationships, threaten and even attempt suicide, as
well as what appeared to me to be an extremely selfish attitude about her own
needs in relation to others, particularly myself.*

*So, when I walk down the street, and my mind begins to fall deeper into
these destructive thought patterns, it is usually because I am growing
extremely critical of myself, of my inability to control my anxiety. Consequently, I say to myself, with each passing year, your specific fears and the
frequency of anxiety and panic has grown more than it has subsided. Instead
of making specific progressions in overcoming specific fears, I have developed new paranoia, fears, and a more consistent anxiety to live with. This
constant and recurring thought only amplifies the inner drama that I
subject myself to, and consequently, it becomes exceedingly difficult to
maintain a coherent pattern that might establish feelings of self-confidence,
self-respect, and the needed energy to build ego-strength.*

About three months later the patient handed me a summary of
his present condition. His progress astounded him, though he is far
from being considered cured.

June 23, 1980

*It is approximately six months since this condition first appeared. And
though it is impossible to relive the depths of apparent despair that I felt for
the sake of this writing, it is possible to reconstruct the regressions and
progressions that occurred by reexamining my writings during this time.*

*This is a frightening moment in itself for me; I am confronting the harsh
realities and experiences of the past six months. What I have come to realize
is that my experience, the complete and utter hopelessness and despair, was,
in fact, very real and frightening. I read my diary of experiences, and one
thought comes across quite clearly. Throughout the greater part of the illness,
my anxiety was so largely enhanced by the anxiety itself. Too often, I found
myself writing and ruminating over the nature of my fears and their
consequences, indulging in the self-pity that seems to accompany illnesses of
this sort. So, as I reread my accounts of the fears, anxieties, and the daily
panics, I clearly see now that my energy, both creative and physical, was
very deeply inbedded in the theoretical aspects of the illness. Rarely did I
understand that better ways of using all that excessive and indulgent energy
could in fact make the anxiety much less overbearing. Ultimately, it was
difficult to allow myself the needed patience and time necessary for really*

pulling myself from out of the depth of despair to a level of rational and more consistent behavior.

Perhaps one of the major turning points in getting beyond the immediate fears of eating, smoking, drinking and the rest of the paranoia was joining a health club, attending almost daily, and thereby channeling a lot of my energy into physical activities such as running, swimming, and exercising. And though the health club did not serve as an immediate and overnight cure, it did serve as an essential starting point for me to expand outside of my detachment for almost everything around me, and bring me outside of my in-depth self-examinations—those tendencies which might appear to serve useful purposes but in reality, only serve to increase the overall level of anxiety.

Also, of profound significance toward reaching a better perspective of understanding was the recognition, through therapy, that to reach any goal, it is absolutely necessary for me to begin feeling better about myself and to allow myself the time it might take to get better. I realized in very real and sometimes ugly terms that I did not have the required feelings of self-confidence and self-esteem that everyone needs. So essential these concepts are that as I acquired more and more knowledge as to the lack of these qualities in my personality, the more I was able to realize the absolute need for them if I were to achieve any degree of betterment. Even now, I am not sure how one goes about acquiring these virtues; I can only say that for me, the eventual realizations of self-indulgence and excessive ruminating over my illness was not allowing me to expand my creative energies, which would in turn give me more of the ultimate satisfaction and confidence I needed to feel good about myself. How profoundly important this concept shall always remain in my life.

In conclusion, I can say that I am living without the constant anxiety and panic of the past few months. I am able to exist much more normally, able to function without the past eccentricity, anxiety, and profound fear that for so long debilitated my way of life. A pervading hopelessness made it very difficult for me to believe that I might ever overcome these feelings of despair. But this is not to say that I have accomplished that which I set out to overcome in the first place. It is a great relief to be over the horrors of the past six months. But problems still remain. Fears that prevent me from living a totally fulfilled life still exist.

So often in therapy, the term "tip of the iceberg" is used to define and illustrate the discovery process which one must go through. For so long, this term frightened me: What might lie beneath the "tip of the iceberg"? But now I feel that I have broken through the "tip of the iceberg," and that I am well on the way to establishing a sense of self-confidence and self-esteem that I will use to the utmost for the total enjoyment of my life.

* * *

To sum up this patient's history, a growing positive outlook on life began to displace his attacks of panic and self-rejection. With the confidence he developed, his work was noticed. A first album of compositions was published. His determination to work on himself was helping him to overcome his passivity. He had experienced the fact that using his energies in work diminished his anxiety and fear of panics while it increased his self-esteem. He comprehended and applied the concept of active hope, realizing that it was a lifelong learning and maturing process. Once this patient experienced the power of using control instead of allowing himself to sink into some of his fearful depths without resisting, it was as if he had found a key. Now that he was not hopeless anymore he began to believe that he had a chance in life to grow into a man with confidence and a sense of direction.

Severe disturbances may result from the constant hammering on a child's brain of the "dos" and the "don'ts." At a recent convention of the American Association of Psychoanalytic Physicians, Dr. James A. Smith (chief psychiatrist of the Child Guidance Clinic, Springfield, Massachusetts), in a presidental address, presented a paper on "Perspectives in Psychoanalysis, Non-Talking, a Symptom. Elective Mutism." It began:

> "Be quiet! You sound like a talking machine," said mother to her twelve-year-old daughter.
> "Gee, mom, I never knew a machine could talk," said ten-year-old Margo.
> "I knew it!" added six-year-old Melanie.
> This pertinent commentary was submitted by the mother of a nontalker. Many child guidance clinics have children brought to their attention who refuse to talk in the school situation. The child's general overall behavior is regarded as shy and inhibited, but at home he is known for his aggressive, demanding, and controlling behavior.
> Attention is given to the dynamics and findings from some six cases of a great number which have appeared at the Child Guidance Clinic over the years. As [Psychoanalyst Bernita] Miller and others have noted, this symptom of nontalking is often seen in conjunction with the so-called school-phobic youngster.
> These cases have been seen and managed in various ways

at the Child Guidance Clinic over the years. In essence, it appears that these children have already relinquished a portion of self so as not to experience the intensity of their instinctual drives, symbolic of disintegration, and the impact of the outer world. Self, thereafter, is experienced through mother or other self objects, so as to maintain a feeling of omnipotence or well-being. This mode of adaptation is presented and appropriate to the child in the first months of life.

—This particular symptom appears in relation, for the most part, to those in authority whose omnipotence is greater than that of the parental figures, particularly the mother. Hence, we note nontalking in the presence of teachers, doctors, dentists, policemen, nurses, etc.—those individuals imbued with omnipotence and who demand of others compliance and renunciation of self.

—The children are aware of sacrificing self and mother's promise of fulfillment if this is done. Hence, they are often angry and demanding at home for mother has promised fulfillment if self is relinqushed or, if not so, mother's edict has been one that they will experience abandonment and be left to the instinctual struggle or the anxiety of fragmentation.

—The children maintain the illusion of a good, omnipotent mother who gives all, for mother's relation to her parents has been a similar one. It is the teacher onto whom is projected the bad imagery, the destructive quality of the child, for she demands that he relinquish his present mode of adaptation to the outer world and participate on a reality basis.

—The nature of the self is really rather weak and the struggle avoided by the very nature of the mode of existence, wherein self is experienced only through others and there is a subsequent need for objects with which to fuse because their picture of the world is a fearful one filled with devils, witches, and the like due to the projection of their own rage.

We see very disturbed children, as young as age six, referred to guidance clinics. These children, are for the most part, from lower-middle-class families striving to conform. They are often bilingual. Their role as adults in a world of reality will be very difficult because they have not learned to develop a meaningful relationship with their world. They are handicapped children, psychologically incomplete, who, in order to survive escape into the realm of fantasy, existing on passive hope or in states of near hopelessness.

Hope, as we said, develops early in childhood. Tragically, neurotic responses to any of the traumatic events the child experiences take place in the absence of any intellectual or reasoned value judgment. By repetition, these neurotic responses form a fixed pattern of the maturing personality.

Pavlov called this process of conditioning "the first signaling system." The signals, millions of them, remain imprinted in the brain, which, when activated, lead to specific, reflexlike reactions.

Sometimes I tell my patients of a scene in one of Charlie Chaplin's films to make the point of conditioning. Charlie, the tramp, becomes a millionaire and suddenly finds he has many friends. They take him to the station and the first-class compartment of the train. The stationmaster whistles. Charlie hesitates to board the train. He waits until the train is in motion, then runs along the train and climbs between the cars until he comes to rest, with a smile of comfort, on the axle of the wheels. This is his "conditioned" idea of how to travel.

Change Is Hope

We psychodynamically oriented physicians believe firmly that human nature can be changed. Indeed, it is in a constant process of changing through school and new scientific facts that penetrate the armor of any cultural integrity. In fact, this author had, upon the request of former President Nixon, developed a project that within a ten-year period would have come close to finding a cure for drug addiction and juvenile delinquency. It was a planned method of prevention. Tragically this Plan was torpedoed by the president's own highest White House staff members who were in oppositon to any outside influence.

In the meanwhile, we physicians who practice psychotherapy have learned how to set free the minds of confused, hostile or hopeless young and not-so-young people, and to undo the harm that was done to the minds of people when they were children. And once we accomplish our work of setting them free from a frightening inner world of devils, witches, angels of death, and paralyzing fears, and make our patients mature and happy people, we as doctors, seek—at least I do—to help them find their way back to the home from which they came, help them to make peace with their parents, and possibly learn to be friends, even if parents are rigid and difficult. As one patient said, "I love my mother because she is my mother but I don't like her. How can I forgive her for abandoning me at age three and mistreating me physically so that I was put under the custody of the state and in despair took a bottle of aspirin to kill myself?" This young woman worked hard on herself and, indeed made peace with her mother, which diminished feelings of guilt and rage and helped her to uncover the many slumbering talents she had.

As a rule, I find children to be more generous than their parents in forgiving, but because they, the children, have learned self-worth, they can therefore afford to give of themselves more and make peace—without pain.

Therapy is only the second-best thing that can happen to humans when they learn, mostly with astonishment, about the people they really are in depth and once free dare to walk with an unhampered gait. The best thing is prevention. But here is the problem: If the simile "just as the twig is bent the tree's inclined" is applicable to humans, who is there to detect the first bending of the twig and who will know how to prevent the making of future conflicts at a time when young brains are forming the blueprint of their future behavior?

True, the world is in turbulence. But it does not have to be, it is not in the basic nature of man. Discontent is the outgrowth of human civilization that demands controls and taboos. Stress must therefore be considered normal. In the American culture it begins at a young age with the will to win. Other people who make up our world, are, for the most part, also turbulent as a result of their own greed and ambition. This leaves the nonaggressive segment of peoples feeling fearful about their survival and powerless to change things. Many of these people dream their lives away, existing from day to day on passive hope. They are the innocent, the ignorant, the passive, and the hopeless, and therefore too ready to follow leaders who cover up their aggression by posing as deliverers from hunger and fear and by posing as strong protectors who display big guns as symbols of their power to impress masses of anxious people from the greatest fear man has, the threat of extinction. For the most part, those people who have put their hope in false prophets remain hungry, because their promises were delusions and their beautiful homes Potemkin villages.

What practical steps can we humans take to make our world a happier and a safer place to live in rather than to exist with apprehension, clinging to passive hope? It can be done only by teaching the young and by putting into their fertile minds the seeds of *uncondi-*

tional love and the responsibility for themselves and their fellow man. By helping children to see reality as it is, and to accept the knowledge that ours is the best and only world we have, we can instill in them the hope that it is within their power to change, without the use of force, what needs to be changed, and permit us to hold on to the one great realistic active hope we have—that the happier children of today will be the architects of tomorrow's better world.

CHAPTER 9

Utilizing Hope

"IT'S PART of the cure to wish to be cured," said Seneca. This maxim can be interpreted in two different ways relative to the different psychodynamic functioning of people. Passive, inhibited people expect the cure to come from without, or to be done for them. Dynamically assertive people want to help themselves.

Patients of the first group might say, "Doctor, I am all yours. . . . I hope you can cure me. . . . I will follow your orders. I will take the pills, the shots and do whatever you say." These patients display their childlike passivity by asking for relief from their pain or freedom from their fears or disturbing symptoms. They put their trust in the physician, who they see as being almighty, as the witch doctor, the healer, the concerned parent who will make them well.

The dynamic, ally, positive patient will say, "I am in trouble." Or, "I don't know what my sickness is. Tell me what it is or why I have gotten into this trouble? I want to know. And if I make myself sick I want to know why in order to stop being self-destructive."

These patients will more readily accept a doctor's reply, "I will tell you all I know about you, but as to the cure, the best I can do for you is to help you cure yourself." These dynamic people will not be content with having a symptom removed, they want to work for the cure. But people are not totally passive nor fully dynamic. They may want to move but don't know what blocks them. They may feel desperate enough to seek help in order to use their energies productively. Whether by themselves or with help, they would like to turn their lives around if they knew how.

Some people know they need medical help but are afraid to ask. Other people put off seeking help until they break down under the stresses of life. They are ready to blame outer conditions for their inner turmoil. And then there are people in trouble who, once they are told the causes for their troubles and the direction in which to move, take off, if not exactly with the speed of a rocket, nevertheless with an undeterred, goal-oriented will.

Turning It Around

Here is an example of an assertive young man who had come to a stop. He was in anguish and caught in a situation he did not know how to resolve. He had come to me upon the recommendation of the gynecologist who treated his wife.

The patient was an alert, good-looking, and outwardly secure man of about thirty years of age. The reason for the gynecologist's referral to me was that his wife had nervous complaints her doctor had diagnosed to be the result of the husband's sexual impotence. My new patient was very embarrassed to talk about an area as sensitive as his sexuality. He emphasized that never before had he had any problem in performing sexually to his or to a woman's satisfaction.

He had married his wife a year and a half ago. The wife was several years younger than himself. It was the first marriage for both. At the beginning there were a few sexual attempts that were moderately successful. He became disturbed when he realized that his wife failed to reach an orgasm. A few months after their marriage he felt traumatized by the experience that he could not sustain an erection. He become more and more anxious and attempted sex timidly and with fear of failure. After a few more months he began to withdraw from sex altogether. He became depressed and had increasing fears that their marriage might not work out.

My questions about his wife revealed that she had grown up in an affluent home and had been very spoiled by her father in all kinds of material ways. She had gone to a good college but could not decide on what to do. She had no particular interest in a career.

My patient described her as being pretty and nice and a little shy. They had met at a party of one of her friends. She was not very demonstrative, yet was responsive to his advances. They started to date, which was enjoyable to both. During that time my patient was

146

outgoing and assertive, though he thought that she was a little snobbish. "But," said my patient, "I thought that would work out once we were married."

The patient himself had also started to go to college. After the first semester his father died. There were five children in the family and since he was the oldest, he had to give up school and go to work to support the others. After a few years he started his own business. He became quite successful and was well liked in the business community.

During my inquiry it became evident that he had put his young wife on a pedestal. There were sporadic references to the fact that she had come from a rich home, an indirect censure that his was a poor family. Further questions revealed that his wife acted in a superior manner because of her college degree and her higher socioeconomic status, behavior which he did not know how to counter. He thought that in due time he would prove to her and her family his accomplishments. He seemed at first baffled by these questions, for he could not understand how socioeconomics could have anything to do with his problems. I asked to see his wife.

The wife came readily. She was a pretty young woman, slightly overdressed, with no particular charm or poise. While her outward behavior was passive, she seemed to be rigid underneath. She answered all questions readily, without displaying any emotional eagerness. However, she was startled when I asked whether she wanted to stay married? "Of course," she stammered. "I love my husband."

There was a short debate about love and the role of a woman in a marriage. Was she aware of any arrogance? "No," she answered. Did she display any affection for her husband or interest in his work or awareness of his needs? She seemed very unsure. I finally indicated that if she wanted her marriage to last, she had to contribute more to the relationship, to give more of herself; and she had to give up her subtle intimidation, which, in regard to sex, was playing the role of a passive, noninvolved partner who tolerates sex because men demand it.

During our discussion on how to show more compassion and assume a more give-and-take attitude, she thought for awhile and then said: "Perhaps I am like mother. Maybe I treat my husband as I have seen my mother treating my father? She is cool. Father is more loving. Mother has her own ideas about how a lady behaves." Now the young woman became frightened of losing her husband. She gave up her brittleness and became interested while I tried to make her aware of her husband's qualities, his character, his superior intellect, and his readiness to assume full responsibility for taking care of his whole family. "Isn't his love for you worth more than a college degree?" Before leaving she asked whether she should come back? I said I didn't think it would be necessary.

When the husband came for his second visit, he stated that he was cured. "Sex is fine, everthing is fine. I don't understand what happened or how it happened."

"You are not cured," I replied. "Only a symptom is cured, not your total personality structure."

"I don't need more."

We then entered into a discussion about a healthy man-woman relationship. "Learn one thing," I said. "Women detest weakness in a man. When a woman loses respect for the man, it generally means an end of the marriage."

The patient came for his third visit. "I almost canceled my appointment. . . . I really feel cured. . . . There are no problems anymore. I came to ask how this magic worked? I can't figure it out and I always like to know."

I suggested he talk more to his wife. However, it dawned on him the degree to which he had allowed his wife to intimidate him because of his submission to her and his confusion about human versus extrinsic values. When he left, he was still shaking his head, wondering how a confusion of values could produce impotence, or how a more assertive behavior could restore sexual functioning. He did not know that his wife's attitude toward him had changed.

Her gynecologist called me and said laughingly, "That was a quick cure. . . . She is fine and seems perfectly happy."

My reply was: "It is the same old story: Women want love and firmness, to be appreciated but also to be made aware of the limits of the man's sphere of responsibility. It is like balancing a fine scale, determined by an open communication and the freedom of expressing each one's feelings and needs. Love is not an impulse. It is a fabric that is being woven or a flower that needs water, sun, and care."

This case may prove that sometimes only little treatment is required to prevent an impending disaster. It may demonstrate that if people become aware—either by their own efforts to talk with one another or by seeking help—of how destructively or sadomasochistically they often act toward one another, they can avoid the breakup of a relationship. Tragically, too often people hurt each other, though they may believe they still love each other. In this case just presented, the two people were quick to grasp, and willing to apply, the basic principles of a happy human relationship and cultivated the love that makes a marriage work. The young man in this case could be cured because he wished to be cured.

The example of another, though more difficult case of a patient wanting to be cured, is that of a young woman who was emotionally an embryo but eager to learn. Through trust and utter devotion, she succeeded in turning her life around. She may speak for a multitude of young people who are at a crossroad in their lives, questioning whether they should just accept the painful fact that they cannot make it on their own and wither away, or embark on a course of therapy which by their immature value judgment, is a sign of weakness, and which carries with it a fear of the unknown and the more frightening thought that therapy could lead to the discovery of a mental disturbance or illness.

This young woman was exceptionally beautiful and acted out the role of the "dumb blond," though she slowly revealed a superior intellect. One day, after she had been coming once a week for a few years, I asked her whether she could give a short, simple summary of what had happened to her and what, as she saw it, had produced her total turnabout, from a lost, frightened, depressed young woman to one who felt happy, secure, and now had none of the fears she had lived with since childhood. She agreed to an unrehearsed dialogue on a tape recorder, which, unfortunately, could not communicate the tone of voice nor the silvery laugh or giggle she had when some of her old feelings of embarrassment emerged.

DOCTOR: What do you think has caused your enormous change, the expression of joy you now demonstrate?

PATIENT: I have become a complete functioning human being.

DOCTOR: Are you aware of the bubbly, happy behavior you display?

PATIENT: Yes (laughing) . . . it feels terrific. . . . I can't believe it. . . . I look at myself . . . I know it's me . . . but I can't believe it's me. I can do things I never thought I could do. I am not afraid. I have no fear. . . . I don't have to think what I will say or how to say something, I simply say or do what I want to do (laughing) with no fear. . . . Do you call this spontaneity?

DOCTOR: Yes. . . . You really believe you have no fear?

PATIENT:	No it's terrific, I was afraid to do anything or everything. . . . I thought I would fail, so why try? (laughing)
DOCTOR:	How did this change come about? Do you say it's great or dramatic?
PATIENT:	It's . . . (giggling) it's earthshaking. . . .
DOCTOR:	How has all this come about . . . a person in fear throughout life and suddenly you have no fear? And now, as you say, you react with spontaneity?
PATIENT:	I am capable, simply capable . . . not incompetent anymore, as my parents thought.
DOCTOR:	How do you think this has come about?
PATIENT:	Your guidance and hard work . . . of course, the trust I had . . . but last time, talking about trust, you said that this was only half the answer. What is the other half?
DOCTOR:	Considering the distrust you have of people, is it distrust more of men or women?
PATIENT:	It's equal but probably more distrust of men.
DOCTOR:	How could you develop trust when you came first reluctantly, having put off your appointments twice?
PATIENT:	I did not know what to expect. . . . I think everybody is scared of going to a psychiatrist. You don't know what to expect. . . . But then after a few, maybe after twenty minutes, I began to feel comfortable. . . . (laughing, a little shy) I guess it's you.
DOCTOR:	What is trust?
PATIENT:	Maybe it's love.
DOCTOR:	Not necessarily.
PATIENT:	Then maybe, like when I sit here, I know I can say everyting and I know I won't be judged. . . . You would make no value judgment, so I feel even if you would say I am incompetent, you would not say it to hurt me. . . . it's just confidence, and I also know you can help me. . . .
DOCTOR:	When I inquired about deeper feelings, how could you have known that there would be no value judgment?
PATIENT:	It took me about six months or so before I became aware of deep feelings. . . . I have never ever told anyone in all my life what I told you . . . my inner thoughts, fantasies, everything.
DOCTOR:	Can trust be built so fast?
PATIENT:	I rather quickly began to feel comfortable. . . . I could

150

say what came to mind. . . . I had no fear you would hurt me and I felt free to say anything. . . .

DOCTOR: To a stranger? I was a stranger.

PATIENT: You are a doctor. I knew you could help me. Before I came I had no human interaction, not even with my parents. I could talk to friends, but not as I speak here.

DOCTOR: What about motivation? What do you want to do with your life? Do you want to go on with postgraduate studies? You were a good student, graduated from college. Why didn't you go on?

PATIENT: I had no interest in anything. It was a minimal existence.

DOCTOR: You didn't care what would happen to you later on? Here you are an attractive woman. Can you accept that?

PATIENT: (reluctantly) That I am attractive? Yes. . . . Now, I can. I thought I had to accomplish this by makeup and other things . . . the way you dress. . . .

DOCTOR: How did you see yourself?

PATIENT: I saw myself as a nonentity. . . .

DOCTOR: What created the change . . . the miracle that suddenly you could move, could get yourself a job, one you wanted, at a place you wanted?

PATIENT: Suddenly I felt I could walk into the place without fear. I understood what had held me back in the past.

DOCTOR: What was that?

PATIENT: My mother . . . the guilt I had about my mother. . . . I would be killing her if I got a job, that's what she said. She wanted me in her business, her salon . . . designing, selling . . . all these vain women gossiping and I would have to listen and everything would be under her supervision. . . . She would watch and be critical.

DOCTOR: Where did the guilt go? You say you have none. It had stopped you from doing something for years.

PATIENT: (giggling) The guilt is gone . . . fully or maybe on a scale from one to ten my guilt is between zero and less than one, close to zero.

DOCTOR: Is it since you feel the chains that kept you from moving are broken that you can walk?

PATIENT: More than that. I can walk into eight offices, eight rejections, and walk into the ninth . . . with confidence . . . or guts. (laughing at that term)

HOPE

DOCTOR: What created the switch? One day you are a prisoner, the next day you can command yourself to move with confidence and freedom. No one turned a switch.

PATIENT: I was ready to grow up . . . to accept the responsibility. . . . I thought of mother saying each time I would go for a job interview that it was killing her. Her words 'It kills me' stopped me. You gave me a definition of guilt. Suddenly everything clicked. Besides then you called me a parasite. That really got me angry. (laughing) At that moment I said to myself, Hell . . . I'll get myself a job.

DOCTOR: Why did you not object to being called a parasite?

PATIENT: I knew, you were right. Sometimes we need that kick in the behind to move. And that was the push I needed. I was angry. But I thought, I'll show him. Besides, I was ready. So, I went out. My father called me a parasite also . . . but that was different. He was critical, he did not do anything for me. You weren't critical. So, when I walked in the door, I couldn't believe it was me. I looked and thought, that is somebody else. I don't know how to explain this . . . it was somebody else with confidence . . . it was me, but I didn't think it was me. . . .

DOCTOR: Now that you broke a pattern and walked into my office with confidence, do you feel happy?

PATIENT: Yes, for the first time in my life I feel happy, because I did something on my own, I never knew how much my parents had overprotected me . . . actually crippled me and then called me spoiled, lazy, a nonentity, and a parasite. I believed I could never do anything and now I can. That's what makes me happy. I never felt how it is to feel happy. From now on I will never ever have fear again.

The jubilant mood of my patient persisted. On another level, the changeover from a passive, dependent little girl to a grown woman had developed on a less dramatic pace. It was not, of course, from one day to another and not only in one area, like getting a job. It was evident in a number of other ways.

A few years before her day of victory over herself she had gotten married. She had thought she was in love. Later on she recognized that it was more a way of escape from an intolerable life of emptiness. Also, it was playing the game of a grown woman. Immature as she was, she was motivated by superficial values, like the man's looks and the way he dressed. He had a cool arrogant air about him. However, what doubts she may have had were silenced by a man who knew how to spell out these three magic words, "I love you," and she felt thrilled. She did not see all the many things that were lacking in the man. Or she projected into the man and into the relationship qualities her vivid fantasy readily produced but which, in reality, her husband did not possess. All she had seen in him were appealing surface behavioral traits. At college, he was the football hero. He still played that role. She slowly woke up to the realization that she had married an overgrown boy, one who wanted to be taken care of. She had to carry the full burden in the relationship. In fact, as she put it, "There was no relationship."

When he came home, he moaned about what a hard day he had had and that he now needed to relax. Relaxation meant reading the sports section of the newspapers and sport magazines, waiting to be served dinner.

It took a few months before she realized that her husband was an intensely angry man. He controlled his anger until after dinner, when he provoked a fight; it was to maintain control, to make her feel insecure. He defended his superior role as a man by doing nothing in the way of helping at home.

After another few months, and before my patient had the breakthrough of getting herself a job in the career she had chosen, she had decided to leave him.

When she discussed that point with me, I told her that she was not ready. I explained that her decision was a cop-out, a running away. "When you leave, you must know where you are going and be prepared to be on your own so that you can meet life as an adult woman." She began to hate her husband. One area to measure the quality of married life, like a barometer, is the frequency and satisfaction or dissatisfaction of sexuality.

Sexually, this patient was as confused, as immature and as frightened as she was in other areas. She was a little girl who had never experienced an orgasm. She considered the whole sexplay as something men used to satisfy their needs. She had learned that from her mother. Her husband was less experienced than he pretended to be. He also lacked the sensitivity to help his wife relax. Upon questioning, she concluded that her mother, a strict Southern Baptist, probably also never had an orgasm. Now in her mid-twenties, this patient had mentally not grown beyond the pretty college girl she had been, who, among many other traditional values, had absorbed her mother's and grandmother's values of sex as being dirty. With her sexually insecure husband, she began to resist sex, replacing her earlier, submissive role with an even more immature one of "love me but don't touch me."

Her husband was in a crisis. He had manipulated his father-in-law into hiring him. This step further depreciated his image in the eyes of his wife. A divorce would threaten his position. His wife postponed leaving her husband on the condition that he would accept psychiatric help. She then would take a wait-and-see attitude. She accepted as valid my suggestion that in their stormy relationship her husband would be helpful as a catalyst that would show up her own immaturities. Only when she found that they could not relate at all with one another, and when she felt secure enough to be on her own, would she leave. As it turned out, the husband began to make progress in his treatment, which his wife respected.

It was a stormy year but with her own anger and fear about the future diminishing, she experienced her first full orgasm. That was an elating experience. From then on her self-acceptance as a woman grew, spilling over in other areas of confidence. The chances for these two people to build a meaningful marriage improved. The growth of one helped the other. They began to respect one another. It still was an uphill battle but one that filled both with the hope that they would make it.

To watch and guide the progress of a patient toward a healthy integration is a doctor's reward for his or her work and patience. It was indeed pleasurable to witness how an immature, frightened young woman, with no self-worth, did, by learning to understand herself better, overcome her fears and inhibitions and turn her life around, to become a beautiful, mature woman, who now is emotionally ready for a meaningful marriage and anticipated motherhood.

Generally speaking, young people are a delight to work with, even if they are stubborn, suspicious, angry, and defensive. Some come willingly, others are brought against their will by a parent. It is then a highly diplomatic game to get such an unruly, volatile young person interested in a dialogue and, beyond this, in accepting the help they need.

One such young man, age nineteen, had been brought into my office. He had flaming red hair and the look of a defiant mule. He sat in silence waiting for my first move. Silence. Finally, I said, "Okay. We both are in an unpleasant situation . . . you don't want to be here and I don't like to spend time with anyone who does not want to be here, so let's make the best of it. We have one hour to kill while your parents wait. . . . I don't play cards . . . what do you suggest? Moreover, why did you allow your parents to force you to come?"

The last question caused him to let loose a barrage of accusations against both parents . . . and we had established a dialogue.

Another young man, also age nineteen, was referred to me by the family doctor because of the patient's drug addiction. The problem became too difficult for the doctor to handle. I saw the patient, an over-six-foot-tall adolescent with pimples, dressed like a hippie. He was unresponsive. There was something threatening about this young man; an attitude like, "Don't push me too hard. I take no crap from anybody."

Finally, he began to answer questions in a bored, defiant, and sluggish manner.

"Why did you come?" I asked. He shrugged his shoulders. He knew that I knew. . . . "So, you are on drugs?"

"Yes," he said.

"What do you take?"

"Everything," he answered. "Even sniffing glue, if there is nothing else."

"Do you want to get over the habit?"

"No," he said.

"Why did you come here?"

"It's her." He meant his mother. "She brought me here. . . . I hate her for that."

"Why do you use drugs?" I asked.

"I need them."

"What for?"

"For kicks."

"Is that the only reason?"

"Yes."

He came back a week later.

"Did you want to come?" I asked.

"No," he said.

"Then why did you come?"

"It's easier."

"Easier than what?"

"Than hassle with my mother."

"Is she with you?"

"She is always with me, like a cop. She won't leave me alone for a minute."

"Would you mind if I talk with her?"

"I don't care," he said.

"I would like you to be present when I talk with her."

He couldn't have cared less, he said, but there was a glimmer of curiosity of how I would handle this mother who terrified him.

Physically, his mother was heavyset, over six feet tall, and weighed over two hundred pounds. She looked stern, rigid, and apprehensive.

"Why do you accompany your son to my office?" I asked. "He is big enough to find his way by himself."

"I have to be with him all the time," she said. "I can't trust him. If I leave him alone for only a minute he is off to get these damn drugs."

"Where does he get the money for it?"

"His father gives him an allowance. He's much too generous . . . we are having fights about it."

The son sat motionless, listening.

"I don't want you to bring him to my office anymore," I insisted.

"I must bring him here, otherwise he wouldn't come."

"Maybe not, but you must let him decide. If you come with him I will not treat him."

There was a mild grin on the young man's face. Evidently he was not used to having anyone oppose her.

"I know for sure," she repeated, "he is not going to come. So, he will go on using more drugs."

I countered her attitude by a general statement that we must neither force nor bribe patients, especially adolescents, to come for treatments they don't want. If their visits are not voluntary any treatment is more or less useless. "As with your son, it must be his own voluntary decision, and, if I may make a comment, please don't threaten him. If you leave him alone he might or might not come."

Afterward I saw the young patient alone.

At one point I asked to see the father. The father was a tall, slim, well-groomed, pleasant, somewhat passive man. He was a vice-president in a bank. I learned that his relationship with his son was a good one. I asked why this was so? He answered, "Perhaps, because I never scolded him. I explained to my son the problem of his drug addiction and how unhappy it was making me. He feels sorry about hurting me but he said he could not help it. The other kids felt the same way."

"Why do you think your son needs the drugs? Is he very unhappy?"

"I know he resents his mother. She always has been very strict with him. He says that his life is so very boring. He broke up with a girlfriend, and since then he is difficult and moody and on more drugs."

I had another talk with my patient's mother and both her husband and son were present. I insisted she must refrain from watching him all the time and searching his room for drugs or, better, never even entering his room. "You must show him respect and that you have confidence in him."

She protested. "But I don't have trust in him. Do you want me to pretend something I don't believe? And who is to clean his room and put his things in order?"

"He is old enough to do it by himself, if he wants it."

"And if he doesn't?" she countered.

"Then don't pay any attention. This is not important at the present time. Our problem is to break your son's dependency on drugs."

The father said he would fully cooperate. He promised to restrain his wife from following her son around.

The son came back himself. It was a kind of test, perhaps to prove to his mother an independent action. During his fifth visit, he spoke about the enormous hate he was harboring for his older sister. As he was becoming more communicative he admitted freely that he still was on drugs, but trying to take less and to use a tranquilizer I had given him.

I then asked, "If you had one wish in life, what would you choose?"

He did not hesitate for long. "I would kill my sister. That would truly be my greatest wish. If I had a second wish I would kill my mother also, but my sister first."

The young patient spoke in a dispassionate way when he made that confession. It was evident that he meant it and that the hate within must have been at times almost uncontainable. He just could not cope with the rising pressures and feelings of violence. It also became clear that he used the drugs to feel giddy, which made him forget the need to murder his mother and sister.

The story had a good ending. Substituting various tranquilizers for the narcotics relaxed him enough to make up with his girlfriend, who had left him when he got involved with a gang that was using drugs. He had missed her greatly and felt the conflict between the relaxing effect of the narcotic drug and the strong need to see his girlfriend again. As he spoke more freely, the blank expression in his face changed into one of more alertness. Also, since he resumed seeing his girlfriend, he was more motivated to break his drug habit. He became very cooperative and determined not only to break away from the gang that used drugs but to build a better relationship with his girlfriend and to resume his studies. One day he came in to tell me that he did not need to see me anymore, that his girlfriend was taking my place and that he had fun without the drugs. And of his sister, "To hell with her . . . she is like mother and I don't care."

This particular story serves two major purposes. One is to give an example of one young person's inability to cope with the problems of adjusting to a mature way of life by controlling his rising hostile-aggressive impulses. The other purpose is to demonstrate the problems of society, symbolized by the helplessness of this patient's parents. The mother, in particular, demonstrates the naive belief in curing an addiction by making it difficult to obtain addictive drugs. As a former White House consultant to the then-Presidential Special Action Office of Drug Abuse Prevention, I had become familiar with this problem in the 1970s and presented plans of drug and crime prevention.

Psychologically seen, the prohibition of the drug traffic is as ineffective as the prohibition of alcohol. Alcoholics find substitutes. Unless we cure the inner hunger we don't succeed. The major problem with drugs is that young, unhappy, angry, or curious children are introduced to a drug at an age of ignorance and then become addicted. Therefore governmental control is necessary. Prevention of and freedom from drug enslavement should start in the home, or, as I had tried to convince the government, by a project that ought to be part of the school curriculum.

Manyfold are the struggles to adjust to stresses in a world that is still greatly ruled by the use of force. And young people are caught between the ambivalent behavior of their elders and an inner idealism of building a healthier and more peaceful society.

The mental depressions in the middle and later years are greatly the result of poor adjustment to the realities of life in early childhood and adolescence. During adolescence an integration takes place between the inner world of feelings, of hopes and loves, and the world of reason—coupled with the demands of an outer hostile world. If young people are fortunate enough to have had two or even only one loving parent or parent surrogate, they can make it on their own. They can adjust with greater ease since they have experienced love. The examples given here were of people who, by accident or will or an innate wisdom, were seeking help so that they could become well adjusted and happy people. They were helped to turn their life around.

Helping Yourself

But what about people who don't have the chance of getting the help they need? Or the mavericks, who refuse help because they must do everything by themselves. Or average men and women, who in their middle years recognize that their passive hope had been waiting for a Santa Claus who never came?

How can they or anyone help themselves from passivity to assertiveness, from wasting time in idle dreams to taking actions that can make their dreams come true?

Each human being is so unique that it is a daring undertaking to present rigid formulas for good health and happiness valid for all. Yet there are a few principles that are applicable to all people who are at odds with life, the young and the old, the hungry and the satiated.

The most important principle to turn one's life around is to learn "to give out." Giving out means to release *energies* our bodies build and store. It may be done in work or play, in love and in sharing. It may be done by building a house or by planting a flower, by writing a song or cooking a meal. Or, it may be recreative, like taking a walk, playing ball, trimming a tree, or cutting one's lawn. We can go to a town meeting and participate in discussing the need for a new school, a town hall, a gym. The idea is in sharing thoughts, feelings, political reforms, on all matters that are instrumental in improving conditions that make for better or healthier lives.

The thought of giving out came to me when I observed a very fat fifteen-year-old daughter of a friend. She was deeply depressed, very self-conscious of her overweight, which, during her summer vacation, made her stay in her room, even on a beautiful sunny day. She stayed in bed with big earphones on, listening to music. Her movements were sluggish, her manner curt and withdrawn. She had a pretty face and alert eyes. Trying to strike up a conversation was difficult at first. I invited her to take a walk with me. She said she was tired, having been in bed the greater part of the day.

The next day I tried again, aware of her sensitivity and mental alertness. While we were walking, I stopped, took a fold of her fatty skin between my fingers and said, "That must go . . . . what a pity . . . such a pretty girl and this ugly fat." I expected an angry response. Perhaps it was my tone of voice or attitude that I was trying to be helpful, that she challengingly asked, "How?" She was preparing for a defense, probably expecting the suggestion of a new diet.

I called her by her first name. "Ann," I said, "watching you I see that you take in all and give out nothing. Nature has a built-in balancing mechanism we call metabolism. When we are overheated, we lose heat by sweating. When we run, we breathe faster to get more air into the lungs, our heart beats faster to bring more blood to the working muscles and brain, supplying them with more oxygen and fuel, prepared by the conversion of food. Animals in the wild state don't eat more than they need, but not so with domesticated animals, like pigs, dogs, and people."

A discussion ensued. "What's wrong with being fat?" she wanted to know.

"Nothing, except the fat people I have seen in my earlier years when I worked in clinics ruined their vital organs by depositing fat in tissues. They may act jolly on the surface, but deep down they don't like themselves. Fat is a defense, like a heavy coat against a cold outside world or a compensation for feeling insignificant. A fat person cannot be overlooked. Women use fat as a cushion against the blow of rejection, like saying it is the fat they reject, not me. Obese people use the psychological defense of denial, so that they don't see themselves the way they really are. It is pathetic to watch all those poor people, who go on diets, spend money on treatments or torture themselves to force a few pounds down, which often enough they gain back as quickly as they lost their weight."

The teenage girl listened.

"You stay in bed because you are unhappy. This means you give out only minimal amounts of energy. You listen to music, which again means taking in compositions created by others. You read, again you take in thoughts or stories or work others have created. These manyfold intakes, without output, is storing fat that cuts short your life and makes you feel unhappy. Not giving out energy is a rebellion against the laws of nature. It is defiance and anger and self-indulgence. Of course music is beautiful. It can be relaxing and inspirational. Reading can be enjoyable and informative. But the enjoyment of these and other art forms, in a healthy state, means to balance the release of energy in the form of work or creativity. After a day of any kind of labor we feel the need for some pleasurable relaxation or entertainment via music, reading, the theater, a concert, a ballet, or a television program."

Ann became argumentative. "What's wrong with escape?" she wanted to know.

"One thing," I answered. "It depreciates one's self-image. It builds no self-worth. When you give out energy in some meaningful way, it produces satisfaction. Whatever you build is visible the next day. What you dream in fantasy is like smoke gone with the wind, without a trace."

Losing weight, like giving up smoking or any other self-indulgence, is a matter of a firm inner decision of wanting to be in control. A decision that lacks that inner commitment is like a New Year's resolution that lasts perhaps no more than a few days. It may not differ from many other resolutions we have made and postponed. Psychodynamically these kinds of wish-fulfillments are like living on passive hope. Executing our decision carries us into the domain of active hope.

Ann, by her own efforts and without further encouragement, put herself on a diet. She was losing weight. The loss of weight was building confidence and a better self-image. A year later, she had grown taller and displayed a remarkable change from a depressed girl into a beautiful, well-proportioned, happier teenager. Ann, like many teenagers, stood at a crossroad. She could have drifted along the path of least resistance and become a plump, discontented young woman who would not understand that her inner anger was eating up the cream of her creative energies. It was a mere accident that I happened to meet this girl at the time of inner crisis, after the divorce of her parents, when her needs were particularly great. Her obesity had gone hand in hand with her need to escape. As she clarified the fundamental difference between living in a fleeting world of fantasy or in reality, her life changed. She became the most popular girl in school, directing, and even writing, some scripts for school plays.

Ann was able to turn her young life around by a decision she herself had made. All she needed, at a time it mattered was for someone to be there who cared to give her some direction about how to proceed. After that, she did the work. She found a life of active hopes and ideas exciting and rewarding. She also found that when you set for yourself a goal in reality there bursts forth a will to pursue it.

Anyone who wants to change his way of life because it has been unproductive, discontent, or hopeless can do it, if there is a will to change and the hope that tells us that we can do it. People make these changes all the time. They change their residence for a better neighborhood, for a warmer climate. They change their jobs for better pay or for more gratification. They change their partnership in love, in marriage, in business, or in any other involvement, if the earlier partnership has turned into a stranglehold or has become outright destructive.

We can change the philosophy of our life, our set of values, in order to become more human, more civilized, or a better person. People who don't change regress. They become less productive, more rigid, and inwardly more alienated and unhappy.

Anyone who wants to turn his or her life around has to begin by asking him- or herself these questions:

Do I know in what new direction I want to go?

Can I structure a road map by myself?

Do I want to take full charge of my life?

Am I aware of how successfully I have resolved the dependency needs I once had on my parents, or parent surrogates?

Have I transferred dependency needs on others, a wife, a husband, a friend?

How free am I as an individual?

Can I give of myself in order to build a meaningful relationship with another human being, especially in marriage; one that could grow into a healthy state of interdependence, one that allows and preserves independence and individual growth?

Finally, we can ask ourselves whether, by turning our lives around, we have, for ourselves and by ourselves, come to grips with the knowledge that we must die? Consequently, have we the clarity about how and perhaps where we want to end our life? Do we have the knowledge and strength to develop a plan for our later years, so that we, on the road to our final destination, can fill our lives with joy and contentment, be it work, study or pleasure, that give us feelings of fulfillment and peace?

The pessimists must ask themselves whether they want to undertake the very difficult task of changing their values and turning their objectives around. That begins with caring about other people and making themselves more trusting and empathetic.

The first and most fundamental principle we must accept is that human nature, which means behavior, can be changed. Underneath our armor of power or fame, of success or propriety, of masculinity or femininity, we either are a passive child that puts its hope on destiny, or we have striven hard to take destiny into our own hands and shape our lives by an inner, escalating power of hope.

Chapter 10

Hope and Marriage

IT IS NOT mere love that holds a marriage together—for many people don't know what love is or confuse love with being in love or lack the capacity to love.

It is *hope that sustains a marriage*, its meaning and its worth. If there is hope, the two partners will be motivated to work out their difficulties and stay together. If there is no hope, then there is no will to wrestle with a conflict situation, and therefore no way for two people to arrive at an understanding of their differences in thoughts and feelings necessary to reach a compromise.

Love in its purest form is an unconditional feeling of wishing to give to another, and of an all-out affection and caring for another human being. Freud says, "Love in itself, in the form of longing and deprivation lowers the self-regard; whereas to be loved, to have love returned, and to possess the beloved object, exalts it again." Love, then, is a state of exaltation similar to a lasting undercurrent of good feelings about another person, of liking to be in his or her proximity, to touch and to allow the eye to take in the other with delight.

"*Being in love,*" Freud also says, "is based upon the simultaneous presence of direct sexual tendencies and of sexual tendencies that are inhibited in their aims, so that the object draws a part of the narcissistic ego-libido to itself. It is a condition in which there is only room for the ego and the object."

The joy of being in love, I tell my patients, is that it is an irrational state, uninhibited by the sober laws of reality, a state of abandonment unrestricted by fear, guilt, or anxiety. That is the beauty of being in love. It is a peak experience, therefore it can't last. It can grow into a maturing process of love. Or, it can fall apart once we recognize the fallacious factors of reality. A woman may learn that her lover is married. She may not have asked and he may have evaded the topic. There can be other problems: socioeconomic, cultural, religious, rational, or an orthodoxy neither one had cared to consider. Being in love takes place on the regressed level of a fairy tale. Returning to reality may cruelly end the dream.

Hope, we said, is a powerful motivating force. It determines will and it determines objectives. Thus every human being, in his or her interaction, has choices when dealing with other people: *To move toward* another human being—which builds love and friendship. *To move against another*—which leads to confrontation and conflict. *To move away from another*—which creates distance, alienation, and, in a last analysis, death.

Finding Fulfillment in Marriage

A marriage that has evolved from a free choice—a moving toward one another—aims at ever-greater friendship. In the healthy state it is a dynamic process of weaving a live pattern of all that is tender and human and caring. This is instinctual. And it is pleasurable. The outgrowth of an integration of two lives is a sprouting of sturdy feelings of happiness that further love and trust.

Marriages of that sort are the ideal. They may not be the average but they do exist. If we deal with an ailing marriage we find that the two partners were immature about the responsibilities of adult behavior. Or that only one of the partners was honest in his or her feelings. The man may have married the woman for her looks, to bolster his weak ego, or to secure his economic position, or out of a need to be taken care of. The woman may have chosen marriage to get away from a restricted, unhappy home, to be taken care of economically, or for social ambitions.

Mature people desire marriage. Immature people are afraid, or are like addicts who want escape and variety. Quantity is a substitution for quality, the giving of oneself, the fear of being possessed, or a faint awareness of inner inadequacy. Avoiding a marriage, then, means avoiding failure.

To two people of good will, marriage is a promise of fulfillment of a man's and a woman's basic needs. It builds feelings of security in knowing that both are there for each another to share happy experiences as well as to offer support in times of need. An intimate man-woman relationship is essential for a state of good mental health.

There is another reason that we seek companionship. Because of our feelings of insignificance as we look up to the heavens, we need not suffer from agoraphobia, a fear of wide open places, or any other phobia to become conscious of our aloneness. Even the securest of humans, if he or she has not found a mate, will experience the pain of aloneness and, in the healthy state, nurture the *hope of finding the missing half without which no feelings of wholeness can be attained.*

Still other fulfillment in marriage can be found in the joy and pain of raising children. It is more joy than pain if parents make it their business to understand their children, which means to understand themselves, as had been pointed out in an earlier chapter.

And then there is the one great fear two people who love one another can face better together than alone: the fear of death or dying. "Who will close my eyes?" said a displaced man, who was without a family and who had been severely traumatized when, at a very young age, his mother died and he grew up an unloved child in a foster home. He was afraid to get married for fear of again losing his wife as he lost his mother or to lose that little independence he had carved out for himself.

Moving Toward Your Mate

Marriage, even under the best of circumstances, is a complex state. It is, after all, the merging of two individuals, each having a past history and possibly, different ideas of how to go about shaping first his or her own and then their mutual future. Each one has stored in billions of brain cells millions of signals with different triggers to be set in motion in each one's own conditioned system of responses. It is the specificity of the mental and emotional personality that makes each human being unique and which, in a matrimonial interaction, requires an adjustment to each other's uniqueness. Many people are not prepared for working toward a bonding of two lives and toward a healthy interdependence that accepts the integrity of one without harming the other's independence and cherished beliefs or needs for creative self-expression.

Thus, marriage is not the end of a courtship with a bag full of enthusiastic hopes but the beginning of a mental and emotional maturing process, a process of hard work with a need for constantly revising one's *raison d'être*, to be matched with and adjusted to that of one's chosen mate. A woman from Iowa recently wrote:

> Our State Medical Library, located here in Des Moines, furnished me your address via the AMA membership list.
>
> I feel impelled to write you after having just finished reading *The Will to Live* (1977 edition), loaned to me by a wonderful and dedicated young nurse who took care of my husband during his two "tours" of cancer surgery.
>
> I first became acquainted with your writing through an article of yours in *Vogue* magazine, January 1972. It so impressed me that I clipped it for my files. I found it to be of comfort and inspiration to me, especially during the terrible year of agony (1975–76) when my beloved husband of forty-four years plus began his walk through the "valley of the shadow." This article, plus a folder of similar articles on related subjects, became a part of my preparatory work (I know now) for what was to come.
>
> My John was twenty years older than I. He was an able lawyer and I was his "assistant." We were never apart, and since we had no children, our love was not shared with anyone other than each other. We had the closest, most compatible marriage relationship possible. His death, although completely anticipated, hit me like the sundering of an oak tree by a bolt of lightning. Forty-four years of one's life is not easily terminated! (He was eighty-six years of age and was active in the office to within three weeks of his final hospitalization.)
>
> I think one of the things that has so appealed to me about *The Will to Live* is that it is not sprinkled with platitudes and *no* theology. It is complete balderdash for anyone to say or write that one does "not walk alone" following the death of a husband or wife (providing one truly loved their spouse). *We are alone!* and no mystical spirit can fill the void.

Because I read the many negative quotations of cynics and misanthropes on marriage, I decided to include the above letter as an example that happy marriages do exist, probably millions of them the world over. The reason that we hear so much more about unhappy marriages than happy ones is, probably, that the whiners and complainers seem to have a louder voice. Even when President Carter spoke of sin and warned the nation to beware against "the lust in one's eye," he unconsciously muttered a little complaint while urging marriage and faithfulness. Said one patient, "Of course I like to look at pretty girls. I remain faithful not out of guilt or out of fear of doing something terribly wrong, but out of not wanting to hurt my wife because of her honesty and fine character."

When two people have made a commitment and continue to move toward one another they will be content enough to resist little selfish lures or the greed and neurotic hunger of others, which, because of their neurotic nature, can never be fully satiated. It is not easy to mature and to work on refining civilized behavior in order to gain control over insatiable impulses and seductive enticement. But respect for other people begins with respect for oneself, which, in turn, helps to build the self-worth and character strength necessary to retain our position of mastery over ourselves throughout the long journey of life.

Dealing with Conflict

One of the instructions I give my patients on how to remain calm in stressful situations, is to say to oneself, no matter how hard someone may try to push, "I won't allow him (or her) to get me out of my chair." It was most effective when I had to appear before the Judiciary Committee of the U.S. House of Representatives, as a sworn witness, to testify why vice-president-elect Gerald Ford had come to my office. When a ruthless congressman threatened me with a charge of contempt, I spoke that formula to myself and answered calmly, "That was a private, confidential matter."

At the sight of an anxiety-provoking signal we might regress and, like a child, defend our pride. This may cause a break in the weaving of a loving marital relationship. Or one partner may hold on to the marriage while the other has lost interest. One partner may have grown up emotionally during the marriage while the other remained static and unmotivated. Such a negative attitude inevitably leads to a disturbance or a rupture of the relationship. The passive partner, the one with little hope, may cling to the other who has the positive hope to build a happier life for him- or herself. This is one of the tragedies that come because the two people never knew each other in depth. Or, if one partner lives in fantasy or in alcoholic escapes, he or she cannot be reached. These people don't listen. They are demanding, narcissistic children who want their way. Such a marriage is doomed.

However, if two people love each other and one matures while the other partner remains passive they can come to an understanding and save the marriage by compensating with other meaningful values. The success of such a case depends on whether the two people have communicated with one another, whether they have used the great human gifts of language and understanding. Not using communication for whatever neurotic reason is a sign of negativism and lack of hope.

Sexual Intimacy

Beside the mental and emotional maturing process of two people, their sexual adjustment is essential for building and maintaining a happy marriage. To become sexually free and intimate is often difficult, due to many causes, primarily cultural taboos and puritanical inhibitions. W. H. Masters and V. E. Johnson, the American sexual specialists, state in their book *Human Sexual Inadequacy and Pleasure Bond* that "a significant sexual dysfunction exists in 50% of marriages." This high incidence of human unhappiness is, for the most part, the result of ignorance about sex and of young—or even not-so-young—people having entered marriage believing that in the course of living together all will work out by itself. It doesn't. A marriage, like a valuable friendship, needs cultivation. Only weeds grow by themselves.

One of the most frequent fallacies in choosing a mate is that people take an attractive facade behavior for the total personality. A child knows from a very early age how to "make nice" to get candy. During the courting period people put their best foot forward. They create a glamorous image about themselves to impress the other because of a need to be loved. Too often they build a beautiful structure in fantasy, which, because it has no basis in reality, is bound to collapse. The result, then, is disillusionment, followed by anger, when the attractiveness of yesterday seems to have given way to the image of a pitiful figure, causing one to say, "Is that the one I had been so madly in love with?"

In an article called "Development of Sexual Intimacy in Marriage," Dr. Raymond Babineau, professor of psychiatry at the University of Rochester, New York, writes, "The fond hope which inspires most couples is that they will grow together sexually as well as interpersonally. Implicit is the commonplace observation that 'first times' are often not wonderful sexual experiences. Each partner approaches the sexual component of married life with his or her own history, inhibitions, and expectations." He goes on to say that, "Physicians often have difficult times deciding whether to counsel patience and the passage of time, or whether to encourage couples to obtain help for their sexual inhibitions."

It is this author's belief that when sexual problems in a marriage come to the attention of a physician, it is already evident that the sex partners have not been able to work out their inner conflict by themselves or they would have done so. The difficulty most people have working out sexual disparity by themselves is the lack of objectivity about oneself and the unconscious transference they may have made to their sex partner. If the transference is positive little help may suffice. If the transference is negative we deal with a more major problem.

Human sexuality is fraught with anxieties and inhibitions that stem from fear, guilt, religious, or cultural taboos. Confused values roam in our unconscious, creating tensions and sometimes more severe neurotic symptoms. Freud's first patient was a young, socially prominent lady who was paralyzed. His analysis revealed that his patient was suffering from conversion hysteria, a disorder of the voluntary nervous system. Her inability to walk was a defense reaction against her unacceptable strong sexual attraction to her brother-in-law. Her cure came when she could relive her childhood sexual fixation on her father.

Simple encouragement may help a couple over a small crisis or perhaps make some surface adjustment but, for the most part, it does not go to the heart of a problem. To talk to a couple like a Dutch uncle is less than cosmetic. It pushes young adults back to the position of adolescence. They may obey for a little while only.

Marriage counseling may also have a temporary effect only. If the two people wish a reconciliation, it helps them to get over a hurdle. But if the two sex partners are passive people they may listen to the advice of the counselor as they had been conditioned to listen to a parent, a judge, a clergyman, or any surrogate authority and, as good children, dutifully obey. In depth one or the other may nurture his or her dissatisfaction, which one day may blow up, especially in the area of sex, by acts of infidelity. Or one or the other partner may withdraw from sex. One patient punished his wife for all the difficulties she gave him by withholding sex, until she, feeling the need for sex, would, with anger and humiliation, approach him.

A surface adjustment may also do grave injustice to an individual's inner sense of freedom and integrity. The result is unhappiness, tension, simmering hostility, and, on unconscious levels, destructive transferences, which, if severely repressed, may cause intense inner stress, psychosomatic illnesses, loss of joy, a decline of vitality, and hopelessness.

Some of these surface adjustments may well contribute to the unhappiness of many people, who, in Thoreau's words lead lives of "quiet desperation." Untreated surface adjustment often diminishes the well-being of people and can become a danger to their mental and emotional health. In cases of marital conflict and sexual incompatibility the wiser course of action is to seek professional help rather than to allow slow deterioration of the relationship.

A case comes to mind. When I was a very young doctor I was honored by the visit of the father of a childhood friend. He was an educated and highly respected businessman, perhaps in his early fifties.

This man complained about pain in his chest. There was no evidence of any organic illness of the heart. Shyly, I inquired about his sexual life. "Maybe once a week," he said. After a long pause he added, "Incidentally, the pain in my chest occurs mostly after intercourse—you are young—you may not understand—it is for the sake of honor that I feel obliged to have sex with my wife."

With my present knowledge I know that he must have resented having sexual intercourse with his wife, a cold, haughty lady. He had married the sister of an enterprising and successful businessman who offered his new brother-in-law a business partnership. I sensed my patient's unhappiness or actual revulsion at having to perform a sexual function he rebelled against. The tension connected with the sexual act had led to the pain in his chest. About half a year later, when I returned from a vacation, I learned that he had suffered a fatal heart attack. This case has stayed with me for all these years and I have questioned the dilemma a man can get into when he would rather kill himself than endure the closeness to a woman he hates. Whether it was guilt, regret, or the inability to adjust to a demanding woman and having no chance of a divorce, my friend's father paid for the wrong choice in his marriage partner by sliding into a state of hopelessness, followed by death.

Communication—Instead of Impulsive Divorce

Recurrent difficulties in a marriage alone ought not be enough of a reason to feel "fed up" and to blow the bugle of retreat. Before considering divorce both people should reexamine why they got married and why they want to leave. If they don't understand the signals to which they react, they may repeat their mistake in a second marriage or a third.

Here is the case of a man who had been brought into my office by his wife. This was his eighth marriage. What precipitated their conflict was a rather insignificant problem that had come up. It concerned their apartment. They had to decide on a new lease within three months. It was an attractive apartment in the upper East Side of Manhattan, which both liked but which, in the case of a divorce, neither one could afford to maintain.

The patient was a tall, somewhat heavyset, ruddy-faced, jovial man in his early fifties, a man who hung around the at-that-time chic Stork Club, a type one meets at any upper-middle-class social affair. He was an alcoholic, who, a few times a year, went to hospitals to dry out.

"I had no problem with women. I met these chicks. I gave them a good time. They liked to get married to me. But then about six, eight months later I would say, 'Honey, that's it—I'll give you ten grand—let's split'—and because I was nice to them I had no problems. But that one," he referred to his present wife, "that one sticks. To her marriage is for real—

"I married her several years back. I thought it was time to settle down. I did not have too much money left anymore. And she was a registered nurse. She was well mannered, well spoken, no raving beauty but fair looking—and I thought that with my heart it's good to have a nurse in the house. But who thought I would have a policewoman in the house, checking the liquor, telling me all about calories and what to or what not to eat. And then this, every day on the scale, taking the blood pressure and listening to the heart. It was enough to make anyone sick. I told her about splitting. She said: 'No.' So, I went to a bar, didn't come home for two days. That scared her. She said, 'Let's try again.' But damn it, a nurse is a nurse. I wake up, find her hovering over me, listening to my breathing, counting my pulse. She thought I was dying. I said there's nothing wrong with my breathing and why do you scare a guy and don't let him sleep?"

In a meeting with her, when she appeared properly dressed with white gloves, she was near tears, admitting she was slowly falling apart. "He is so uncooperative." "But he is not your patient," I told her. "But I'd hate to be alone again."

I felt that if I advocated separation it might have a twofold effect. It would bring the stark reality close to them but also it would defuse in the man any doubt that my hidden plan was that of a marriage counselor just trying to keep them together. Almost at once after I suggested separation she displayed more anxiety. We decided on a joint session that ended with the two people leaving arm in arm and thanking me for having saved their marriage and the apartment.

People find it difficult to understand that when they are angry or feel hurt they regress and act out their feelings from a childish level. That accounts for the screaming temper tantrums and the whole array of psychosomatic symptoms that aim at making the other person feel cruel or guilty or whatever defense reaction they have learned. Therefore, decisions made in such a state may be regretted once a person's mind returns to reality.

I discouraged an attractive young woman from running away before she knew where she was running to. "You are not prepared for a life by yourself. Grow up, prepare, and then, when you have worked out your own conflict and gained clarity and wish to leave, by all means leave. Be careful not to call a situation hopeless before you have become aware of your own image as it appears in the eyes of your partner or opponent." In a quarrelsome situation a wife or husband can sometimes serve as a catalyst for one's own neurotic behavior and we can learn from it. Said Edmund Burke, ". . . my opponent is my helper . . ."

When it comes to a first confrontation or when there are a series of marital battles, the eventual survival of a marriage may well depend on the structure and strength of hope that may emerge in one partner or the other. One spouse, in response to an angry encounter, might be able to overcome the incident and then "forget" the whole thing, like children who quarrel and then make up. The other, more sensitive, partner, because of his or her weaker ego, cannot get over a hurt and may react with withdrawal.

Some of these people remain on an emotionally immature level and behave toward their spouse as they did toward their father or mother, which amounts to reliving a childhood existence. This is functioning on two levels. On one, the reality level, they display the semblance of normal behavior, fulfill all marital and social obligations dutifully, but live up to an inner resolve of giving nothing of themselves and of keeping bottled up all their feelings and emotional experiences. They are prisoners who don't dare to revolt. They may have wish-dreams of their spouse's going away, disappearing, or dying and then being free. Or they escape into neurotic activities, embracing a fad, a cult, a good cause, in which they spend their energies mechanically without joy or satisfaction. Or they may join the 10 or 12 percent of the population who are alcoholics, drug addicts, or gamblers.

A woman in her mid-thirties, childless, came to my office. Her husband had threatened to divorce her because after eight years of marriage he was no longer willing to tolerate her erratic mood swings, her constant screaming, and her whining about the little daily crises that happened only to her. The husband was an attractive man who had worked hard on himself to learn the self-discipline and to build the self-esteem he had not learned in the home in which he had grown up. Of superior intellect, he had built a successful business. Often strained by stress in the office, added to by having to drive for nearly an hour every day through heavy traffic, he wished for a peaceful hour at home to relax. It was then that his wife almost never failed to approach him with one of her little woes: that the plumber had not come or that the cleaning woman had said she was sick.

The woman had a brilliant intellect, which she used quickly in sharp, caustic attacks on all that was said and in questioning methods or values of the kind of therapy I would be using. Referring her to someone else would have been an easy way out, except that she had undergone several unsuccessful attempts to obtain psychiatric help. The main reason for her previous failure and the resistance I encountered was that she lacked any genuine motivation. She came only because of the fear of being divorced and of losing the position of being taken care of.

During our initial sessions she sat either stone-faced, giving no indication whether she had understood an explanation, or with her head looking down, expecting the doctor to do something, like magic, to make her well. She would contribute nothing.

As physicians we may think that a particular patient is a real pain in the neck but in the therapeutic process we cannot allow ourselves to express any value judgment at all. Enjoying a warm, human rapport with almost all of my patients, I felt that occasionally I should take on a challenge, even if the prognosis was not too promising. Nevertheless, this patient, as I anticipated, strained my patience to the limit. It was her way of releasing some of the turbulent hostility with which she had grown up and which had stayed with her. She did not know any other way of dealing with people, except with her husband and a few friends with whom she could communicate on a thin layer of friendliness.

The only way to succeed in this case was, at the very beginning, to lay down a first demand. I would take her on as a patient only if she would cease screaming. When she began to argue the point that this was precisely what I had to cure, my answer was, "If you can't control the screaming and whining, you can't come back." After a week she reported, somewhat amazed, that she had not screamed. But removing this symptom, less than one-eighth of the iceberg, was necessary to save the marriage. Then the real work began.

She began to talk and she understood well. But when questioned the following week about whether she had made any progress, she answered, "No." Now, a therapist does not tell a patient what to do, he or she makes a point by questioning or by making a suggestion. Yet each time a suggestion was made about how to break her self-destructive behavior, this patient would, without allowing a minute of thought, reply curtly: "I can't do it."

To make her aware that I did not take any of her angry assaults personally, but saw them as part of an illness, I read her the following paragraph from my earlier book, *The Drive for Power*:

> Pavlov created behavior in dogs that resembled that of persons who live in fear and who have no incentive or ambition. They exist in a state that is like the somnabulistic phase in hypnotism: a limp, ambitionless twilight zone. Beyond this, Pavlov produced *paradoxical* behavior; that is, by crossing signals he induced animals to show an exactly opposite reaction. For instance, by the exposure to prolonged stress and a mix-up of signals, a dog would walk away when food was presented and, when food was taken away, return to look for it. We find this in persons we call oppositional, those who automatically must do the opposite of what is demanded.

I left out reading the following sentence: "This is an indication of a serious mental condition."

This patient functioned extrinsically by contributing the minimum necessary to run a home efficiently, to keep it clean, prepare the meals, do the shopping, and other necessary chores. Though extremely talented, she resisted producing for fear of failing and to appear as incompetent as her mother had sarcastically pointed out she was.

On intrinsic levels, where deeper feelings were involved, she repressed affection, and it was the patience of her husband that made the marriage work. This difficult case would take a very long time to be helped. We had to clarify signals, break her early conditioning, and diminish her anger by channeling her negative energies into more meaningful pursuits. To the credit of this very unhappy woman it must be said that she did begin to cooperate, though in her own peculiar way. For instance, when she described days of utter despondency and hopelessness, I asked her to write down her feelings. Her first response, of course, was "I can't write." But when I said, "I want it," she would not argue any further and returned for her next session with a beautifully written paper that gave a lucid description of her anguish and despair, her agitation and her rage, but mostly her hopelessness. Because of its honesty it brought out my empathy and further will to help.

The dramatic depth of human suffering and the first signs of an upturn to a more positive outlook and new hope cannot be presented because it would require the permission of the patient, who felt reluctant to give it. All that can be said is that the two and a half years of hard labor paid off by this patient admitting that she now had hope that she could be helped.

Sources of Strife

Most problems, as they occur in marriages more so than in any other human interaction, are the process of transference, which, as stated before, can be positive or negative. In problematic situations we deal with the power of negative transferences. Risking the danger of oversimplification, we could say a man may react to his wife as he reacted to his mother or the way he saw father behave toward his mother. By identifying with his father his attitudes and his emotional signals may be indeed similar to those of his father. This means if father had been passive he, as a husband, would most likely also be passive.

Another frequent difficulty in marriage is caused by the fixation on a strong parent. The previous case of the woman who was so angry that her husband wanted to divorce her was a case of fixation. The woman had experienced a severe trauma at an early age that arrested her psychosexual growth. It kept her "fixated" on her mother. Though cruel and merciless in beating the child, the mother was, in the absence of a father, the only close relationship she had and the only tie to life. By the process of identifying with a mother who was always angry, the daughter became an angry lady herself. She grew up heavily censoring all her own actions for fear of severe beatings. Though she hated her mother, she tried, in order to avoid punishment, to please her. Pleasing meant not doing anything that could annoy her mother or provoke one of her violent criticisms. It was, therefore, safer not to do anything at all, which, in turn, led to her fear paralysis whenever she had to take independent action. The difficulties in therapy resulted from transferring the authoritative fear of her mother to the doctor. This created an automatic ambivalence that was not entirely negative. In the depth of her mind there was a little positive feeling. "Help me. I can't help being nasty. I don't mean it. Don't give up on me." Against this small voice of hope was a louder, negative, inner voice saying, "Do nothing for him because he will only criticize you and find fault with you whatever you say or do." By this unconscious dynamic interplay she would see people as critical authorities and, therefore, be on the defensive.

There are marriages in which, though both people are dynamically passive, they have nevertheless managed to coexist peacefully for many years and, in time, learned to communicate. If, however, in the life of passive people no free communication develops, a sudden eruption of buried rage and anger and fury may occur.

A situation comes to mind of a man who was Germany's greatest actor and, therefore, offered by Hitler and Goebbels the position of a Reichsführer of the Arts, even though his wife was Jewish. He refused. Switzerland made him an honorary citizen. After the war, he came to New York, where I saw him professionally. He was nearly eighty years old and I marveled at his face, for never before had I seen such peace and serenity. One day his wife came to see me sobbing: "Tell me—what is his illness?" she wanted to know. "He always had been the most gentle, the most kind and considerate man. And now he is angry with me. He pushes me away. He does not want me to come near him and has said a few ugly things about me—"

I could not tell his wife what he had told me, namely, that all his life she had been sitting on him, controlling him to the point of tyrannizing him. Now, as he sensed being near death, he rebelled, daring finally to express the anger he had repressed for the greater part of his life.

An incident, more amusing than dramatic, was published years ago in the *New York Times*. A couple were in court in front of a judge who was hearing their divorce case. The judge, turning to the plaintiff, asked, "How many years have you been married?" "Forty some years," answered the man. The judge shaking his head asked, "After all these years you want a divorce?" "Yes, your honor," replied the plaintiff. "Enough is enough."

If in a marriage one partner is the optimist, and the other a pessimist who always anticipates disaster, a relationship also can be worked out, if the person with more positive hope has enough strength and love to tolerate the drag of the other. In one such case the man came for help. He loved his wife but was too passive to leave

176

her and unable to resist her quarrelsome nature. As he came out of his withdrawal she responded with more respect, and since neither one wanted a divorce, they worked out their lives together.

Manyfold are the problems in marriages, because manyfold are the games people play with one another. Indeed, honesty is a rare commodity, and without honesty there can be no firm basis for an enduring positive relationship. Too often people torture one another because of the unresolved hates and sadistic impulses deep within themselves.

Why do people marry? Becasue it is conventional, cultural, and because one's parents got married? No, the need goes deeper, as we pointed out earlier. A life alone is half a life. So, it is a selfish need to get married. Why then do we not stick to the bargain we made?

Is it disappointment, greed, lust that makes people in increasing numbers break the commitment they have made? Or is it the immaturity, the child's need to get, to demand, to want all the attention, all the love, all the care, failing to be consciously aware of the needs of the other? The follies of the parents are too readily laid as a burden on the children, who one day may do the same to their own, unless they learn how to break the curse of the continuity of their lives of confusion and ignorance.

Here is an example of the passivity of a man who was emotionally crippled by his father, a Southern gentleman, so that he preferred to lie rather than to be truthful and to escape responsibilities rather than to have the courage to act. Thus six people suffered, three adults and three children, while, superficially, the problem did not appear to be extraordinary. On the surface the man was honorable, president of clubs and charitable organizations, and a kind, civilized, and helpful person, yet within himself he felt like a colossal failure.

This man came to my office in an acute crisis, when his wife discovered that he was carrying on a love affair with another woman. The wife was in a rage, demanding he break off at once the relationship with that "phony Italian countess" or she would divorce him, disgrace him in the community, and take him for everything he had. Under the impact of her threats the husband promised not to see the other woman. However, it was not too long after the first reconciliation that he was seen again with his mistress. Now the wife was fuming. She came to see me, pleading with me to cure him from his "sick obsession" of being attracted to women with foreign titles.

My patient was scared of a divorce at that particular time because of the scandal it would cause in the prominent North Shore Long Island community and because of problems with his health. He was nearing his sixtieth birthday and was expressing anxiety about aging.

During our initial interview I learned that he and his wife had seen a marriage counselor but, as he said, with no success. It was then that the husband—we shall call him Ted—upon the urging of his wife, had come to see me. The wife had also been urged to see me, by a friend who had been a former patient of mine. She came for a consultation because of her nervous state and possibly to engage my sympathies. She was an attractive woman, in her late forties, with reddish blond hair, green eyes, and conservatively dressed. Her friend had made her believe that I probably could rid her husband of his obsession with European aristocracy. The wife knew the other woman, who, she admitted, was pretty, married, and lived in the same community. Both couples belonged to the same country club and, therefore, met from time to time at dinner parties. "Besides causing me great grief," said the wife, "my husband, as president of the club and a respected member of our society, is jeopardizing his reputation and is humiliating me." I told her I would be glad to listen to her but that in this case I could only treat him. Also, an obsession, if that was the husband's problem, is not just cured by telling him not to see the other woman. I had to get the full story from her husband, including his problems, before I could form an opinion. But even then my impressions would be kept confidential. It was necessary for the man to gain clarity about himself and his need before he could arrive at a rational decision. The wife demanded more reassurance than I was able to give her at that time, but she accepted my explanation.

Ted was a tall, slim, slightly graying businessman. In dress, speech, and manner he reflected the Ivy League image. "My problem is," he said, "I am a disturbed individual—primarily a coward. My wife is wrong when she believes that the Italian lady, she called her a whore, had seduced me. I have always lied to my wife—I have always had a mistress."

"Why?"

He did not know. Why had he married her? He was not really sure. "She was very good looking—an all-American girl, a great tennis player—and I was considered rich, the man about town and a good polo player—a good catch, I assume. When I think back I did not have the faintest idea what love was. Silly, we looked good together. Everybody liked us as a couple. Now, I realize, we played a game with one another and for other people. For a few years all went well, but more and more I discovered how unhappy I felt and how little communication we had—my wife and I. Sex was never really good. I should have known then that she was cold, at least toward me. Sex got worse. She faked orgasm. Soon enough I did not care. We should have divorced then but I did not have the guts to act. So, we stayed together with little joy and no appetite for sex, until I had the first affair with my ladyfriend. This was an electrifying experience—she made me feel young and masculine again and at a time when everything else in my life, especially the economy, was going wrong. Now, I am eaten up by guilt—guilt about lying to my wife and guilt about lying to my mistress about getting a divorce. I am so depressed that I sometimes wish I would have another heart attack, one that would end it all. I really believe that everybody would be better off. My wife would get all my possessions plus my insurance money, my mistress would adjust to her marriage and her unhappiness about my indecision, and my guilt would end. I would have peace. I could not think of death before, but now it isn't so terribly frightening—the thought of freedom from the constant bickering of my wife, who now disgustingly and clumsily plays detective and follows me everywhere. Indeed, if I die all my worries would be over."

A triangle situation is one of the dilemmas a doctor occasionally has to deal with. It puts him or her in the middle of two warring parties, in which he or she must maintain scrupulous objectivity and live up to the full trust of the patient. In the heat of an argument or during the pain and depression of the patient, the doctor must be on guard, at all times, against any moral value judgment that might creep into his or her discussion or line of questioning. Freedom from pain and the physical and mental well-being of the patient remains, as it always has, one of the doctor's first and uncompromising principles.

Guilt can have a severely depressing effect, as evidenced in another case. I think of a patient, a leading Brazilian industrialist, who consulted me once a year, when he came to New York. He had suffered a heart attack and since then had lost his zest for life. He was depressed, mocking his getting old and bemoaning the loss of his sexual powers. He found relief in just talking philosophically about life, and the futility of man's existence. In the meanwhile he kept on making a great deal of money. He would return the following year, when again he would be in New York. During our third meeting, he said that he had been looking forward to our meeting. He was finally ready to share a secret with me. "I love my wife," he said, "and the five children we have. I love them very much. But I have a mistress and I love her and the five children I have had with her. They are my children, too," he said with emphasis. "Every afternoon I visit my mistress and play with the children until it's time to go home to my wife for dinner and then I play with our children. They are older now and we talk more. I know I am depressed. All the pills the doctors in Brazil have given me have not helped much. My friend, who sent me to you, said you would come up with an answer. So, this is my worry. If I die, my mistress and her children will be poor and hungry. They are *my* children." He now had tears in his eyes. "That's my constant worry, the woman and the children being hungry, plus the guilt—that makes me sick." I asked whether he trusted his lawyer. "He's the best," said my patient. "Well, then, why not put your mistress and the five children also in your will?" He seemed perplexed. "I can't do that," he replied. "What would my wife say?" He groaned until he slowly grasped the reality. "Will she be mad?" he exclaimed almost with a trifle jubilance. "Of course, she will be mad—but then I will be dead—and she can't scold me because I am dead—and both women and all my children will not be hungry and my wife will console herself with all the money and possessions I leave her." He was jubilant when he left. I saw this patient only one more time, a year later. He said he came to say, "Thank you. I am a happy man. I don't feel sick anymore. I changed my will and now my doctors in Brazil say that my heart is better."

Now, back to our patient whom we left in a state of depression, wishing he would die. He had suffered a first heart attack, which he believed was the result of his constant state of stress, brought on by living in an unhappy marriage, lying to his wife, having a mistress, feeling guilty about that and too much a coward to say anything or to do anything about it. It became evident that this patient had lived with an undercurrent of depression the greater part of his life, which he managed to cover up by activities and escapes. His loss of physical vitality and lack of motivation was explained by doctors to have come from circulatory disturbances. He knew that he had some of his father's "doomsday" philosophy. He even had an inkling that his lack of motivation and his lack of will to win were protests against his father's domination and hostility against him, his son. There was nothing he could do that would please his father or make him proud. And now he understood that he was hurting himself. Having learned how to put on a brave, considerate, gentlemanlike facade was a nice image for other people but did not help him. Actually, he was a gentle and thoughtful man, but whenever he was alone, he felt overcome by a cloud of negative thoughts, a sense of futility and a depression that paralyzed his ideas and future plans.

It had been at a social affair when he met his new ladyfriend.

From that moment on life became beautiful. "I may be crazy getting involved with that woman and hurting my wife—though I don't love her—and running the risk of being ostracized by the community. Even more so, to be discovered by her jealous husband, to say nothing of the upset of my children, who defend their mother. And I know how demanding and immature my ladyfriend is, but being with her makes me feel relaxed and at ease. And sex is the best I have ever experienced. Away from her, I feel anxious and miserable. It's incredible, though I know how cleverly she plays the role of an innocent child, she is devious, irresponsible, and lies with a smile. In spite of knowing all this I keep on loving her. It's probably sick on my part. But against all reason, when I watch the grace of her movements, the elegance of her life-style, the witty manner of her speech, her magnetic seductiveness, I can't help but think of the clumsiness of my wife, her lack of taste and refinement. I keep on asking myself why I am such a coward, why I cannot act, give up my big home, let my wife take whatever she wants, and start a new life with a woman who makes me feel alive."

Later on, after many sessions, he could answer the question. Could she ever be loyal? Would she not betray me as she was betraying her own husband? And would she be content once she becomes my wife? Is she not just strong in the pursuit of her game to get the guy and then, when she has to settle down to an everyday routine, regress to a passive life-style, waiting to be entertained, to be catered to, to structure a frivolous life-style with fun but little substance, while now she enjoys the game of winning over another woman?

My patient continued having the affair with his mistress in utter secrecy. Then he was caught. His wife stood there, like the archangel of death in pain and rage and condemnation. This time, after the initial anger, there was a serious discussion between him and his wife about a separation.

Then, the wife, with the permission of her husband, came to see me. She stated how disappointed she was that I had not cured her husband of his obsession with false glamour and his infidelity. My answer, as always, was that therapy means helping a patient gain insight, independence, and freedom of action, so that the patient can then decide which route of action he or she wishes to take. I also explained that it was not up to me to tell her husband what to do. A doctor does not play the role of God nor that of a parent. Perhaps the role is more that of a guide, who, as a good listener, and who by the choice of his questions, can lead a patient to self-awareness and clarity about the reasons he or she had gotten into a jungle and the ways of getting out. A patient must gain clarity before he or she can make a healthy decision versus a lethargic, passive one, which only perpetuates a life of indecision and hopelessness.

If a man cheats on a woman, then there is something basically wrong with the relationship. If the woman is unaware of the infidelity of her husband, then either she has failed to be aware of his insecurity or discontent or she does not care. A sexual problem may have existed from the very beginning. Or she was too insecure to talk about it. Or she had not given enough of herself to make the man feel secure and wanted. Of course, the reverse is equally true. Most of the time the sexual interaction is a good barometer of one or the other partner's role in the relationship and the degree with which two partners like one another. In sex it becomes evident who is the passive partner and who is the aggressive one, and who gives and who only takes, and who is using the other. Does a man use the woman for his sole sexual satisfaction with little regard for her feelings, needs and fears; or does she use the man for whatever she may wish to get out of a relationship?

My patient's wife had to recognize that her basic rigidity had affected her sexuality, which, in turn, did not make her husband feel relaxed with her. Her answer that she never refused her husband sounded defensive and was further proof that she lacked the subtleness and art of lovemaking. In the session she had with me she was in a cooperative mood. She could finally accept the possibility that she may not have paid a great deal of attention to the quality of their sexual intercourse and that she considered it normal that after a few years of marriage the sexual interest would diminish. Nothing was done about that. And my patient, against all warnings, kept on lying to his wife about breaking off the relationship, while she kept on threatening, snooping, and following him. It turned into an ugly drama, increasing the stress of three people while diminishing their self-esteem.

One day, after a serious circulatory complication and the warnings of my patient's specialists, he said in a voice of desperation and sadness: "I really don't care about life anymore. I finally have come to realize why I could not give up my mistress—I know now that without her I would have already died. With all her failings, her trickiness and immaturities, *she is my only source of hope* and the only reason for me to go on."

Treating this man was difficult because he could not make a decision and because of the almost complete transference he had made from his father, whom he hated, to his wife, who was as cold, as rigid, and as critical as his father had been. Consequently, and without any awareness of the underlying dynamics, he was as afraid of his wife as he had been afraid of his father. A reconciliation with his wife was difficult, because of her lack of softness and her rigid Victorian values. She demanded an either/or decision.

Also my patient had developed a revulsion against even the thought of sex with his wife. Good sex and anger don't go together. My patient's hope for freedom and a happier life had grown increasingly dim. He realized that when he had come to the few significant crossroads in his life he had always been too frightened to make a decision. And when he had to act he closed his eyes and allowed an opportunity to pass him by. His problems at this time were the same as those that had been with him ever since he entered life as a mature man and which he avoided facing.

Generally speaking, most problems in old age are the same ones we have failed to resolve when we were young. Every compromise we make to evade making a decision interferes with the growth of security and self-esteem. By the same token, every action we dare to take strengthens our ego and our confidence in our judgment and self-image. When we surrender deep beliefs we cut short life itself.

As to my patient, he was in a vise. His failing health made him increasingly more fearful of acting. The economy had reduced his considerable fortune and the cost of a divorce would wipe him out. His wife kept on threatening him with a divorce but her hate of the mistress made her stop for fear that the mistress might then succeed in marrying her husband.

There was a later meeting with my patient's wife. She was in acute conflict. Her pride and outrage at being cheated on made her want to divorce her husband. On the other hand, she did not want to lose him to "that other woman." Again, she wanted advice I could not give her, but winning time was, because of my patient's circulatory problems, desirable. It also allowed his weak ego to grow stronger at the same rate as his fears about a possible divorce diminished.

This patient was gaining insight, though he regretted that it had come so late in life. He had learned to understand, and thus control, his periods of depression. His moods still fluctuated between despair and hope but in an overall way he was more cheerful. His mental state had shifted from an almost completely passive-negative, at times hopeless, state, to a less frightened and somewhat more positive frame of mind. There were even days when he was free from his feelings of hopelessness and actually had a more hopeful outlook, though nothing had changed and he still had not made a decision.

It was a pathetic sight to watch a grown, well-bred, well-educated man being torn apart by the ruthless possessiveness of two selfish women, which, of course, was possible only because of his weakness. He was not brought up to be a fighter but to respect women almost to a point of submissiveness.

In his mind he saw clearly that his wife represented the austere tradition that life was not meant to be enjoyed. The mistress, on the other hand, was a source of pleasure and a light, somewhat frivolous way of life. To my patient she was an added source of reassurance against the anxiety of aging and of sexually still being a competent man. He was aware that he paid heavily with his health and money to fight on both fronts: his wife's constant little acts of castration and his mistress' punishing him for his broken promises by her making him buy her luxuries he could not really afford anymore.

When questioned about why he wouldn't take a firmer stand toward either woman he replied with a shrug of his shoulders, "I was not brought up to fight, nor to hurt anyone." The real reason for his passivity was his fear of losing his mistress, and with it the uplifting feeling of a satisfying sexuality.

Because of his conflict and hesitation to make a decision, the help I could offer him was supportive therapy; that is, encouraging the man and repairing a wounded self-esteem. The passivity was part and parcel of his life philosophy. His improvement was moderate, for he said he was too tired and too old to change. What this meant was that he felt it did not pay anymore to go through upheaval and pain to change. He also had the constant, very real fear of another, perhaps fatal, heart attack.

In Summary: As with Life, So with Marriage

Marriage, with all its difficulties, may well be as Heinrich Heine, the poet, put it, ". . . the high sea for which no compass has yet been invented." My own experiences as a physician have taught me that most people live their married lives the way they are structured in their specific psychodynamic interaction with people. Those motivated by active hope will deal with conflicts in their marriage positively and assertively, with the aim of preserving the relationship, or, if betrayed by their spouse, end it rather than continue to play the game. People with passive hope will escape into fantasies of wishful thinking. They may suffer, endure abuse, harbor inner rebellion, take little revenges but stay more or less put, feeling unhappy until they break or their relationship dies from wear and tear.

Poets, who in verse and rhyme express their own or other people's feelings and follies, write about matrimony the way they write about hope. The poet who is an optimist says, "The hopeful man sees success where others see failure, sunshine where others see shadows and storm." Or, as Shelley put it, "Hope will make you young."

The pessimist, the narcissistic cynic, laments about marriage, saying it is a state of being "coupled together for the sake of strife." Or, as a Danish proverb says, "A deaf husband and a blind wife are a happy couple."

These poets let out their pain and self-pity in beautifully structured verses, but psychodynamically seen, they are adolescents, who, if they could love and give of themselves rather than complain, would either write nothing or more positive and cheerful poetry.

In marriage, as in all other aspects of life, people who can hope will strive for happiness, while people who remain passive in their hope will emotionally remain immature and unhappy. And all a person's brilliance, talent, and intellect may be of no avail. As life has taught me, knowledge is power but the know-how of applying active hope is superpower.

CHAPTER 11

Hope and Sexual Fixation

"SEXUAL LIFE does not begin only at puberty, but starts with clear manifestations soon after birth." This statement of Freud's, strongly attacked at first, but more and more accepted during the following five decades of scientific investigations, has given us a deeper understanding of human sexuality. The nonpsychoanalyst can hardly assess the pervading power this human function has in all areas of mind-body interaction, human behavior, ranging from the normal to the perverse, from the sadistic to the masochistic, from the libidinous inspirational will to create, to self-punishing tortures, to expiation for one's sins.

Sexuality has played a paramount role in producing neurotic behavior. Freud's dramatic cure of a woman's paralysis of her legs—due to conversion hysteria, as reported earlier, brought on by the severe repression of her illicit wishes to have sexual intercourse with her brother-in-law—made psychological history. Since then sexuality has been found to permeate all areas of physical, psychological, cultural, and artistic life. Sexuality, in various forms—as erotic impulses, driving needs, or exciting fantasies—maintains throughout life a motivating power for all human activities. It colors our mood swings, inspires our works, or produces various degrees of anxiety. Insight into the power of our sexual instinct depends on an individual understanding of oneself. It may also be denied or forcefully repressed and then it becomes an element of pressure, a time bomb in our unconscious.

Sexuality then, is more than the mere sex act. Sexuality produces tension that increases when this need is denied or willfully repressed. By the same token, the satisfaction of sexual hunger, sex-play, and the sex act go beyond a mere release of tension. In a compatible man-woman relationship it becomes a source of uninhibited pleasure. It produces feelings of gratification and well-being.

Sexual satisfaction also produces feelings of enjoyment. It uplifts the self-image of a well-functioning male or female, thus reassuring a person of his or her role as a sexual animal. And, as indicated, sexuality can be inspirational, triggering creative ideas. For varied lengths of time, the sex act makes humans feel at peace with the world.

Inhibition of sex causes tensions. Its denial is a disruptive force of normal instinctual needs, producing irritability, sleep disturbances, discontent, psychosomatic symptoms, and even more serious illnesses such as hysterical blindness or deafness, impaired muscular coordination, paralysis of limbs and a host of other physical disturbances. Any severe repression of sexual activity is incompatible with the freedom of dynamic hope.

Disturbances in the field of human sexuality are a by-product of the inhibiting demands or confusions about its role in modern civilization. Different from all other bodily functions, sexuality is a bilateral operation. Sexual satisfaction, except for masturbation, requires a partnership, the union of a man and a woman. It began, as a cynic put it, not with an apple on a tree, but with a pair on the ground. And because of the involvement with another human being, we must understand not only our own attitudes toward sex but those of another—attitudes that may produce possible conflicts, different depths of feelings, different degrees of freedom or inhibition, conscious or unconscious fears, which are sometimes neatly covered up by a mask of normal or casual behavior. Thus, the neurotic overlay or inner ambivalence about sex, if it is not an initial problem, might become a complication in the man-woman relationship that affects all areas of emotional interaction, and emerges as a disruptive force in the building of trust and intimacy, and a positive transference to a sexual love object.

Understanding Transference

It seems that to most men their mother remains the ideal of all womanhood. A boy in the body of a man may fervently search for the ideal woman, who he now can possess, a wish thwarted in his youth by the fear of his more powerful father. If unfulfilled, the need to be loved by one's own mother can remain an unconscious motivating force to prove oneself worthy of mother's love and possibly surpass the power of his father. These secret wishes have long been "forgotten" but have, nevertheless, remained a motivating force that has driven man on, throughout the ages, in a never-ceasing quest for power.

Many women speaking about their husbands or other men state that many of them still have, and display, strong emotional ties to their overidealized mothers. The image a man has of his wife may merge with that of his mother, and his wife would then be punished for all the failings of the man's mother. Or she may be expected to carry the heavier burden or greater share of the responsibilities. These negative transferences are frequently not understood and lead to breakups of many marriages.

Transferences that are unrealistic produce misjudgments and failure. We can all read into another person qualities and virtues that don't exist. And yet, we may blame the other person for a rejection or an inability to love that was never there to begin with. We may bathe in the warm glow of being in love, while the affection that seems to come from the other may not be more than the projection of our own love, similar to the reflecting rays of the sun.

A woman also imprints into her brain the image of her ideal man, based on the image of her father. How a woman sees her father may have built trust of men or instilled fear or hate. Similarly to the boy and his feelings for the first love of his life—his mother—little girls, in the absence of a developed critical judgment, also accept the father as a paragon of power and protection. The early vibrations of feelings may produce pleasure or pain, trust or distrust, ease or frustration, love or hate, or any of the other corroding conflicts that result in the need to withdraw or to gain domination of one sex over the other as a means of self-protection.

The process of identification with one or the other parent builds guidelines for the man-woman relationship and concepts of happiness that stem from either passive or active hope. The girl with passive hope will wait for the knight on a white horse to rescue her and to love her. The passive man may dream of Venus, the goddess of beauty and the mother of love, who will greet him with a warm and loving embrace. Such a man may sail the seven seas to find the ideal woman who can love him unconditionally. The man, in his hunt for this ideal to fill his lonely existence, may, in his state of excitation, find a near-ideal, which he then, in a Pygmalion fashion, might try to reshape into his preconceived ideal image only to end up with a woman who may turn out not to be what he wants. The man who cannot accept a woman the way she is will be chasing a phantom, like Peer Gynt, who cruised the world for the ideal woman capable of fulfilling his adolescent fantasies of love, while Solveig, the woman who truly loved him, was growing old waiting for him.

Women or men who have gained maturity can make a realistic adjustment and find a partner they can share life, love, and sex with because their outlook on life was positive and their human interaction inspired by dynamic hope.

But not too many people work on themselves hard enough to develop tolerance and goodwill. Those who don't remain rigidly passive or aggressive, submissive or domineering.

Rigidity in one's adjustment to another human being and the confusion about one's sexual role in modern life turns a relationship into a battlefield. Feelings run high—from excitation to dashed hopes, from ecstasy to jealousy, from joy to despair—always determined by a person's passive or active hope: One person may helplessly wait and dream; another may evaluate a situation realistically and move to action by fight or flight.

A distorted concept of sexuality can lead to a fixed aberration from the normal to the abnormal. Hope for sexual fulfillment in states of sexual aberration are the result of an arrested sexual maturation in severely inhibited, narcissistic personalities. These in-depth passive and emotionally immature people, unless treated, remain deeply discontent. A great deal of their energies goes into controlling their inner anger while their outer defenses are an obsessive-compulsive compensation. Many of these men and women can separate sex from an involvement of feelings. This, in turn, can become a source of sexual dysfunctioning.

Men with confused or immature value judgments can, as we said, have uninhibited sex with a prostitute but be impotent with their wives or women they put on a pedestal, especially if these women are beautiful and bring out in a man feelings of inferiority. Motivated by a need to compensate for feelings of unworthiness, a man may seek out famous or beautiful women to cover up his arrested sexuality. Such a man may depend on a woman's beauty, fame, or socioeconomic position to bolster his inner weakness, which he covers up and balances by keeping the woman insecure, playing the role of the macho male. Such a man is vulnerable. There are many with an inflated ego who manage to present to the outside world the image of an irresistible sex idol but who could suffer a crushing defeat by a woman whose power may lie in the weakness of such a man's ego and his unconscious transference to his own manipulating and controlling mother. As a boy he may have hated her but nevertheless his need to possess her remains. Such a pathological dynamic interplay can lead to sexual perversions in men or women. One case of such perversion, sexual enslavement, or bondage, shall be presented:

The Professor's Story

That patient was a brilliant intellectual, a teaching professor at a university. He was in his late forties. When asked why he came to see me he said he was a "nervous wreck." He also said how difficult his decision had been to seek help. He described himself as a maverick, a man who had a ferocious sense of independence. He emphasized that he was confident of handling his own affairs by using clear, cold logic. Coming to see a doctor for emotional problems was an admission of weakness he greatly detested. An even more embarrassing weakness was his need to admit his inability to free himself from an obsessional fixation on a woman.

This was his story: On one of his trips to Europe he had met a woman and, though he had found her not to be particularly attractive, he had nevertheless become sexually involved with her. She was married. Her husband was an internationally prominent political figure. What was even more humbling to him was that he had met the woman's husband personally. Worse, he had to meet him from time to time at certain corporate board of directors' meetings.

My patient was abhorred by this discovery and decided to break off his unpardonable involvement at once. He thought this would be no problem, since it was not even a sexually gratifying affair. He was angry with himself for not having investigated the woman's social position. It did not occur to him to go into any background study because he thought that with the end of the trip the affair would end.

Back home in New York, the woman began to telephone, displaying her wit and charm. She insisted on seeing him, inventing different reasons. Each one of their meetings in his apartment ended up in having sex, which afterward caused him revulsion, followed by feelings of depression. The woman, on the other hand, became increasingly more demanding. She wanted to be reassured that he would not leave her. She was wise enough not to talk about love nor to ask whether he loved her. He countered her demands with evasiveness and sometimes could muster enough courage to say that he disliked her and that there would be no further meetings.

My patient began to hate the woman and found himself being

afraid of her phone calls. He almost decided to keep the receiver off the hook. But he had to keep the phone operational, and she would reach him.

Like a man who makes a New Year's resolution, he had decided to use all his willpower to resist her demands to visit and say, "No." But then, when she got him on the telephone, she kept him on until he was overcome by a strange sensation, as if he were losing control. He would feel drained of all energy, and the decision to use willpower would vanish. Like a Pavlovian dog who reacts to a given signal, he reacted to her demand of wanting to come by saying, "Yes." It was, as he said, "against my will. . . . I hated myself for having become party to an ugly triangle situation. But I felt helpless to resist." He hated her to visit, he hated to make love to her, and he hated himself for this heretofore unknown abominable awareness to be possessed. Above all, he was torturing himself to find out where his iron will had gone.

My patient was a slightly built man and, as he put it sardonically, "not exactly a matinee idol." Yet, he said, he was enormously successful with women. "It's my mind, I suppose, that fascinates women. The most glamorous and most beautiful women fall for me and I make them go to bed with me. Some call me a Svengali, others say I hypnotize them. And I had been in full control, always with all of them, until now."

My patient was confused, angry, depressed, and deeply ashamed of this relationship and the knowledge that there was a woman who controlled him. He knew it was neurotic. "Crazy," he said, a psychopathological case of a man's total sexual submission to a woman, a mystifying bondage he could neither understand nor break. He read literature on the psychopathology of sex, yet all his intellectual knowledge could not stop his reflexlike blind reaction. The woman on the phone, his meek reply to visit, then sex. Finally she would leave and he would sink into a state of depression and self-hate.

In the meanwhile, the husband of my patient's ladyfriend had become aware of his wife's intimacy with my patient. There was no scandal. The diplomat had chosen to ignore the matter. This cool, civilized behavior made my patient feel even more wretched and lewd. The mixture of shame, guilt, and self-hate became unbearable.

My patient was a man of great knowledge. He had a sharp, critical mind. "I could analyze other people down to the tee," he said. "I could quickly perceive their problems and weaknesses. But in my own case, I am helpless. I know what answer to give to a friend in such a weird situation, but with this woman I am putty in her hands. I am not different from an alcoholic on a binge. When the telephone rings, all my firm intentions fizzle away. I struggle and struggle and finally say, 'Yes.' "

The interviews with this patient were intense and, because of his strong intellectual defenses, difficult. He pondered why he spoke in a calm voice, why he did not argue, or display any cynicism. Though he said I was the last hope he had to be helped, his unconscious resistance was stronger than his wish to be cooperative. He knew he was fighting for his life and that the key to his cure lay in unconscious experiences in his early childhood with a mother who had made him passive and submissive and of whom he had been afraid.

We approached his stormy childhood. The patient displayed little emotion; his voice remained flat; he repressed the emotional vibration. He was desperately holding onto his logic and his mental defense of intellectualization.

Little by little my patient's reaction formation emerged. His mother was all power and control. Only from her could love and feelings of worthiness come. This demanded total submission to her. It also produced a power drive to make himself worthwhile; to show off his intellectual brilliance and his accomplishments. As a human being he was a cold and uninvolved man who was motivated by a need to prove his masculinity by new conquests of beautiful women. He could bring out their insecurity and thus make them dependent on him while he remained cool and in control.

One day, in a state of utter despair, he arranged for an appointment and went to see his ladyfriend's husband. It was a humbling journey, a humiliating experience. He needed to expiate some of his guilt and shame. The diplomat was polite, reserved and said coldly, "Sorry, that situation is your problem. In my position, I can't afford a divorce . . . or a scandal. . . . Moreover, I do not wish to be helpful."

My patient left this meeting like a whipped dog. It had been his last attempt to resolve his conflict by himself. It was then that he made the appointment with me. From then on he concentrated on his therapy with me. He came once a week for five months. His unconscious sexual fixation on his mother became clear to him, his ego became stronger, and he could now comprehend his compulsion to dominate women as an act of revenge. By rendering them dependent he gained superiority and lost his fear of being hurt by any of them. His passive hope to find a mother substitute who would love him unconditionally remained a fantasy, since he kept all women at arm's length. Yet projection of his own ardent need—the intensity of his love-play—had the effect of disarming women, who saw him as being strong, a master, and kept alive an illusion of having found an ideal or mature love. My patient and his women had been playing an emotionally highly charged game that because of its erotic excitement had the lure of a dangerous fascination. It kept my patient on a course of hoping to find one day a woman who would be like his mother and love him. This then would set him free.

This was his first breakthrough. The second breakthrough came when he realized that by the power of transference, I had become his father. Different from his natural father, who was cold and critical, the image of his new father substitute, the doctor, was kind, understanding, nonjudgmental and most important had "forgiven him" for his Oedipal fantasies. The meeting with his lover's husband had been an attempt to seek forgiveness for his unconscious crime of having taken a mother figure away from a symbolic father substitute. After this dramatic meeting, he felt free and cut the knot of his paralyzing entanglement.

Shortly after that meeting, he was surprised by his inner calmness when he firmly told his ladyfriend that the game was over, not to visit and not to call and also not to write another of her long, witty love letters, for he would throw them, unopened, into the wastebasket. He was cured. His passivity had slowly given way to enough self-assertion that he could extricate himself from a strangling entanglement. This first step as a more secure man was also a first step toward building self-worth. With the new hope that existed in his mind he felt he could muster his life in a world of reality and move toward becoming a more mature man. The day he could express that feeling was the day we decided to terminate our sessions.

The Plight of the Passive Male

Submissive sexual behavior in the male is a source of unhappiness to both partners. The passive male who performs poorly in the sexual act is bound to have a low profile of himself. If he attempts to compensate for his inadequacy by driving for the acquisition of extrinsic values, such as money, possessions, or a position to impress his wife, or women in general, he is trying to reassure other people, which means he is trying to reassure himself of his worth. Yet it will not earn him respect from his wife nor from others, because on a deeper level he does not respect himself. He sends off vibrations that other people pick up. Often, as time goes on, women feel deceived and trapped in such ungratifying relationships. They either leave or take subtle revenge for the uninvolvement, inner alienation, or absence of sexual satisfaction.

Among my patients I had treated two women, both celebrated beauties. Each had gained social prominence, one in Washington as a known hostess, the other in a jet-set setting of New York. Both left their husbands after a few years of marriage and both refused any alimony or the million-dollar settlement both husbands had offered, though both had no money of their own. For these two women, freedom from insecure and passive men was worth the price of giving up a mansion and a secure position. Both ended up having financial problems but both cherished their independence and self-esteem. Both, however, as I came to know them, also hated men as they had hated their fathers.

Women who lack sexual satisfaction or a gratifying human inter-action will take revenge for their frustration and dependency. They are very clever and imaginative in the way they go about punishing or castrating the male. One woman patient admitted that whenever she knew that her husband wanted sex she would delay going to bed by finding chores she had to finish, such as doing the dishes or wanting to see the end of a movie on television, until she heard her husband snoring.

In an article called "Sexual Revenge," in *Human Sexuality* (February 1979) Dr. Nathan Roth, assistant professor of clinical psychology, New York University School of Medicine, writes:

> During sexual relations people are very vulnerable to injury to their self-esteem by a partner wishing to hurt. When gratifying sexual activity is highly prized, as it generally is, a target for vengeful actions is readily available. . . . Since she [the patient] felt contemptible, she tried to take revenge by visiting contempt upon her husband in sexual intercourse. This she did regularly by eating an apple or dialing her bedside radio while her husband had intercourse with her.

A young patient of mine was very unsure about his masculinity. He had been drawn into a homosexual involvement he did not quite enjoy. He was too frightened. He liked the companionship but was too passive to resist a kind of lovemaking that left him with discomfort and guilt. Only his need for human closeness and his fear of being close to a woman made him endure the homosexual involvement.

This patient's depression reached a point of such despair that he came for help. During the first interview with this patient I learned that he felt insecure with women and was frightened when they made sexual advances to him. He was a very attractive young man. When asked what he feared, he said, "They are so powerful." Upon further inquiry he gave a description of the home in which he grew up as a teenager.

"When I came home from school, I found mother resting on a chaise lounge, watching a TV program with a box of candy next to her. Before leaving his office, my father would call to ask what she wanted him to shop for for dinner. Mother would give all details. Later on, when he came home, he would go into the kitchen to start cooking dinner for all of us. Sometimes mother would criticize this or that dish, which we children often felt was unfair. But nobody said a word. After dinner, we children would clear the table. Mother would do nothing and I thought, really, it is no fun to be a man. I thought a woman's life is a much better one, no rushing off to work, possibly having a difficult boss, and then work again at home. These were my first questions about whether a man would not get more out of a life in a homosexual relationship in which he is being taken care of and is freed from responsibilities."

The deeper problem, as it turned out in our meetings, was that this young man's psychosexual development was not arrested, as is the case with most homosexuals, but that he had suffered homosexual panics due to anxiety attacks and confusion about his own masculinity. To him the area of male-female sexuality was indistinct and bewildering. His father's passive or even submissive behavior created the confusion about normal male behavior.

In the natural process of growing up he, as a boy, had emulated his father's personality, a normal process especially when it comes to forming an identity. In his adolescent years his father's weakness and readiness to submit to a woman became evident in his own behavior.

Later, in his profession as an art teacher, he could unfold his talent as an imaginative painter. He was liked and respected by his students. Being very critical of himself, he felt no particular attraction to male students but shyed away from developing relationships with young women because of his fear of sexual involvement. It was a stroke of good luck that he met a sensitive and understanding young woman who fell in love with him. She was patient, kind and reassuring. Her awareness of his fears caused her to be on guard against ever playing an aggressive role, except in their sexual encounters when she tried to help him overcome his inhibitions.

He left my treatment when he decided to get married. The respect the two young people had for each other as people, and for each other's talent and similarity of their values helped the man to overcome his passivity and to form a new image of himself as a more assertive male. Both the man and the woman entered married life with confidence and the hope of being able to share the good and the bad and to fulfill each other's needs.

Clarifying Sex Roles

The women's liberation movement, with all its merits, has produced a great deal of confusion in the area of human sexuality. It has been my observation with the men and women I have treated that rather than clarifying each other's role, it has caused uncertainty in their sexual life.

A clear point must be made that this author is not intending. to make any reference to the women's struggle to attain equal rights in the socioeconomic, political, educational, or any other sphere of work, profession or activity, but restricts himself only to the area of sexual interaction and the psychological affect the striving for dominance has. The fact is that ignorance or confusion about one's role has been causing a great deal of needless suffering and breakdown of relationships.

Sexuality too often becomes the battlefield of dissatisfaction two people may have in other areas. A woman may feel used or restricted to Otto von Bismarck's three K's for the role of women: *Kirche* (church), *Kinder* (children), *Küche* (kitchen). But that was a century ago, when women had no rights. Today, we have the domineering wife who is driving a sexually insecure husband deeper into passivity. Or a controlling male, who wants a slave rather than a mature wife.

Flying south to a psychiatric convention, I saw on the plane the much talked-about movie, *Kramer vs. Kramer*. Though somewhat overemphasized, perhaps, to make its point, it nevertheless showed effectively an area of conflict in modern marriage, leading to an actual reversal of the traditional roles: The father, not the mother, bringing up a child. This then is the scenario: The husband, a young, ambitious vice-president of a company, is not aware of the emotional needs of his very attractive wife. In her quest for "fulfillment," she

197

chooses to leave her husband and her young child with seemingly no previous quarrel. She goes to California, sees a psychiatrist, has several affairs, and after about two years returns to New York and sues for custody of her child.

The husband-father struggles hard to cope with the needs of a little boy, who wants his mommy, needs to be fed, to be brought to and picked up from school. He loses a good job in favor of taking care of his son. As the divorce proceedings are about to begin, he has to take less well-paid jobs hurriedly, in order not to appear unemployed.

The divorce proceedings in court clearly establish a mother, probably in her late twenties, abandoning her young child, then, when she makes more money than her ex-husband, returning and fighting for the custody of the child. At present she is living with a man, which indicates that she does not hesitate to expose her young child to a new father substitute. She also might replace him as she has before, since there is no mention of permanence.

The judge awards the mother custody of the child, a decision that is cruel and void of humanity. It seems almost a routine procedure to award the custody of a child to a mother, whether she is psychologically fit to rear a child or not. As of late some judges show understanding and compassion in their decisions and move away from earlier verdicts that were cruel, stereotyped, and void of any psychological awareness of the child's needs or interest in finding out who of the two parents would serve in the better interest of the child. Children of divorced parents enter adult life with one stroke against them.

The mother is triumphant. Under her sweet facade she chooses the aggressive masculine role of a liberated woman over motherhood and the man she had married. Her acts of castration are further demonstrated by her life of sexual freedom, as symbolized by taking a playboy bachelor lover and engaging in a career in which she overtakes her ex-husband by making more money. If that is in line with the psychodynamics of her personality, then why does she commit a second traumatic blow to her child by tearing him away from his father, with whom he has now developed a secure and loving relationship?

But then comes a dramatic change of heart. Perhaps seeing the pain in the defeated ex-husband (or is it a flash of guilt or magnanimity), she allows the child to stay with the father.

Far from wishing to be a critic of this film—it is beautifully acted—I must nevertheless make a few remarks, because it reflects a modern trend that corrodes, if not the sanctity of marriage, then at least the deeper meaning of a commitment.

Why did this woman marry this particular man? His looks? His future that seemed secure? Did she use him for a start in her own life? And why did she not talk to him if she felt dissatisfied? Both were educated people. Why, instead of trying to communicate and come to an understanding, did she, like an angry and irresponsible child, run away to satisfy her own selfish needs? Was it for survival or simply a power play? True, the man pursuing his own American Dream was so busy building his career that he perhaps did not notice his wife's dissatisfaction. Evidently they did not communicate and thus were unaware of the other's needs and feelings.

It is the story of many people who thought they were in love, which dynamically means they moved *toward* one another. But contrary to usual experience, when people begin to fall out of love, for whatever reasons, they move *against* one another. That is, they either fight or make adjustments. In the film they move *away* from each other—a breaking away or, symbolically, death.

In a psychoanalytic meeting, a known female psychiatrist presented a paper on the women's liberation movement from antiquity until the present. The theme was that throughout history women had been dominated by the male. At the end of the lecture I was drawn into a discussion of the paper. Since the psychiatrist was a friend, I did not want to be critical but put my sentiments into one question: "There is an old adage that says that the hand that rocks the cradle rules the world. My question is who, in America, is bringing up the children?"

A Tragedy of Sexual Fixation: The Actress's Story

Freud named six points of impairment of sexual functions:

1. The mere turning aside of libido, which seems, most easily, to produce pure inhibition;
2. Impairment of the execution of the function;
3. Rendering it difficult through the imposition of special conditions, and its modification through diverting it to other aims;
4. Its prevention by means of precautionary measures;
5. Its discontinuance by anxiety, when the initiation of the function can no longer be prevented; finally,

6. A subsequent reaction of protest against the act and a desire to undo it if it has actually been carried out.

Sublimation, the unconscious defense mechanism of diverting unacceptable sexual drives into socially acceptable activities, may lead to positive, creative works or to negative, destructive plans and behavior. Substitutions for strong sexual needs lead to a vast variety of abnormalities and mental disturbances. Loves and hates run into extremes, sparked by renewals of hope of finally finding an ideal sexual partner, but as with all neurotic hungers, they never can be satiated.

Similar to the case history presented earlier, of a man who had a deep psychosexual fixation on his mother he could neither understand nor break by himself, is another case that comes to mind. I had treated a woman, whose fixation on her father was so intense that not only did it ruin her chances for a happy man-woman relationship, but in the end caused her own tragic destruction. The police could not determine her cause of death, whether suicide or murder.

The patient was a dramatic actress, at the peak of womanhood, a striking appearance with a charisma that captured everyone's attention as soon as she entered a room.

Her father was a giant in industry. The home she grew up in had gained the fame of being a meeting place of international personalities well-known in high finance, politics, the arts, and letters.

Men with money, titles, yachts, and castles did not impress her. Only men who had reached a pinnacle of success in the arts fascinated her. In a first eye-contact with a celebrated superstar, she explained the strange sensation that overcame her, first a feeling of excitation, followed quickly by a losing of her will that led to her unresisting submission to such a man's magic spell. She did not know that it was not necessarily the power of the man, but her own reaction of "swooning" into a floating erotogenic masochism. The psychodynamics in her lust for pain by surrendering to men of fame were a conditioned and thus unconscious transference from an overidealized image of her own famous father to exalted father figures. In her obsessed mind she assumed a fully submissive role before she was to meet her hero. Her strong-willed defense of integrity, her compassionate or discriminating value judgments, her search for honesty, all the facets of her distinct and sparkling personality became enveloped in a haze. She regressed into a love-struck little girl who had only one overriding wish: to please and surrender to the vivid image of her father.

To be singled out as a love object of this woman was a mixed blessing to the men. I had treated one of her lovers, an internationally famous actor of film and stage. She was devouring him as she would all of her chosen men, while at the same time acting like a slave at their feet. Her love was an all-consuming blaze of giving all and demanding all, regardless of social discernment or considerations. Public figures could not afford an avalanche of her affection. She would follow a man wherever he went to give a speech or a performance. She would send costly presents that would cause suspicion, rumors, and fierce jealousies. This woman was a renaissance figure, with her Greek profile, her black hair, her long neck and her emerald green eyes.

Her uncontrolled self-offering inevitably led to a rejection of the men she was obsessed by and made her prefer the company of homosexuals, who consoled her during the subsequent periods of depression. Torn apart by severe doubts and the pain of anxiety of losing an idealized lover, she would seek out psychics, gurus, mediums rather than come for consultations. She supported a small army of unemployed actors and musicians and a few homosexuals she liked because of their talents, their wit, and sensitivity. One of her homosexual friends extended his short visit by moving into her apartment permanently, then having his own lover move in also. They began to control her life by becoming her chief advisers. Eventually they occupied her master bedroom while she moved into a small guest room. During this period she also went on drugs.

Her erratic life exhibited increasing breaks with reality. She was drifting in and out of fantasy living. Her many friends felt more and more neglected and were deeply concerned. She made dates which she broke or did not keep and visits to my office became rare because of her fear of being discovered to be on drugs. She had always fought being committed to a hospital.

In the meantime she had gotten engaged to her first homosexual friend, who now acted as her future husband, making decisions concerning her money matters and a change of her will. One morning at dawn, he called in a panic. His fiancée was dead, he said. He did not know what had happened. Perhaps an overdose of sleeping pills. When I saw her some fifteen minutes later no rigor mortis had set in. I called the police, advising her fiancé and his friend not to enter her bedroom or bathroom nor to remove any medication until two detectives arrived. The detectives came later in the day to my office to gather more information. I could not determine a cause of death. The homicide detectives were very careful in expressing any of their suspicions. Even the autopsy was not conclusive about whether she had taken or had been given the overdose of drugs. The brilliance of this woman's life and her tragic death was colored by a ceaseless and irrational search for a replacement of her dead father. As her mental state deteriorated and her obsessional transferences became irrational she would, guided by the stars, pick a night and dress in boy's clothes, having imagined that her father had been disappointed in her being a girl. On such nights, she would climb over a fence into the garden of her demigod lover, in her childhood hope to see and be embraced by him. These expeditions ended with states of total exhaustion followed by deep depressions.

Psychodynamically, this unusual woman of great beauty and talent was a manic-depressive who suffered episodes of schizophrenic breaks with reality. She was a lady of the world at one time and a child at another, when she escaped into the beautiful world of fantasy inhabited by elves and good fairies. She had had several hospitalizations, including several electric shock treatments. It was the time before the discovery of psychotropic drugs and also before I had changed my practice from clinical medicine to that of dynamic psychotherapy. Even so, it is questionable whether this woman would have been helped because she lacked a basic motivation to integrate into the world. She did not know what a healthy life was nor how to live it. Hers was a life of passive hope, always anticipating that a new exciting miracle was about to happen. Then she would sink into her cyclic depressions. Today's chemotherapy, far from being a total cure, nevertheless is quite successful in helping disturbed people to maintain a fairly even temperament and to prevent episodes of psychotic breakdowns. Psychodynamically, this woman's mood swings from manic highs to deepest lows of hopelessness. In such a numb state, void of hope and will, all innate power is turned against the self, which, without medical help leaves a person only one route of escape from pain: suicide.

CHAPTER 12

Hope and Cults

IN 1978 the world was shocked to learn about the most incredible mass suicide in recent history, an event so gruesome and, in its circumstance, so bizarre that ordinary people's minds could not comprehend how nine hundred Americans, all dreaming about living out their lives in a manmade paradise, would instead drink a lethal potion of cyanide, thus rounding out a circle of hope, hopelessness, and death.

As program chairman of the American Association of Psychoanalytic Physicians, I decided to present for our scientific meeting on January 30, 1979 a paper on "Human Failure: Motivation for Mass Suicide and Mass Murder." Because of the circumstances of the then-recent spectacle of Guyana, I invited two distinguished members of the mass media, Jim Jensen, anchorman at CBS, and Squire Rushnell, vice-president of ABC and producer of "Good Morning, America."

What were the feelings of seasoned reporters to such a human tragedy? We, as physicians, are often confronted with tragedies and have an empathetic approach to every loss of life; as scientists and phychoanalysts we never cease to search for the deeper motivation of a human tragedy in order to widen our knowledge on the behavior of people so that we can learn to cure and perhaps even prevent repetition of human catastrophes.

Jim Jensen, a brilliant commentator and a compassionate man, denied being moved by any stirring human feelings. He said that otherwise he would not be able to report events with objectivity. He indeed presented the abominable reports in a cool and professional way; only his voice betrayed some of his controlled horror and empathy.

Squire Rushnell, a warm-hearted man and a dear friend, who has a keen interest in the welfare of children—he produces children's programs—also gave his views with objectivity. However, he too could not cover up the depth of human sentiments. It was also he who had helped to determine the format of the evening's program.

I began my paper with "A Word About Human Failure." As a psychological term, human failure means any deviation from the concept of "normalcy" or conditioned behavior. It is basically a destructive or self-destructive response to life situations, ranging from minor accidents to an acting out of obsessive-compulsive drives or acts of violence, the extremes of which are suicide and homicide. Chapters in the ongoing story of human failure are incidents of mass suicide and mass murder.

A case in point is the massacre in Guyana in which over nine hundred people died.

The public responded to the reports with utter disbelief and demanded more information. Indeed, for weeks, many explanations of this gruesome event were given but, as far as I know, none, including a book by an eyewitness reporter who survived, did fully explain the psychodynamics of the self-immolation and murder. We, as psychoanalysts, by the very nature of our work, feel challenged to examine the bizarre circumstances in order to provide a scientifically satisfactory explanation of the motivation of the massacre that took place in Jonestown.

What seems puzzling and indeed inconceivable to many people is the paradoxical quality of this event in which nonviolent, believing people, who had joined the temple in the hope for a better life, could then be led to such a state of blind submission that the majority would, without revolt, follow the demand of their mentally deranged leader to kill themselves.

Mass suicide and mass murder are no mystery to psychiatrists, and Guyana is not without precedents. Throughout history, people have died for the glory of an idea or a faith. When I was a student, our two upper classes in Berlin, students seventeen and eighteen years old, volunteered at the outbreak of World War I, only to die a short time later, when drunk with nationalistic excitation they ran singing into the fire of the French machine guns. They died for the glory of their country. About thirty-one years later, Adolf Hitler, before he himself committed suicide, ordered everybody to defend the burning capital. Thus, ten-year-old boys of the Hitler Youth threw themselves in front of onrushing Russian tanks and blew themselves up with the tanks. The Kamakaze pilots of Japan committed suicide attacks in World War II as a self-sacrifice for their emperor. Another incident of mass extermination was the children's crusade, motivated by the belief of serving Christendom by liberating the Holy Land. Caligula, the Roman emperor, wore military boots as a small child. When he came to power he turned into one of the most ruthless and cruel autocrats regretting that all of mankind did not have one neck that he could sever with one single blow. Through the centuries sadists have paraded as saints, as saviors or as liberators in order to attract followers, whom they exploited for their own megalomania and their own mad drive for power.

Mass suicide is possible only if people possess no ego strength and no self-worth and therefore hope to gain security and self-esteem by embracing a worthy cause and submitting blindly to a leader who promises to give them a reason for their existence, a position of self-importance, or, in a religious sense, to deliver them from the sin or guilt that may plague them.

Mass murder is also motivated by vengeance, as related in the legend of the Pied Piper of Hamelin. When the city fathers refused to pay him for having freed the town of all the rats, he revenged himself by playing his flute, putting the children in a state of trance so that they followed him everywhere and finally into the river where they drowned.

The Pied Piper of Guyana, the charismatic Reverend Jim Jones, put the followers of his People's Temple in a state of hypnotic trance by the lure of creating a new, ideal society of justice and true brotherhood.

How can such a "spell," or state of mass trance, be produced? What happened to the critical reasoning power of the educated followers of the People's Temple? Why did they, like the poor and disadvantaged temple members, obey Jim Jones's command to die?

The answer that is scientifically acceptable is based on two factors. Both are the result of studies done by Ivan Petrovich Pavlov, the Russian physiologist and Nobel Prize winner.

The first factor necessary for an understanding of the phenomenon of mass suicide and mass murder is rooted in the various types of personalities of the people involved and their interaction. Among these types there is structurally one that makes a follower and another one that a produces a leader.

The second factor is based on the knowledge of what happens to the brain cell under the bombardment of extreme stress.

The Dynamics of Cult Personalities

In 1959, the same year I visited the Pavlov Institute in Koltushy, near Leningrad, I published a paper in the *Ohio State Medical Journal* called "Health and Wholeness." There are two paragraphs of this paper I would like to quote because they contain Pavlov's four types of personality, which correspond approximately with the four temperamental types Hippocrates had described about two thousand years earlier. Pavlov conducted experiments, first on dogs and then on people, that led him to arrive at observations that closely approximated Hippocrates' four temperaments: the choleric, the sanguine, the phlegmatic and the melancholic.

In my paper I substituted psychodynamic terms for the Pavlovian types calling Pavlov's

1. Strong, excitatory type the *hostile-aggressive personality*;
2. Lively type the *aggressive adjusted personality* (Pavlov found this type to show purposeful and controlled reaction to identical stresses);
3. Calm, imperturbable type the *passive dependent personality*;
4. Weak, inhibitory type the *regressive withdrawn personality*.

This last type, the inhibited and withdrawn personality, is the one that would most easily become a follower of a cult like that of the People's Temple. People of that type have a weak ego and often lack roots or a real purpose in life. Insecure, confused, often in conflict about their sexual identity, they would feel inspired by the promise of the security of a communal existence *like a family*, something they perhaps have not had. They would also, for the most part, accept readily the rule by a strong "father" who would take care of his "children."

Types two and three, because of their ego strength and adequate self-worth, would not easily submit to an authoritative figure like Jim Jones nor would they be likely to join a cult. They would most likely resist the pressure of religious or political conversion. People of that group might give up their lives but if so, it would be in defense of their personal freedom and independence. And they would not commit suicide or homicide.

Type one, the hostile-aggressive type, is a restless and angry personality with a fragile ego. People of that type try to cover up their insecurity by a constant need to prove their strength. This type often suffers from a sense of sexual inadequacy, which they compensate for by striving for extrinsic values such as positions of power, control, possessions, and money. Under prolonged stress or failure, they may break down—or they may escape an acute breakdown by suddenly switching from a behavior of aggression to that of an idealistic, spiritual way of life and by adopting new, intrinsic values, such as brotherly love and impeccable moral virtues. A leader like Jim Jones comes from this type of personality.

Here is an example of the paradoxical switch of behavior that can take place as the result of intolerable stress. The husband of a patient of mine called me one Sunday, very early, in a state of panic. His wife had just died from an accident or suicide by drying her hair in the gas oven before going to mass. The man, tortured by intense guilt, anxiety, and grief, then quit his job and left for a prolonged vacation. When he returned, he displayed the behavior of a religious fanatic. He became an evangelist, having turned from his hostile-agressive behavior to that of a pastoral preacher. This switch is reminiscent of Chuck Colson, called Mr. Nixon's "hatchet man," who, as a result of his misdeeds in the Watergate case, underwent a religious conversion and switched from killing careers to a new job of saving souls.

Another route of escape of the hostile-aggressive personality after a severe defeat is the switch from having been a belligerent aggressor to becoming a loyal follower or a fervent disciple of a revered leader. The killers of Congressman Ryan and the other people in Guyana came from this type, the converted hostile-aggressive personality who blindly carried out their master's orders to kill.

The leader of a cult is usually a psychopath who generally possesses a special gift of persuasion, or charisma. *Charisma,* from the Greek word *caris,* means to favor or to gratify. In Christian theology charisma is a divinely inspired grace, gift, or talent to prophesy and to heal. And, according to Webster, it is a special quality that captures the popular imagination and inspires unswerving allegiance and devotion.

Brainwashing Explained

The second factor to explain mass suicide is the deliberate process of changing the individual personality of a follower. Once a cult structure is in existence and has a sufficient number of followers, the cult leader can, with the aid of group pressure, proceed to systematically break down the established pattern of behavior of his followers and shape them in his own image and to his own needs. A new conditioned reflex system will make people react automatically according to the newly set signals in the brain. This process, in its abused form, is commonly called brainwashing. Here is the theory behind the mysterious process and how Pavlov came to discover it. But while Pavlov had hoped to be able to produce the "ideal man," using his theory, his method has been abused for sinister political or cultist purposes to break the will of people who would otherwise resist coercion.

In 1924, the rising waters of the Neva River caused a great flood in Petrograd. It reached Pavlov's laboratories and flooded the kennels in which he had been keeping his conditioned dogs. The water rose dangerously close to the ceiling, and the dogs swam in utter terror, seeing no route of escape. At the last moment an attendant rescued the dogs, and, when Pavlov later examined them, he found that some of the animals had switched from a state of acute excitation to one of complete inhibition. These observations puzzled him and led him to a systematic study of the causes that had brought about the disappearance of the carefully conditioned responses—as if the brain had been washed clean.

Pavlov came to the conclusion that when an overstimulation of the brain becomes so strong that it threatens the functioning of the brain cells, inhibitory processes take place and bring to a halt their functioning in order to protect the cells from exhaustion or destruction. He called this process *protective inhibition*. He found this protective act to be a regulatory device and a crucial factor in all struggles an animal must wage for its survival.

Later on, Pavlov and his school confirmed that a man's reflexes correspond exactly with those of a dog and that the act of protective inhibition leads not only to a decline of vitality, but is also the condition found in mental illness. In a remarkable paper the then-eighty-year-old scientist published, he gave the reason why, he, as a physiologist, had undertaken the "excursion into the field of psychiatry." He said that not only had he been able to produce neuroses in his animals, which were analogue to human psychosis, but he knew their treatment.

Inhibition, he explained, plays the role of a guardian of the most reactive and irreplaceable cells of the organism—the cortical cells seated in the outer layers of the brain. Inhibition protects these cells against excessive pressure at times when they have to meet extraordinary excitation. Protective inhibition secures them the necessary rest in the form of sleep. Sleep, after intense stimulation, spreads over both hemispheres of the brain. The brain cells recover.

Here is a further part of Pavlov's experiments that explain the methods by which protective inhibition can be produced or how for political reasons a free will can be broken. It also helps us to understand the agony and fear some of the people of Guyana must have suffered, particularly the mothers who resisted killing their babies with cyanide.

We stated that after the first conditioning had been broken, animals and people would react automatically to the new conditioned commands and to only those. Nevertheless, such a new conditioning may require reinforcement. This is carried out by creating conditions that lead again to a state of protective inhibition. There are four ways of accomplishing this:

1. An increased intensity of the signal;
2. A change in the time interval, frequency, or regularity of the signal;
3. Contradictory signals, as when, in rapid succession, positive and negative signals are given and the dog becomes confused about which one to follow; and finally
4. Fatigue, by overworking the animal, by exposing him to a variety of stresses, whether chemical, thermal, or mechanical. There is also torture, which can be physical or psychological, calculated to cause fear, anger, despair, and similar prolonged emotional irritations.

Jim Jones used all four methods to break down any resistance to his followers. He used terror, hunger, beatings, and fatigue, to which must be added states of hopelessness, fortified by the isolation in a jungle that provided no escape. Jim Jones, pressured by his own paranoia, increased the fear of the people by warning them that sinister outside forces, such as the CIA or racial extremists, would kill anyone who tried to escape. With their will broken and their bodies overfatigued, the people in Jim Jones's temple were doomed.

Guyana, then, is an example of how people can be lured into a cult at a time when they are confused, lonely, insecure, sexually frustrated, or in any other way dissatisfied or unable to cope with a reality that is frightening or which they simply don't understand. In

209

a state of regression, aided by group pressure and with no logic and intellectual controls to guide them, these people will follow their master, whether he is a messianic leader or a charismatic dictator. He can then live out his own madness at the expense of his brainwashed followers.

It was not within the scope of my paper to speak about the prevention of the Guyana massacre or any other cult-inspired holocaust. However, if I were allowed three words in regard to prevention, or cure, they would be GOOD MENTAL HEALTH. As to the mass murderer Jim Jones, I would paraphrase the words of the tragic figure of Mephistopheles in Goethe's *Faust* when he said, "I am part of that power that always wants the good and creates the evil."

Religion or Perversion?

Another study on the psychodynamics of cults had been presented by George J. Train, former assistant professor of psychiatry at the New York University Downtown Medical Center, a friend and a man of great knowledge. In March 1979 he gave a scientific paper on "Cults—Loss of Autonomy Dynamics," saying that the purpose of his paper was "to explore the possible theoretical psychodynamics that motivated the tragedy [of the People's Temple] and to point to some generalizations."

By definition, says Dr. Train, "A cult is in any religion regarded as unorthodox or even spurious or even involved in excessive devotion to some person, idea, or thing." It must be differentiated from the established religions. By established religions this author assumes Dr. Train to mean beliefs in a superior being and a spiritual faith or a dogma laid down in scriptures such as the Bible, the Koran, the mixture of Eastern Hinduism, Buddhism, and other philosophies.

Disregarding the abuse and distortion of religion, it has deeply affected cultural development (as our Western Judeo-Christian morality indicates) through worship in a divine power. Western religions, while prescribing *adherence to specific life-styles, have not*—especially since the separation of Church and State—*worked at isolating members* from the mainstrain of secular activities.

There we have a fundamental difference in the practice of the main cults of today, be it the Unification Church (the Moonies), the Church of Scientology, Hare Krishna, the Divine Light Mission, Children of God, Love Israel, Church of Armageddon. All demand unflinching loyalty to their leader and to the institution, the church, as did Jim Jones and his People's Temple.

How Can It Happen?

The question has been asked over and over: How is it possible that a wide spectrum of people—young, educated college kids, educated older people, and the multitude of those in their autumn years—would fall victim to a messiah or a demigod, numbing any of their rational abilities of judgment, to surrender to a Christlike deliverer of mankind, offering to him or the institution he leads all their labor and all their earthly possessions?

The answer is as complex as it is simple. The simple answer is that all these people have lived a life of no hope. The complex part is the technique by which people have been robbed of their last bit of rational thinking and made utterly dependent and believing.. Before going into the technique itself, one must discover the mystery of the psychological potion that performed these astonishing conversions. It is an enslavement of the human mind by first convincing people of their empty and perilous existence, the futility and hopelessness of their existence, and their chance to be saved.

As to the techniques: Who has not been approached at an airport—as this author has been many times—by young, attractive, soft-spoken women, who, while they are greeting you, are already attempting to put a flower in your lapel? While appearing alluringly charming and passive they display a subtle aggressiveness when you refuse the flower, following you and trying to convince you that the flower is a symbol of love and that they want no money.

"They all use coercive persuasion," said Dr. John G. Clark, a psychiatrist, writing in the *American Medical News* (May 9, 1980), a paper issued by the AMA. Dr. Clark's patients were harassed after he testified to the Vermont legislature that "cults pose a serious danger to the health of their members." In his article Dr. Clark writes that several female patients received bizarre telephone calls. "Did Dr. Clark make sexual advances to you?" the anonymous caller asked the women.

"Someone of the Scientologists must have been watching the patients drive up to my office," said Dr. Clark, "and tracked them down through their license plates." Following his testimony, "They wrote me threatening letters, called my neighbors, spread rumors about my children, disrupted my speeches, even wrote to the dean of the Harvard Medical School demanding that I be censured."

The continuous praying and dancing and speaking of love for one another combined with exhaustive commune activities are meant to leave no time for thought or reflection and to break down any last inner resistance or memory of their earlier life.

As pointed out earlier, Pavlov could demonstrate not only the making but also the breaking of an earlier conditioning. The question that baffles people the most is the total subserviance to the leader or the doctrine of a cult. Young people, who had previously been rebellious and angry, are now totally obedient and speak only of love. The only scientific answer I have that explains the total change of personality is found in the earlier description of Pavlov's protective inhibition—the wiping out of any earlier conditioning due to extreme fear—combined with the utilization of the previously mentioned four methods of reinforcement. Once a brain is washed clean, any new conditioning can be established without resistance, as if the brainwashed people are puppy dogs. Pavlov found that this second conditioning is almost impossible to break, as evidenced in cases of religious conversion. A new belief is being defended with self-sacrifice or utmost obstinacy, as if one's life depended on it. In a psychological sense, this is so: because new conditioned responses form an individual's new patterns of behavior, its reactions remain automatic. It allows people to get through the demands and chores of a daily life strengthened by repetition and—in a commune life—by a watchful group insisting on strict adherence to a code.

Dr. Clark describes the life of a Bostonian physician's twenty-six-year-old son who had gone to Hare Krishna meetings while still in high school but joined when in college. He then lived for seven years in a commune. This is how the young man described life with the sect:

"The routine was the same. We were awakened at 3:30 A.M. for cold showers. The next five hours were spent attending religious services and classes and chanting, singing, and praying. At 9:00 A.M. we have breakfast, usually a paper plate full of rice, bread, a vegetable, and a sweet. We'd spend the next twelve hours—with a break for lunch and dinner—walking the streets to solicit money. When we got home at 9:00 or 10:00 P.M. we'd be ready to drop."

This Krishna follower lived with thirty or forty others, spending almost the entire seven years going to different towns in Massachusetts to raise money.

"I got to be pretty good in sizing people up, deciding what approach to take so that they'd give me money." When stories about cults appeared in newspapers and people began to ask questions, this young man decided "to pose as a deaf-mute and sell miniature American flags." He used other tricks equally successfully.

"Although proud of raising funds successfully, I became increasingly disillusioned that the group was not living up to its promises of real happiness, of trying to help other people." He began questioning who the Krishnas were really trying to help.

After several years he became dissatisfied with the rule of remaining celibate. He then asked the president of the Boston Hare Krishna to find a wife for him. The president selected a woman and both were allowed to talk for a few minutes every day to determine whether they'd get along. "I was so brainwashed at that time that I didn't realize how absurd this all was. There was no other alternative, so we got married." Nothing changed, husband and wife had to remain in their separate dormitories. According to the Krishna rule sexual intercourse was allowed once a month for half an hour, to be preceded by five hours of chanting.

"The group had been very supportive in my court battle to gain control of my trust fund. Immediately after I turned my money over to the group, my wife stopped talking to me and moved to a Krishna farm in West Virginia."

Once he decided to move out, the group seemed almost glad to get rid of a dissenter. He found a good job with the management of the Boston University Hospital and regrets that he did not leave the group sooner. "It was hard to admit how wrong I had been all along. At least I've got my freedom back and I'm not a slave anymore."

The Lure of Cults

In our study of the motivation of young people to join a cult, we must emphasize a point: *the fear of growing up* or *the fear of meeting the real world.* Whatever the confusion in a parental home or lack of love, the *idealism* of searching for and finding *real love and real happiness* have an enormous appeal to the emotionally immature. While life in a commune may turn out to be hard, it is *the promise to be taken care of* and the hope of finding a family life many of these kids never had—or, if they had it, it was void of genuine love and the feeling of security adolescents need to build an identity—that motivates them. And for these illusions and hopes young people sign away their freedom and the chance to grow up in a real world with an opportunity for real love and real fulfillment.

Cults are a sad testimony of the confusion of our time and confusion about real values and honest beliefs. Cults offer an escape, such as the drug cult or any other cult that builds a protective wall between a weak or passive ego with little hope and an assumed cruel world outside. *Hopelessness* then becomes the motivating principle for longing for a protective childhood setting, with brothers and sisters and a parental authority to protect the passive and fearful young person. To the older people it is a return to a family structure that also may not have been too happy.

Breaking the Hold

This author agrees with Dr. Clark that the cults abuse the first amendment for living out the irrational and megalomaniacal power drives of the cult leaders. Psychodynamically, the love these leaders preach—and these are well-spoken words only—is a mechanism against their own deep-seated hostilities and/or self-hates. The dynamics are to gain *hope and power* through their Godlike control of lost human beings.

The cure, of course, is the activation of positive hope to build a strong ego through work or gratifying actions. This develops self-worth and love. The aim is to develop individual independence. The controls parents have had and which emotionally disturbed adolescents have transferred or surrendered to another authority or a "loving group" that is bound to stifle independence needs to be broken in order to attain inner freedom. Only by assuming control over our own lives can we attain maturity and freedom that will readily allow us to assume the responsibilities of adulthood. Cultist life is a subexistence of fearful, lost, and emotionally immature children.

In our chapter on children we outlined some of the dangers that, if unchecked, produce neurotic behavior. Dr. Train stresses, as this author does, the need to build self-esteem and confidence, feelings the Moonies and the Hare Krishnas don't want their followers to develop.

The psychodynamics of preventing people from being enslaved by a drug or a religious cult are similar to a plan this author has developed as a method of drug-abuse prevention, which is presented in the closing chapter of this book.

CHAPTER 13

Hope and Compulsive Gambling

ON WHOSE SIDE is hope when two people throw a pair of dice? And what is it about people that compels them—since antiquity—to try their luck, to take a chance, to gamble away their waking hours or their estates, to risk bankruptcy and jail—all in the hope of winning? Or is it only to win? Sometimes, as we shall see, there is an unconscious will to lose. But even that is not a full explanation of what motivates about 80 million Americans to gamble. According to a survey of the National Council on Compulsive Gambling, in 1974 88 million Americans participated in some form of gambling, wagering a figure that has grown to over 17 billion. About 80 percent of respondents in a nationwide survey favored some form of legalized gambling.

What kind of fever is it that is so widespread and has grown beyond a form of entertainment to involve supervision by individual states and the federal government?

There are three aspects of compulsive gambling: *legal* gambling, *illegal*, or criminal, gambling, and the *psychopathological*, or compulsive, gambling. While we shall briefly examine the first two activities, it is the third—the psychodynamics of the compulsive gambler—we shall explore in greater detail. We shall also explore the role hope plays as a trigger for igniting this particular compulsion.

"Gambling is inevitable," writes the Commission on the Review of the National Policy Toward Gambling, in its introduction to its final report. "No matter what is said or done by advocates or opponents of gambling in all its various forms, it is an activity that is practiced, or tacitly endorsed by, a substantial majority of Americans."

The pervasive and inevitable nature of gambling was, according to the report, "the simple, overriding premise behind all the work of the commission."

Legal gambling has taken two forms: One, legal gambling industries have undergone substantial expansion; and two, new forms of legal gambling have been created. During the past fifteen years, six additional states established parimutuel horse racing and the total number of horse races run increased from 6,000 to 12,000. Nevada's casino industry also underwent significant growth: taxable casino revenue increased almost 600 percent, from less than 200 million in 1960 to more than 1 billion in 1974. New Hampshire established a state-operated lottery in 1971; New York legalized off-track betting in 1971, and New Jersey established the first legal numbers game in 1974.

In order to study gambling as it exists in the United States, the Commission on the Review of the National Policy Toward Gambling was created by Congress in the Organized Crime Control Act of 1970. The commission prepared some thirty research papers and held forty-three days of hearings across the country. "It is now the task of Congress to take the next step in developing a fair and reasonable national policy toward the existence of gambling," declared the chairman, Charles H. Morin, a Washington attorney.

"This report and the recommendations will surprise many Americans and *may startle* some. But those who are surprised and startled should carefully reflect on the significance of the fact that a pastime indulged in by *two-thirds of the American people*, and *approved* by perhaps *80 percent* of the population, contributes more than any other single enterprise to police corruption in their cities and towns and to the well-being of the nation's criminals.

"Most Americans gamble because they like to, and they see nothing 'wrong' with it." (Original italics) It is this statement that leads us into our own study of the psychodynamics of gambling. States and governments are in a dilemma with regard to effective law enforcement, calling it "impossible" to write a law *prohibiting what 80 percent of the people approve of.* Indeed, how can a government based on democratic principles devise a law that is meant to deal with a human passion, the very nature of which it does not even know. The United States had tried to solve the problem of alcoholism by the Prohibition Act,

216

which Congress, in 1933, appealed by the Twenty-first Amendment. This attempt to control a vice had to fail because it could not deal with the psychodynamic and psychochemical factors that cause a neurotic need for alcohol. Only in a most rigid political or religious state, such as Iran, could such a law work, because human rights, the way we know them, need not be considered.

An incident comes to mind. In 1959, as the chairman of the psychiatric group of the United States Committee of the World Medical Association (now not open anymore to membership of individual physicians but only to autonomous states), I was involved in a dialogue with Professor Timofev, who was, at that time, vice-director of the Bechterev Mental Hospital in Leningrad and chief psychiatrist of the Soviet Army. When I inquired about homosexuality, he answered curtly, "We don't have homosexuality in the Soviet Union because it is illegal." (From paper, New York Academy of Sciences, June 1960, pp. 585–588.)

Unless we know the medical and psychological causes of a neurotic aberration or a compulsion, we cannot take rational steps to deal with such a problem effectively—and this goes also for compulsive gambling.

Why Gambling?

What is it in people that drives them to a gaming table or to indulge in any other form of gambling?

First let us describe the term *compulsion* as defined by the American Psychiatric Association. Compulsion is "an insistent, repetitive, and unwanted urge to perform an act that is contrary to the person's ordinary wishes or standards. Since it serves as a defense substitute for still more unacceptable *unconscious* ideas and wishes, failure to perform the compulsive act leads to *overt anxiety*. Compulsions are obsessions that are still felt as impulses."

Consequently, gambling is not necessarily neurotic for people who are out to have a good time. For them, going to the racetrack is having a day of fun, of experiencing the mass excitement—the sharing of an emotional experience with others—of taking in the ambiance, the colors, the sight of beautiful horses. All this contributes to having an enjoyable time.

Compulsive gamblers are like chronic alcoholics who cannot stop after a second or third drink. Their drive to gamble is pathological. The American Psychiatric Association has offered new diagnostic criteria to clarrify pathological gambling as a disorder of impulse control, as an illness evident in every field of human endeavor; and to classify the gambler as a sick person who is in need of rehabilitation rather than incarceration.

Here is an example of a gambler who was unaware of the neurotic nature of his compulsion and suffered physically and emotionally by attempting to sublimate his inner drives.

The patient, a man in his late thirties, tried to conceal his anxieties, which manifested themselves in physical restlessness and sweaty hands, behind a pleasant jovial facade. When asked about his reason for coming, he said his cardiologist and his wife had urged him to seek help, a notion he disputed by saying that except for some heart trouble there was nothing wrong with him. Questioned about his heart he said that he was suffering from a tightness in his chest, a fast heart beat, and an oppressive fear that his heart might stop at any minute. This was causing him great apprehension and panic. His doctor had given him nitroglycerin capsules that would stop or prevent an attack.

The problem with his heart had begun over a month before, when a friend of about the same age had suffered a serious heart attack. From then on he began to "feel" his heart. He "heard" his heart pumping and his pulse running fast. He had gone at once to see a cardiologist but felt reassured only for a few hours after the doctor told him that his heart was normal. He speculated that the pathology of a heart attack might not show on the cardiogram until a day or two later. So he went back for new tests about twice a week. Yet his anxieties did not disappear. He was irritable, could not sleep well, got up in the middle of the night to watch TV, but could not concentrate on the program.

After some initial hesitation he began to talk about himself. There was a dramatic quality in his voice, as if he was finally coming to life.

As a teenager, one day he experienced seeing his father strike his mother. This upset him greatly. He avoided an answer to my question about whether he did not want to hit his father or kill him. He repeated only how terribly upset he was. "We were very poor and there was never peace, so after father beat mother I felt so devastated—I could not stay in that home any longer—I felt so helpless—so like nothing. From then on I lived by myself."

"You said you were sixteen—where did you go? What did you live on?"

My patient got somewhat embarrassed. "I gambled," he said. "I had worked out a formula—I was always very good in mathematics—my teachers called me brilliant."

"You lived by yourself since you were sixteen, without working or having any support from anyone?"

"Yes, my gambling got me through school and college—in the fifties the dollar was worth more than what it is today. My yearly income averaged around $20,000."

"From gambling?"

"From playing the horses. Then, when I graduated from college I wondered what to do next, go on and become a math teacher or go where gambling is an honorable profession: the stock market. That's where I went. The day I made my first half a million dollars was the happiest day I remember. I had no choice but to go on. Today, I am successful. I doubled that amount several times over."

"You never lost?"

"On and off. It never upset me. I would figure out where I made my mistake and quickly regain my losses."

"How did you feel when you lost? Were you upset?"

"Not really. I felt I owed something to fate or whatever it is—so, I did not mind losing. Losing money is something like paying off a debt—unconscious—or maybe guilt—"

This patient was not merely a compulsive gambler but emotionally a severely disturbed man. He had great difficulty controlling his inner hostilities, efforts that left him always feeling exhausted.

"I maintain beautiful offices at Wall Street but getting through the traffic strains my nerves to such a point that I feel they might snap. So, I have a direct line from the Stock Exchange to my country home and a TV set in my limousine in case I have to go down to the office."

Though this patient professed to have confidence, he never fully lost his distrust of people, but admitted that he had told me more about himself than he had ever told any other person, including his wife.

Through his wife, a lovely, bright young woman, I learned how inwardly alienated this man was. His mood swings were extreme, predominantly depressive. In these morose states he would go to bed and sleep, read and sleep more. After he gave up his anxiety about his heart, I suggested that, when he felt utterly exhausted, he play tennis.

He looked at me in a very peculiar way. "So, you want to kill me—you just want me to drop on the tennis court—did my wife suggest that?"

I reassured him I had not discussed this with his wife, that it was entirely my idea and he should do it.

When he returned the following week, he expressed his amazement at how well he had felt after having played tennis for two hours, first fearfully, waiting for his heart attack, but then with vigor. The explanation was, of course, that the aggressive energies he had been repressing and turning against himself, causing his feelings of fatigue, were now channeled into a physically enjoyable game.

One day, he finally opened up. "I'll tell you why I gamble. I know of *two real feelings only: anger, and the excitement when I gamble.* I overcontrol my anger, which, I know, makes me tense all the time, and I try to do things and help people, to be a better person, but it does not change my fears and tensions. But when I gamble I come to life. I don't gamble to win. Of course I want to win, but that is secondary. I gamble because of the excitement, because of the *exhilarating experience of feeling*—I really feel." The inner hope to recapture these precious feelings made him the compulsive gambler he basically is. The fear of losing this one chance "to feel" had caused him to put up resistance to any psychotherapy.

The Compulsive Gambler Defined

What then are the deeper psychodynamics in compulsive gambling? A New York psychiatrist-friend of mine, Dr. Harry Perlowitz, gave a psychoanalytic paper on "The Compulsive Gambler," which he has allowed me to quote from:

"The compulsive gambler is a psychoneurotic with obsessive-compulsive features. He is an oral-receptive and anal character constantly looking for supplies not attained in his formative years. He had reached the genital state of development and regressed to the ano-oral stage, taking a part of the phallic stage with him. As the phallic stage was incomplete, it is obvious that his motivation pertaining to this stage will be impaired. Separations and divorces are common. Metaphorically, life with mother and father was hazardous, and becomes a way of his own motivation, usually with few exceptions. His father was passive and his mother dominant. In reviewing one hundred cases, less than five percent of fathers were dominant. The mother lacked major mature feelings, thinking, doing and saying in her unconscious epistemological strivings. Demonstrative love, praise, attention, and proper protection were lacking. Through the process of introjection the compulsive gambler became unconsciously hostile, narcissistic, megalomaniacal, dependent, and inferior, along with the other oral and anal components.

"In the majority of cases the father was a compulsive gambler and the son identified strongly with him. In one aspect of his mind the gambler unconsciously figures that as long as his mother accepted his father, he too, unconsciously will gamble in order that the mother accept him, as the compulsive gambler is strongly entrenched with her in his Oedipus complex.

"In considering the entire gamut of psychological disturbances, ambivalence is probably more marked in the compulsive gambler than in any other psychological condition. He can be kind and helpful or cruel, stubborn, obstinate, stingy, and he often has psychosomatic symptoms that may end up in organic pathology.

"What has been said thus far involved the personality structure of the compulsive gambler. We will now deal more with his need to gamble. Compulsive gambling is a reparative process and as such it is a very poor one. It leads to the degradation of the person, which is, unfortunately, encouraged by city, state, and county. The city and state especially remain as inanimate professional gamblers who will profit while the compulsive gambler sinks into a state of narcissistic mortification. Having been unable to attain the needs of his formative years he struggles in his maladaptive structure to gain them. His needs are infinite. Money to him is symbolic of love. He borrows from his family members, friends, relatives, and Shylocks to gain more money through the act of gambling. Placing a bet produces in him a state of elation. He is then unconsciously involved with his Oedipus and castration complexes. The placing of a bet represents foreplay with his mother or a surrogate and making 'a killing' represents the unconscious sexual act. Losing is followed by a temporary state of dissatisfaction, which is soon followed by a period of pseudorelation. The money he won is adulterated. He will unconsciously be severely punished by his superego if the money is kept. The struggle is now between id and superego. He will continue to play until he loses his gains. In an obsessive-compulsive way he repeats the same act until further money is not available. The compulsive gambler, therefore, plays to lose.

Summary

1. The compulsive gambler is a psychoneurotic with obsessive-compulsive features.
2. The compulsive gambler is an ano-oral and partial phallic character.
3. The introjected love of the compulsive gambler's mother was essentially based on her unconscious selfishness and cruelty.

In turn, the compulsive gambler unconsciously reprojects hostility and unlawful acts toward family and friends, is often a philanderer.

4. In his partial identification with his father or a surrogate he, too, becomes a compulsive gambler.

5. The compulsive gambler lacks ability to reason. He has no interval of reasoning between stimulus and response. As soon as he places a bet he has already assumed that he has won.

6. Most bets are made on horses. The horse is symbolic of the compulsive gambler's mother. Masturbatory orgastic responses are consonant with the fury and labor of his racing horses. Masturbation is aimed at his mother or a surrogate and his goal is unconsciously the genital area.

7. Because of superego restrictions the gambler consciously plays to win and unconsciously plays to lose."

A Cure Based on Hope

Compulsive gambling then is a severe neurotic disorder, that, in the International Classification of Diseases has been given the diagnosis of *pathological gambling*. As Dr. Perlowitz pointed out it can be traced back to an incomplete, or *psychosexually arrested*, state of development. Thus, a cure will depend on a patient's awareness of his or her illness and an activation of the hope to build a more secure, meaningful, and rewarding life.

In an earlier chapter on neurosis of children we said the "purpose" of the neurosis is to achieve unconscious goals, *therefore there is a strong resistance to give up this purpose.*

Every obsessive-compulsive drive has a neurotic basis that keeps on urging an individual to perform certain acts to satisfy the unconscious neurotic need. The alcoholic must have his drink to regress into a state of oblivion or to remove the inhibitions to release anger or to feel free to talk about love. The drug addict escapes an intolerable reality and rises to a position of omnipotence in which he has the godlike power to be master over another human's life or his own (homicide and suicide).

The compulsive gambler needs the *excitement and euphoria* that elevates him or her above the trivial demands of an everyday life filled with responsibilities he wishes to escape. By the mechanism of *irrational hope* he fantasizes attaining lots of money and power to glorify his ego, which he knows smarts from being weak and ineffective.

The cure for compulsive gambling is similar to the treatment of other neurotic illnesses and possible only if the need for excitement can be substituted by a *new active hope* to attain in reality what they feel when they gamble. For the most part, compulsive gamblers need to overcome depressing feelings of being deprived and need to be accepted by people so that they can integrate in a social group as honest, working and giving people. Helping a neurotic ego to be cured can be accomplished by developing self-worth, confidence, and an interest beyond one's own egocentric needs.

The gamblers I have seen are sick people. Their lives are empty and life itself has, in spite of their social or business successes, not brought them the fulfillment that gives an individual feelings of inner peace and satisfaction.

I am reminded of a scene at the Aristotle Onassis Sporting Club, an exclusive gambling club in Monte Carlo. Since I don't gamble at all, I had ample time to watch the faces of the rich and a few superrich in states of highest excitation. Some of these faces, in spite of exhibiting masks of cool, controlled, pokerfaced indifference, had the eyes and tension of birds of prey, ready to swoop down to devour their victim with greed and lust. It seemed to me to be similar to the feelings my previously mentioned patient had described, that gambling produced *real* feelings and a sense of *real* passion.

Dr. Robert L. Custer, who is an active contributor to the newsletter of the National Council on Compulsive Gambling, has developed a chart that is shaped like a big V and which depicts the stages of decline and recovery of a compulsive gambler. The descending leg of the V consists of three phases, the *winning*, the *losing*, and the *desperation* phase. It begins with occasional gambling becoming more frequent, with fantasies of winning. Then in the losing phase: losing episodes, lying, losing time from work, borrowing money, unhappy home life, inability to pay debts. In the desperation phase: increase in amount and time spent gambling, remorse, blaming others, panic, illegal acts—finally reaching the bottom of *hopelessness*, with suicidal thoughts and attempts, arrest, divorce, alcohol, emotional breakdown.

The upstroke leg of the V also has three phases: the *critical*, the *rebuilding*, and the *growth* phase. It begins with honest desire for help, stopping gambling, thinking clearer, decision making, returning to work. The second phase shows accepting self, weakness and strength, improved spouse and family relationships, new interests, returning of self-respect, resolving legal problems, less impatience, more family time. The growth period shows insight to self, facing problems promptly, giving affection (interest) to others, and finally reaching the peak of recovery called New Way of Life, reinforced by a stable and constant support by *the inner power of active hope.*

In a speech entitled "Treating the Compulsive Gambler," Dr. Sirgay Sanger, a psychiatric consultant to the National Council on Compulsive Gambling says that "the compulsive gambling problem has its origin in childhood." As Dr. Perlowitz pointed out, "it's not the sort of thing that suddenly starts, anymore than alcoholism is something that 'just happens.' "

Dr. Sanger writes: "For the majority of Americans gambling is a diversion, and a socially acceptable form of amusement—[however] in real life compulsive gambling accounts for a never-ending saga of heartbreak, not only for the individual gambler, but also for the ten or twenty others, including his or her family."

Dr. Sanger refers patients to Gamblers Anonymous, recommending it because of its experience and the positive effect of its group therapy method. But when people reach a plateau, they need to be led to the origin of their unhappy personality structure, to the events that made the child they were turn away from healthy growth to an escape of passive hope, the wishful thinking of the child.

The increase in gambling will remain a problem as long as individuals are ignorant about their inner self, their inner needs and their unresolved conflicts. These confusions create tensions, anxieties, and states of boredom—inner pressures which can be diminished by escapes such as an excessive need for sex, alcohol, food or compulsive gambling.

If we think of the economy of our own daily production of energy, we find that probably less than ten percent is being used to live creatively and thus joyfully. Margaret Mead, the anthropologist, estimated that people in our culture use something like five percent to six percent of their potential. I would hope it is higher. The unused energies are spent in different ways, ranging from self-amusement or various escapes to long periods of sleep, to attempts of actually killing life energy by excessive intakes of tranquilizers, drugs, or alcohol. This numbing of energy causes loss of interest and promotes fear of doing anything that could reveal incompetence, which in turn increases depressions and ends up in hopelessness.

All that has been said previously about turning one's life around and of *mobilizing hope* to provide the incentive and imagination necessary to create attainable goals goes for the attempts of curing compulsive gambling.

All gamblers are motivated by one kind of hope or another—but it is always a passive hope. The compulsive gambler is psychodynamically a man or woman who suffers from all shadings of self-rejection leading to a sense of futility and hopelessness. Again, its cure lies in the mobilization of the power of active hope.

CHAPTER 14

Hope and Cancer

As I sat at the bedside of my dying mother, holding her slender hand, two realizations began to evolve that had a profound influence on my medical thinking. One was that when a man or a woman has made up his or her mind to die, there is little a physician can do to save them.

The second realization was that on deep unconscious levels, people determine when, and sometimes even where and how, they wish to die.

As to my mother, then in the seventy-seventh year of her life, an event took place, minimal in the eyes of the world but decisive concerning her feelings of independence and pride, that was like a final signal to let go of the battle for her life.

The event was a decision that had been made by my brother, myself, and our parents for them to spend the long, hot summer of 1949 away from the city in a cool mountain resort area. Our main concern then was our father's physical condition. He had developed a cancer of the prostrate gland that with a treatment of estrogen, a female hormone, could be kept under control for several years. However, due to his very light skin and insufficient pigmentation many blue-eyed people have, he had been advised against being exposed to the sun on an ocean beach, a resort mother would have preferred. Mother did not care about the mountains and because of the distance she dreaded being cut off from social contacts and visits from her children. She nourished an undercurrent of resentment against the summer plans as if she were being forcefully banished into exile. However, it was not her way to fight openly against a decision. She was a lady who detested arguments and, indeed, as children we never ever heard her raise her voice. On the surface it seemed that she had quietly surrendered in consideration of father's needs but had hoped for some compromise. As matters stood she must have felt that her opinion had been more or less ignored, and feeling hurt she then reacted with a silent withdrawal. And this must have been that significant moment when, on conscious or unconscious levels, she probably had made her final decision, the one, that in less than two weeks summoned me to their cottage.

She had developed an acute case of jaundice. Recognizing the danger of that illness, caused or aggravated by inner grief, I pleaded with her to go to a hospital. Throughout life mother never had been decisive. This time she was firm. In a sad and soft but determined voice she said, "I want to go home. I want to be in my own bed." I knew the meaning of these words. They meant I want to *die* in my own bed. We took her and father back to New York. While she had her own physician, she wanted me to be her doctor. The following day, as I was injecting a needle to hook up a bottle of intravenous blood serum, she looked at me with unforgettably sad eyes and said in a half whisper, "Let go of this—there is no purpose anymore—" She was saying it's too late. It was a last good-bye.

Her doctor and I agreed that a malignant growth must have been in process for some time and that the feelings of hopelessness mixed with intense repression of enormous inner anger had probably produced a spastic blockage of the bile duct causing the life-threatening jaundice. Mother refused an operation, which might have been too late anyway. Father accepted the other doctor's and my opinion to respect her wish to leave her alone. Mother's quiet way always commanded respect.

It is an agonizing experience to play the double role of physician and son at the deathbed of one's own mother. The sound of each breath is evaluated by the trained ear of the doctor, touching at the same time an emotional cord. The conflict came home to me: Do we physicians obey the Hippocratic law to fight for the last breath or do we refrain from giving the life-prolonging hypodermic needle and obey the wish of the patient who wants to die? Mother died peacefully because she wanted to die.

Reflections in a state of acute grief are a peculiar mixture of memories, of pain, guilt, and love on one level of human function-ing—and yet rational actions that have to be taken, such as funeral arrangements, on another.

As to mother's wish to die, beside the factor of reality—her ill-ness—was the thought of the deeper emotional causes. The glory or meaning of her life was over. Her pride had always been enormous. Before she came to the United States she lived in her circle of friends like a ruling queen. Father adored her, fulfilling every wish she would ever express. Mother had a way of escaping the roughness of reality by telling an amusing story or by escaping into her own world of fantasy. In the summer she would manipulate father to take her to Karlsbad for a cure, and in the winter both, on her insistence, would go to Italy. Wherever she went, she had a circle of women who would do everything for her and listen spellbound to stories of ghosts and devils and gnomes and pixies she made up, in which she discharged her own anxieties and problems and the ones of those around her. In New York, she felt displaced and unfulfilled. She did however enjoy the success of her children—until the summer day when she realized that father was seriously sick and that she could possibly be left alone without his protection, concern, and care. Father had spoiled her terribly. From the moment she knew about father's illness a new element of fear had come into her life. Mother had always lived with hope. Now father's cancer totally destroyed this hope. Her sentiments had always been: If one of the two had to die she wanted to die first. Indeed, she died *when* she wanted to die and significantly before the mental torture of being with her life-long mate alone for a long, anxious, and depressing summer.

And father? When mother died it was evident that his life was over, that he would give up and die also. All his life he had been a man whose first duty had been to provide for mother and her comfort and the needs of his family as well as the many relatives mother had had. Now there was nothing anymore for him to do. Heartbroken, grieving and feeling lost and embarrassed to depend on others, he gave in to his children's urging to live with his oldest daughter, his favorite. But not for long. His cancer now began to cause disturbing symptoms. A life-saving operation was performed. He never recov-ered. He had marked his time. Exactly one month before the first anniversary of the death of his mate of fifty-eight years he too died when he wanted to—perhaps believing he would be reunited with her.

I dedicated my first book, *The Will to Live,* to the memory of my mother. In it I wrote the significant chapter "Man Dies When He Wants To Die," which eventually led to all the studies that followed on death and dying. Since then my own thoughts and observations about death and the interaction of cancer and hope have deepened. With more observations through my psychoanalytically oriented detectivelike curiosity, I began to search for the deeper mental and emotional causes that contribute to the dreadful disease of cancer. And while many factors must come together to produce a malignancy, the one human emotion I noticed standing out was *hopelessness*.

Patient Behavior

In a chapter, "Personality Factors in Dying Patients," I contributed to Herman Feifel's book, *The Meaning of Death* (McGraw-Hill, 1959), I wrote in regard to cancer patients: "The most arresting characteristic of these patients appears to lie in their attitude toward their illness. With the exception of a comparatively few personalities who exhibit an enlightened, scientific, and sometimes martyrlike attitude, most cancer patients are evasive and rejective of their illness. This can be observed in their lack of interest concerning symptoms, clinical findings, therapy, and marked attention to details. Most of them even avoid the direct question Do I have cancer? Neither do they appreciate the honesty of the physician who volunteers this diagnosis to them. From a medical viewpoint, most of these patients, in their outward behavior, are 'good patients,' if we consider 'good' a submissive, cooperative attitude, and one that does not give the doctors and nurses any trouble. They can become, nevertheless, rebellious and hostile if they feel themselves rejected or slighted. Son e, having come to the end of their trail, may now dare to release pent-up hostility against members of their family or friends in a desire to retaliate for previously suffered hurts and rejections; others, freec from lifelong conflicts and self-centeredness because they already live on another plane, are now capable of displaying touching courag＜ and unselfishness. From a point of psychological evaluation, these patients appear to be immature, dependent, and often regressive personalities.

"A brief case history experienced during my early years of medical practice may illustrate this type of patient: A fifty-nine-year-old male patient came to see me because of his 'neurosis,' as he ,ut it. His case history revealed that nine months prior to this first cjnsultation, he had suffered a terrific pain in his chest and back. He Lad seen a local doctor who treated him for anemia and a spasm of the esophagus. He was unable to swallow food, even cereal, because cf the 'nervous bubble in my upper chest.' Since the start of his illn ;ss, the patient had lost twelve pounds, but added quickly that this was natural since he was unable to eat properly. The question as to whether he had received a radiological examination was answered affirmatively. An X-ray taken two months earlier, apparently only a flat film, had not shown any organic disease. He concluded that the stabbing pains across his chest and stomach were new symptoms of his neurosis.

"The family history disclosed that both parents had died at the age of fifty-eight; his father from a cerebral hemorrhage and his mother from cancer. One sister had also died from cancer. The patient himself was a shy, soft-spoken, melancholic man. He had never married. He had no relatives or close friends and lived by himself, pretty much withdrawn from the rest of the world. His emaciated body and history aroused my suspicion of a neoplastic involvement. A radiological examination revealed, indeed, a malignant growth in the esophagus with perforation into the bronchial tree. This diagnosis was confirmed a few days later at New York's Memorial Sloan-Kettering Cancer Center. There the patient received a course of supervoltage X-ray therapy.

"About two months later the patient returned to my office stating there had been some initial improvement but that now he had a constant pain in his back and across the gastric region. He was losing weight rapidly. It was apparent that metastases had invaded all his vital organs and that he could live only a few more weeks. Throughout the illness his behavior, outwardly at least, remained gentle, friendly, and cooperative. He was anxious to win approval and to relate to the physician as if he were the authority in whose hands his future fate rested. Though Memorial Sloan-Kettering is known to be a cancer hospital, this patient, when he inquired about the duration of his hospital stay and his type of treatment, did not once ask about the nature of his illness.

"In summary, we see the patient as a passive dependent personality whose predominant attitude was a deep sense of futility and hopelessness. He was a lonely and pessimistic individual who, apparently, had been unable to establish any meaningful relationship and who had no purpose or ambition in life, nor any significant work that could serve as a sublimation for his creative being. Consequently, there was no reason for this man to continue an existence that had become intolerable. He may have unconsciously longed to be reunited with his mother, the one and only symbol of protection this man apparently had known. One may speculate, therefore, whether it was just an accident that this patient's illness began at about the same age at which his mother had died.

"If we wish to assume any relationship between his emotional life and his illness, we must attempt to answer two questions: one with regard to the time of illness; the other, as to the nature of illness. In my own practice, I have long since learned to take into consideration and even, to some degree, to correlate somatic crises with a psychic trauma due to the loss of a parent. Depending on what the relationship with the parent had been and on the patient's personality (degree of integration or maturity), one patient will live through the critical period of a serious illness and another may become the victim of his or her own fear, love, or guilt, which are causing states of stress, somatic symptoms of illness, and, eventually self-destruction. The contributing role of genetic and psychodynamic environmental factors in repeating a family disease as a cause of death is far from clear at this time. It may be assumed, however, that both exercise influence in a continuous interplay. This is in accordance with present concepts of psychosomatic thinking. In a preliminary report LeShan and Worthington found three factors that differentiated the protocol of cancer patients from control subjects:

1. The loss of an important relationship before the diagnosis;
2. An inability to express hostile feelings; and
3. Tension over the death of a parent, usually an event that occurred many years previously.

While no position can be taken here as to the validity of the method applied in this study, the third factor, tension over the death of a parent, appears to be of pointed significance.

"As to the second question of the nature of the illness—in view of the growing evidence that continuous emotional stress can cause changes in human biochemistry, a correlation between psychogenic factors and malignancies cannot be simply dismissed. This important problem needs further intensive study and more attention than it has received during the past years. Writing on the phenomena of carcinogenesis, Szasz states that frustration of instinct leads either to a progressive or regressive adaptation and that while the primitive systems tend to adapt progressively, complex organizations tend toward earlier, more archaic patterns of behavior. He assumes, therefore, that the development of malignant growth is due to complex systems living under stress and to the regressive tendency in highly developed organisms. Karl Menninger, referring to the above-mentioned LeShan and Worthington report, stated, '. . . one of these days the cancer research people who have had such enormous financial support and who have worked so frantically and intensively on the problem for the past thirty years will wake up to the fact that *psychology has an influence on tissue cells,* a proposition which they have consistently regarded even until now as a preposterous heresy.' "

In 1952 I developed a research project to examine whether there indeed exists a relationship between a cancerous growth and a specific type of personality. The plan was to examine two groups selected according to their age, sex, and location of their illness. One group would be patients with a diagnosis of cancer, the other group would have a functional or organic, not cancerous, illness in similar organs, such as the bronchial tract, the lungs, the stomach and intestinal tract.

Since Laurence Rockefeller was president of the Memorial Sloan-Kettering Cancer Center and interested enough to back the project, I put together a research team. The project was voted down by the director of the hospital, who was against that ". . . mental stuff . . ." We are about to turn the corner, he said, in regard to the discovery and a cure of cancer. That was nearly thirty years ago.

Cancer as a Manifestation of Hopelessness

No claim is being made here that my work and thoughts on cancer satisfy the criteria of scientific medicine. The concept of a psychosomatic process in regard to cancer has been strengthened by nearly thirty years of observation coupled with an insight into the patient's area of unconscious thoughts and feelings. Human beings handle their lives the way they want to live—aggressively, greedily, humbly, fearfully, hopefully, lovingly, angrily, passively—in short, more or less according to their conditioning but also to a measurement of the intrinsic and extrinsic values that motivates them and the feelings that ensue.

Cancer, I believe, is a wear-and-tear disease triggered by a variety of noxious agents that cause irritations that can be chemical, thermical, physical, and continue to exercise their destructiveness on certain types of cells. The mental and emotional reactions to irritating agents are specific for each individual. While most people resolve stress by fight or flight, there is a wide group of people in between, who live with fright, of not being able to decide on a course of action. The physiological-hormonal-chemical responses to an alarm reaction—a rise of the blood pressure and an outpouring of adrenalin and other "fighting" hormones—is severely repressed in the future cancer patient. The mental defense mechanism of denial is strictly applied to preconscious awareness that there might be something wrong in a

233

person's physical functioning. But the denial is scrupulously applied in the area of mental and emotional functioning. There is a multitude of people who are structured to be aggressive or passive, to be activists or dreamers who live out their hostilities, fears, resentments, and frustrations not in reality but in the deepest depth of their mind. These people's mental state will therefore be under stress, though they take great pains to conceal their true inner feelings, by cultivating a pleasant, unconcerned, friendly, or even pseudoaggressive facade to fool other people, but primarily themselves, for fear of showing how they really feel. The question of the *reason for one's existence* cannot be answered by simple or sophisticated formulas or platitudes. Cancer strikes me as a form of suicide in the unconscious of many people who, in reality, would never dare to express or to admit any thoughts on suicide, which they may reject for moral, religious, or other reasons.

A case in point is the story of a woman who came to see me first about two years ago. Mrs. O. is a sophisticated lady in her mid-fifties, a successful fashion designer, now retired. She grew up in two cultures: in Europe, at first in her native Vienna, later with further artistic schooling in Paris; and finally in the United States. After the Germans conquered France she was put into a French concentration camp and after the war she came to the United States where she married an American with whom she built a successful business; she had the talent and he had the business sense.

Her medical history revealed that fourteen years prior to her first visit to my office she had undergone a mastectomy because of a cancerous tumor. Twelve years later a malignant tumor was discovered in her chest that could not be operated. The specialists in Massachusetts put her on chemotherapy, which caused unpleasant reactions. She had decided to consult me because of a deep depression she could not shake.

When I asked what she thought was causing her depressions, she answered: "My present life is not worthwhile living."

"Is it because of your cancer that you feel life is not worth going on?"

She did not hesitate long before answering, "My husband and I are worlds apart. Also, since my first operation and the new illness, I feel I am not a woman anymore."

As to her childhood she said her father had shown her newspaper pictures of children being killed. She was not sure whether that was meant to warn her or whether it was an expression of his sadism. The parents talked about divorce but Hitler's entry into Vienna changed everything. She had been left since chldhood with a fear that someone would break in and kill her.

After her third visit, she said that our talks stirred her up greatly but that she wanted to continue to come.

To a question about life she answered, "I feel hopeless." She said that for several years before her present illness she'd had "a fear of death—life is not worth living." And then she made a most significant statement: "I wished for a sickness to appreciate life."

After her fourth treatment of chemotherapy she had thoughts of suicide. She thought of cyanide, perhaps because her mother had been gassed in Auschwitz.

Two months after I had seen the patient first (because of the distance she came only twice a month), she said she was in a fabulous mood. "I feel good every day I am getting better—*I have a strong drive for survival, an undeterred will to live.* And I am not even angry at my husband when I say I am coughing [she thought because of the tumor in her chest] and he answers, 'I cough too.' "

Four months after the beginning of her chemotherapy her *cancer had stopped growing.* Her mood was more optimistic. She now suggested having our sessions recorded on tapes, so that she could listen to them at home.

She began to vent, and increasingly so, anger against her husband, who was very matter of fact, displaying neither sympathy nor affection. Several weeks later she began to assert herself more and fought her husband's resistance to taking an apartment in New York so that she could go to concerts, the ballets she loved, and enroll in a French cultural group. They would spend weekends at their home by the sea.

A year after she started her chemotherapy a rib-scan was taken which showed "activity" in the ribs. This upset my patient greatly. Her new specialist in New York minimized the process in one diseased rib, reassuring her that it was nothing to worry about.

She continued to listen to the tapes that had been done in my office saying, "Listening—I find it very helpful." Her mood improved and several weeks later she said, "I am in a good fighting spirit—I feel strong—but *I can't forget for a moment my disease.*"

As her insight increased she exclaimed, "Fundamentally I want to die to start a new life without my husband."

"A morbid-childish fantasy," I dared to interject. "You could accomplish this without risking your life by having a divorce in Reno."

Mrs. O. was very self-critical. "Why?" I asked.

She answered, "I don't like myself because I made the decision to marry my husband—it was safe, he loved me—it was a compromise."

She was encouraged to make attempts to seek a rapprochement, for certainly unless she was cured it would be unreasonable to leave. At this time, she needed her husband perhaps more than she realized. Her serious attempts to be more thoughtful of him were rewarded when both went to France and had "a wonderful time."

Several months went by when she remembered vividly a stormy love affair that took place before she decided to get married. It went on and off for three years. "When it broke I wanted to die—after that I had my first cancer."

About two years after she had started the chemotherapy as well as seeing me, new tests showed no trace of cancer. The tumor was gone as well as the involvement in the rib. She was on an emotional high. "I made peace with myself—I feel great—I like myself more—I love living in New York."

One night she woke up and wrote the following: "I feel something new—something I had before, when I was young and successful. I'm beginning to feel good about myself, proud of what I have accomplished. I've climbed the mountain again—I am up on top—keep on reminding myself that staying on top needs constant vigilance—never forget fighting—I've got a lot of my old strength back, moving more quickly, working more quickly—T [first name of husband] out to play tennis—I don't feel neglected anymore—I feel tolerant—in the mood of shopping—buying clothes for next season—things I haven't done for a long time."

Recently, I had a personal meeting with her cancer specialist. Because of his outstanding competence as a physician and his compassionate human concern about his patients, Dr. John A. Finkbeiner, associated with the Memorial Hospital for Cancer and Allied Diseases, must be mentioned. He contributed greatly to this patient's recovery. I related to him that now that Mrs. O. is less preoccupied with dying, she has more problems meeting the challenges of living.

Dr. Finkbeiner, referring to our recent conversation, wrote: "—not only with Mrs. O., but *with many patients, I have noticed that they may be psychologically prepared to die, but somehow the treatment has been successful. When the patient is faced with the fact that she or he is going to live they have considerable trouble handling the fact psychologically—this is not an isolated occurrence, at least in my experience.*"

236

Where There's Hope There's Life

The lesson of this case, reinforced by the experience of Dr. Finkbeiner, is that a successful medical treatment of cancer should perhaps consider a combination of chemotherapy with psychotherapy. *If patients are not aware of what emotionally made them give up the fight for life*— we must exclude victims of nuclear accidents and other toxic chemical poisoning—and *if patients don't make an adjustment in changing their inner feelings of hopelessness, a cancer may reoccur* as was the case with Mrs. O.

In a series of articles "Coping with Cancer," which the pharmaceutical company of Hoffmann-La Roche published, a part reads: "How patients cope with cancer—with its diagnosis, treatment and terminal stages—varies greatly, depending on personality makeup and the coping style and manner they have used throughout life." This is a thought similar to those expressed by this author at a convention in 1956 and in the previously mentioned book *The Meaning of Death*.

As in the case of Mrs. O., one of the Hoffmann-La Roche articles advocates the need of maintaining self-esteem and interpersonal relationships. The most valuable part from my point of view is one under the heading, *"The Role of Hope."* The article says, "[The] *Key to Coping with Cancer is having and maintaining hope. What they* [patients] *fight their cancer with is hope*—hope of a cure, hope of a chance to live longer. In a study of two hundred cancer patients, it was observed that each and every one maintained at least a little hope. People without hope see no end to their suffering but *those with hope have 'confidence in the desirability of survival.'* Hope for cancer patients stems from possessing a good self-image, healthy self-esteem, and the confidence that they still can exert a degree of influence on the world around them. *Hope depends more on how patients regard themselves* than on deception, denial, or illusions of cure and indefinite survival.

"The key to coping with cancer is having and maintaining hope. Hope can give cancer patients a sense of a special mission in life, which, in turn, enables them to endure more tests. Hope can convince them that this new treatment will cure them and perhaps others. Hope can spring from news of someone else who was cured or relieved of pain. Except for good news about their own illness, cancer patients like to hear this most. It buoys their sense of hope, nourishes them in cruelly difficult times.

"While hope often supports denial of the full impact of having cancer, hope springs too from the reality that cancer obeys no laws.

Who knows how long a person with cancer may live? An eight-year-old boy in California was operated on for cancer of the thyroid; two years later he developed metastases of the lung and was virtually given up as dead by his physician and his parents. Yet ten years later, this same boy was running the two-mile race for the University of California track team.

"Physicians and family alike need never assume a totally hopeless attitude toward a patient with cancer. The bare possibility of one chance in one thousand of surviving may help that patient psychologically endure what might otherwise be an intolerable burden. Even if the illness is not curable, death is by no means always immediate. The patient can continue to be active and participate in work and social activities. Hope can be maintained but it must be focused around control—around preserving a state of comfort with minimal pain rather than around expecting an unrealistic cure."

Patients may be first traumatized by an awareness that they have cancer. Some may not want to know. Others may realize that they had toyed with the idea of death and almost swam out too far. Shock may make them wish to return, and many do. For some it may be too late.

The Hoffmann-La Roche article also reports, "A seventy-two-year-old widow in Florida—who swims, flies a plane and is very self-assured—noted pains in her rectum three months after her husband died of cancer of the esophagus. She immediately saw a doctor and was diagnosed as having cancer of the colon. The woman was not seriously threatened by the experience. She confronted it openly. She was able to talk about her concerns and worries—and to cry frequently for a few days postoperatively. But she had full confidence that she would resume her previous life style when she was discharged. And she did."

Besides the depression preceding a life-threatening disease such as cancer—the depth of the dialogue about one's role in life, one's needs and growing doubts of having them ever fulfilled—the realization of the illness is traumatic. While a person, as our Mrs. O., thought of dying, in the bright light of day it is frightening. Some patients may suddenly have second thoughts about throwing away their lives and begin to fight, when medically it is too late. Some patients remain nihilistic, others have to cope with another form of depression, a preparation for an impending death; it is a final good-bye to people we love, to people we have worked with, even to the daily little chores.

A person who commits suicide impulsively in an acute state of panic is on such a deeply regressed level of human existence that he or she cannot think rationally. The cancer patient who wants to live must deal with the thoughts about dying and with all that had meaning in his or her life, the joys, the pains, the hopes and the battles lost, and hopefully those that could be won.

It is tragic that in our culture we are terribly "private" and don't talk readily about our innermost feelings. This also goes for the patient who has cancer and the family who tries to encourage the suffering husband, wife, parent, or friend. We grieve before the official grieving time.

The Trying Time of Anticipatory Grief

Several years ago I was asked by the president of the Foundation of Thanatology, Dr. Austin H. Kutscher, to write a deposition paper on "Anticipatory Grief" to be presented at a convention in conjunction with the Department of Psychiatry of Columbia University Medical Center. It reads:

"Anticipatory grief is a profound emotional response to an impending and irreversible loss through death. Because of its element of absolute finality, the anticipation of the loss of a beloved person may arouse a heightened sense of anxiety, or pain, regret, and depression, depending on the intimacy and meaning of the threatened relationship.

"Anticipatory grief may be felt by both the dying patient and his survivors. The dying patient may feel the pain of parting and of leaving behind those he had cared for (a spouse, children, close friends) with pangs of anxiety whether they will be able to manage life without him. There may be feelings of regret and guilt of perhaps not having provided well enough for his surviving dependents. Also, there may be a sense of unfulfillment of not having finished his life work, or the bitter sense of failure of not having finished using his potentials and having thereby wasted his life. And then, there may be, of course, a cold fear of death, of grieving about the cruel reality of having to die—just as there exists, on the other end of the scale, a wish to die. As a rule, death is desired when a longing for final peace outweighs all other affects and when the daily battle for survival is becoming too troublesome to be endured.

"Anticipatory grief may vary in depth and intensity, for at no time does the total personality reveal itself as fully as in the face of death. The loving and responsible person may experience deeper grief because of his concern about those he leaves behind while the selfish individual may adopt the French motto: *"Après moi le déluge."*

239

"Anticipatory grief of a dying patient may be replaced by rage and anger. An immature man may die with a curse on his lips, as Beethoven did, while a mature man may meet death the way he has lived, with an acceptance of the grim reality that has made him make peace with himself. Such a person may experience inner anticipatory grief but may display outwardly little sadness because of his concern not to make the parting more painful than necessary.

"There will be little anticipatory grief in the mentally sick, many of whom had been suicidal and had wanted to die and seem glad to leave a world they did not understand and considered a sea of never-ending troubles.

"Now, as to the survivors, anticipatory grief exists in the face of losing a dear or important love object. Mixed with the sense of loss, there may be a fear of losing a source of security, of dependency, or protection, or of a cherished companionship. There may be an upsurging of love one may not have fully displayed. As a consequence, there often exist fear and states of panic and depression. Or there may be a Freudian 'sympathetic response,' a pain that physically resembles the one of the dying patient and that emotionally causes anxiety and a purely neurotic anticipation of one's own end and of dying a little bit with the person who is actually dying.

"Independent of but frequently mixed in with anticipatory grief is conscious or unconscious guilt. Conscious guilt often stems from a feeling of not having done enough for the dying person. Unconscious guilt has its basis in ambivalent feelings toward the dying patient (Oedipal or moral) or it may be rooted in the religious concepts of some people's anticipatory judgment by God or other people's belief that Christ has given his life so that they may live. At any rate, anticipatory grief is a trying time for both the dying patient and the people who will be left behind."

In Summary: Lowering the Odds

Cancer, the dreadful disease of our time, appears, in the light of our present medical knowledge, to be a wear-and-tear disease produced by specific stresses that affect different people in different ways, except in cases of a thermonuclear catastrophe when it destroys all life. More and more, however, do we physicians try to understand the relationship of human beings to themselves and to other people, come to the inescapable realization that *we ourselves*, in our deepest unconscious and at a time of hopelessness, *give the signal to cease a battle of defense*, which, under normal conditions, is a constant repairing of injured tissue. The cells have been the target of our stresses, be they physical, chemical, or thermical, but primarily *a ceaseless pounding of unresolved* exacerbating *emotional conflicts* that finally produces a first lesion in the soft tissue of an organ.

It is not that a body ceases to fight but that a dispirited mind unable to make peace interferes with the production of new healthy cells necessary for healing, and instead produces a most primitive cell, the cancer cell, to heal the lesion. And because it is primitive— that is, not as highly organized as the healthy cells—it grows faster. Like a destructive weed, it grabs the food and like a ruthless army invades unopposed the healthy tissues.

True, human life is limited. The question then is its quality. Do we wish a life of unending conflict and torment or a life of joy and creative work? Hope plays the role of compass and barometer.

Losing hope means to allow, unopposed, the forces of destruction to ravage our bodies. Building hope, by engaging in meaningful action and filling the hours of our lives with the passion of work and a love for another human being, *produces a sense of fulfillment and is, I believe, the best bulwark against executing ourselves by the disease of cancer.*

CHAPTER 15

New Hope for Mankind

"THE GREATEST REVOLUTION of our generation is the discovery that human beings, by changing the inner attitudes of their minds can change the outer aspects of their lives." These thoughts of William James, reinforced by remarkable gains in psychology during the past three decades, have grown into a solid basis on which our new hope for a better world can be created. The momentous works of Pavlov, Freud, and their schools have finally done away with the orthodoxy of the immutability of human nature—reviving the ancient Greek formula of *Panta rei*, everything flows. They have opened greater depths of understanding of human behavior, its origin, and methods of changing, first by Freud's process of free association and more recently by the use of scientific principles in studies of human interactions, by laboratory experimentation, research projects, and the newer discoveries in biochemistry. Human nature can be changed; so much so that Pavlov, a most critical scientist, was dreaming, as we stated earlier, of creating the "ideal man," by means of carefully conditioning a lively human to be free from ancient fears and depressions. We in the Western world prefer a slightly different method, *education at the earliest possible level*. One such plan shall be presented later on in this closing chapter.

But change does not come easily. In our cnapter on children we stated that the purpose of a neurosis is to achieve certain unconscious goals—a reason why many patients offer strong resistance to changing their pattern of behavior. Similar resistance goes for the group as well. A group, especially on a national level, is bound together by common tradition, ancient customs, and similar beliefs. Like a family unit these inner forces transform a group into a cohesive mass that resists deviation from established customs as individuals resist change. A group tends to fight for the preservation of the old and traditional, having no conscious awareness that these values may have long outlived their original usefulness. Yet they are rooted deep and are defended because they also provide a sense of belonging and security.

When we evaluate the reaction of a group of people in regard to human events we find, disregarding specific individual differences, two basic emotional responses: One group of the population is passive, the other group is progressive; one is holding back and living on false hopes, the other is moving forward spirited by active hope.

A large segment of the passive group is suspicious of change, as suspicious as the peasants who fought the first vaccinations against smallpox. Many feel too powerless and helpless to fight City Hall. They frequently display a doomsday philosophy and the belief that everything is up to the government anyway. They pay their taxes, go to war, because Big Daddy says so.

The second group responds to new events with keen interest and renewed hope in the betterment of the lot of mankind. It has been people of this group that have tirelessly struggled for progress and, indeed, have advanced civilization to a point where they succeeded in pressuring their governments to build such monumental institutions as the United Nations and adopting universal policies of human rights. Frail as these first steps may appear, in the history of mankind they are giant steps. When we consider the relative shortness of time since the rise of civilization, these milestones are a far cry from the time of burning witches or a world with no law, ruled unopposed by brute force.

Moving Forward

Progress is like a fever that goes up and down, hope versus hopelessness. We can only deplore, but must not despair, painful events of regression, as for instance, the recent (1979) action of a government that claims to be civilized but in a fit of raging fever reverted to ancient barbaric methods of kidnapping and stoning people to death—with a judge throwing the first stone.

In the chapter on cults we tried to show that psychopaths don't know that they are mentally sick and people don't know why they follow them. The people, for the most part, are passive and helpless. Therefore they believe the promises of their Pied Pipers. In the case of the people stoned to death their crimes were sexual transgressions, normal in one society at one time, a mortal sin at another place at another time. Does an event of deep regression mean that there is no real hope for human development? On the contrary. These acts of "temporary insanity" have come under the sharp searchlight of psychiatry on individual and now on psychopolitical levels. They have not diminished but rather strengthened our need and our hope to find answers to human problems such as violence.

History is full of periods of stormy progression. We need only think of the time during which one of the noblest of human documents was written: the American Constitution. But history also has produced the deepest regression of humanity: methods of slow torture, the use of science in the negative to sadistically design gas chambers aimed at the destruction of millions of people. Executed not in a heat of passion but laid down in a document written in more primitive than legal language, these Nuremberg Laws were conceived and signed by Rudolf Hess, a psychopath, Hitler's deputy and the only one next to the Führer himself who was allowed to sign a document into law. What he did makes him one of the greatest mass murderers who ever escaped the gallows, by his plea of amnesia.

And yet, in spite of setbacks by people who are motivated by hate and have dedicated their lives to death and destruction because of their own inner self-hate, human progress has marched on. Even at its darkest moments and at times of utter despair the light of hope has never been fully extinguished. It has kept on flickering in the minds of men and women who psychologically have been structured to approach life with hope and thus have the moral strength to endure catastrophes, resist torment, or be lost in the trivial—even if resistance means personal pain and deprivation. These people have carried the torch of civilization forward because of their strong beliefs and their visions of a happier destiny for mankind.

As science is slowly winning its battle against superstition and man's ancient lust for blood, the ghosts and evil spirits begin to vanish. With more education grows the hope that the never-ending search for greater knowledge, better methods, and newer discoveries will make mankind more free, teach us to be more just, and to become more civilized.

The Role of Physicians

While scientists in all fields contribute to the deeper understanding of our world and the nature of man, it will be the job of physicians, especially those whose work concentrates on the functioning of the human mind, to develop methods of better prevention of illness (be it physical or mental, as long as we make that division instead of speaking about one wholesome individual). *Only sick minds use their brains to figure out how best to destroy what healthy minds have labored to create.*

Years ago I made the point that we physicians can no longer remain in the safety of our ivory towers—be they our offices, or clinics, or laboratories—like the learned men in the Middle Ages who conversed in Latin. We must talk to the world and assume our full responsibility for the welfare of mankind. We must extend the frontiers of our work in all areas of human interaction. Our jobs must go beyond the interest of our patients and our studies must reach into all areas where there is human interaction. As I wrote in 1955, in my book *Love and Hate in Human Nature*, speaking to a delegate of the United Nations, "If you diplomats cannot achieve peace, perhaps we doctors will—when they [diplomats] fail, it is the physician who is called upon to heal the victims of their defeats, either on the battlefield, in mental hospitals or in institutions for the crippled and disabled."

The time has come to address ourselves to "the prevention of war instead of patching up human wreckage that it leaves." A few decades ago the AMA came out with a fundamental statement that is worthy to be remembered: "We doctors are equipped for the first time in history *to help mold citizens of tomorrow and influence the trend of human destiny.*"

As a result of my past studies about the mental health of political leaders I introduced a new term, *psychopolitics*, that was to widen our psychodynamic studies on the mental health of political leaders. This contains the nucleus of a hope that we will eventually succeed in building a healthy leadership that will work not for power but for peace and a happy brotherhood of man. Because of this special interest of mine it gave me pleasure to read the address of the outgoing president of the American Psychiatric Association, Dr. Alan Stone, and I wish to salute him for his forward stand. His address took place at the APA's annual meeting in San Francisco, 1980. Dr. Stone, professor of law and psychiatry at Harvard University, referred to psychiatrists having overcome the tyranny of narrow orthodoxy by turning toward pragmatic eclecticism. Psychiatrists cannot isolate themselves but must deal with today's issues of racism, homosexuality, and the situation of women. "It is no accident that each [issue] invites psychiatry to take a stand on human values. Human values after all are a crucial link in the chain that binds the self to society. To take a stand reveals something about our own selves, our own relation to society, and our own vision of what it means to love and to work."

Whom Do You Trust?

So we must go on with confidence and hope. But are all people who say they want better lives really our helpers? Let us turn to our lawmakers, brilliant men and women who defend the rights of all people. But do they? To what degree can we trust our political leaders to progress humanity in general and our great nation in particular? How was a Joe McCarthy possible? Have not others also failed us and our trust? Have they lived up to their great mission to give "advice and consent" to a president who, because of his own disturbed mental state, exercised disastrous judgment, unhampered by our protectors, the members of the Congress?

The latter failure this author is referring to is the Tonkin Resolution. That a president (Johnson), in a flash of anger, ordered air raids against Communist North Vietnamese PT boats that attacked American ships may have been justified or may have been a human error, but that Congress, with the exception of three senators, within a record time of a little over twenty minutes, gave the president full powers of action, without investigating the facts, strikes this author as being a sign of mass hysteria and irresponsibility. It helped to cause this nation the longest, bloodiest, and most controversial war that succeeded only in America losing prestige throughout the world.

One Man's Plan

In quest of what an individual can do when confronted with mass depression and a country polarized because of this unfortunate war, I gathered all my courage to write and eventually went to see President Nixon in his Oval Office. On my mind was a plea for peace by suggesting the establishment of a Department of Peace or, in order to avoid another bureaucracy, an Agency for the Exploration of the Psychodynamics of Peace. The visit ended with a job the president gave me to present my ideas of how delinquency could be prevented.

My report, personal and confidential, had a dramatic impact. Sudden praise from European press agencies, total condemnation and ridicule by the American press. Why? The Ehrlichman staff, possibly to disrupt my relationship with the president, released a viciously distorted version of my report that said that my plan was aimed at sending six-year-old disturbed children to camps. And since juvenile delinquency was prevalent in the black ghettos, the insinuation was that my program had a racial undertone. The great hope to make a valuable contribution was destroyed by a deceit concocted by a group of men around Nixon to maintain their control. Even a man like Robert Finch, then secretary of HEW, ignorant, innocent, or being part or perhaps a victim of the conspiracy, had the arrogance to sneeringly state on national TV, on "The David Frost Show," after I myself had appeared the night before on that same program, "after all we don't want to send six-year-old children to camps." That ended my chance for a plan of helping "our children in trouble."

After the storm of the press died down, the *New York Times*, to the credit of the vision of the creator of its Op-Ed page, Harrison Salisbury, recognized that possibly some double-dealing might have taken place and thus invited me to write about this particular story and other editorials on psychopolitical events. Thus I carried on my struggle to make the public aware of the need for methods to secure sane minds at the highest levels of government. In the midst of this it came as a surprise to receive, over a year later, a phone call from the White House asking me whether I would consider the president's request to be a consultant to a new drug abuse prevention center the president was about to establish.

In 1971 President Nixon was then under pressure from the public because of the high rate of drug addiction in the military, an evident sign of the widespread hopelessness of young men involved in what they came to see as a most merciless and hopeless war.

After the telephone conversation the president sent a deputy, a White House lawyer, to explain and discuss the project. The president had thought of me because he knew about my interest in preventive medicine. I made it clear that prevention had to begin with helping children. I outlined that we had to use the only still-functioning institution dealing with children, our schools. I quickly learned about the fear some parents would have in some parts of the country if psychiatrists or psychologists were to appear in their schools. Therefore, I had to think of another plan and asked for one weeks' time to consider the president's offer. Also, I wanted to be reassured that my boss would not be some bureaucrat, and was told that my boss would be the president himself. After a week I accepted, and on September 10, 1971 I went to Washington, where the new offices opposite the White House were being painted. With Mr. Jeffrey Donfeld, the White House lawyer, and Dr. Jerome Jaffe, a psychiatrist who would supervise the use of the treatment with Methadone—a synthetic narcotic as a substitute for heroin—I was asked for some ideas I might have. Based on my earlier studies on the plan to curb juvenile delinquency I presented an off-the-cuff outline of a plan that would affect all forty million school children all over the United States from age six to sixteen. Only on a uniform national basis, without interference from local politics, could I see a successful solution to the drug problem as well as other problems of children. If my plan would be implemented we would, in ten years, bring down the crime rate almost to a trickle. If we would do nothing more than rely on law enforcement alone the drug problem would flourish and juvenile delinquency would increase.

This then is a condensation of my plan as I presented it on September 23, 1971 to the president:

In order to keep psychiatrists away from schools, social workers and volunteer teachers should be trained in a technique of *role playing*, during which children, free from criticism and reassured of *no judgmental* treatment, could act out their feelings, impulses, thoughts, fears, angers, etc. *The basic idea was that not teachers but the children themselves would be the therapists.*

Children like to help one another. Children care to listen to other children's troubles and as a group children would discuss their or someone else's problems. It would build interests and open up an arena of discussion a family could not provide. Feelings of compassion, understanding, empathy would build small cohesive groups that in an air of friendship would pull in a loner, withdrawn child, or prevent an angry child from acting out his or her anger destructively.

Troubled children need hope. They need the reassurance that whatever their problems are or their background may be or what home difficulties they may have, they have a chance to be heard, *that they have a second family* that does not judge them or scold them but that is genuinely interested in them as people.

While it is not the government's job to undo the failures of parental influence or inadequate education *we all pay the price for these failures.* Surely, it is not easy to teach children love, but with patience we can teach children tolerance, responsibility, respect for their fellow man and for our free society. We would then end up with fewer mental hospitals, fewer prisons, and a diminishment of the present violence and polarization in this country and other countries as well. In cohesive groups of eight, children would practice their therapy and learn to trust and to love and eventually to look at their world with confidence and hope.

The cost of the program—I was shocked at first—when Dr. Jaffe estimated it—was $3 billion. "This is not much for the federal government for a program of that dimension," he said. Actually it is a small price and a fraction of the cost in lives, and in the billions of dollars being wasted to repair vandalism, theft, arson, and other acts of destruction, not to mention the fear of people walking their streets at night.

This plan became a victim of Watergate, as were many other tragic casualties that resulted from this national disaster.

Did this failure discourage me? It did.. But while I was deeply disappointed I never really lost hope. Ideas sometimes float in the air. Perhaps someone else might come up with a similar or even better plan. Perhaps another time may be more opportune. Or perhaps another president with wider vision may see the merits in *a plan that aims at prevention of crime without interfering with the individuality of children* and decide to implement such a plan. My firm hope is that one day a plan like that will be integrated into the school system.

The hope that we can attain a world free from crime and hopelessness is no idle dream to me. It will become a reality not because crime does not pay but because, like good health, living with hope simply makes people feel good about themselves. It is the principle of maturity to do out of one's free will what others do for fear of the law.

With deep admiration I wish to refer here to the work of one man who, in the face of opposition, almost single-handedly changed our world. He was Johann Heinrich Pestalozzi (1746–1827), a Swiss, and the man who is the father of our modern school system. In a small room he started to teach children the three R's and laid the foundation of modern elementary education. Having studied theology at the University of Zurich, he was forced to abandon his career because of his political activities. At the turn of the nineteenth century he retired to his farm, Neuhof, where he conducted a school for poor children. In his writings he widened his system of school education.

250

It is the purest form of active hope of one man. It profoundly affected the cultural development of the Western World and laid the seed of an educational system that has grown into being the cornerstone of teaching and learning of our modern world.

This man's work grew out of a hope that what he wanted to do would be done, not by some rare or singular princely act of generosity or tutoring of the very privileged, but with the belief that all people have a right to learn. Pestalozzi proved that hope will make a wish grow into undreamed dimensions.

Today's hope for mankind lies in the fact that the vast reserves of psychodynamic psychology have not even been tapped, except where it applies to the welfare of individual people. Our hope for a better world is so unshakable that once the United States begins with programs—be they role playing or similar methods in our schools—the world will follow, leading to the road to peace and justice.

We can look ahead with a fullness of hope because science cannot be stopped any more. Neither can the power of wider programs of education that grow with each new piece of knowledge. Teach a child of five what love is and it will grow up to love the world. And teach a child never to be afraid and look ahead with confidence and it will grow up helping to build a world of trust, peace, and justice.

The sustaining power in the process of building such an ideal lies in this book's message that *hope sustains life*, that from it spring all of man's creations, his conquest of new worlds as well as his own human development, and self-fulfillment.